Participatory Learning in the Early Years

Routledge Research in Education

Participatory Learning in the Early Years

Research and Pedagogy

Edited by Donna Berthelsen, Jo Brownlee and Eva Johansson

Routledge
Taylor & Francis Group
New York   London

First published 2009
by Routledge
270 Madison Ave, New York, NY 10016

Simultaneously published in the UK
by Routledge
2 Park Square, Milton Park, Abingdon, Oxon OX14 4RN

Routledge is an imprint of the Taylor & Francis Group, an informa business

Typeset in Sabon by IBT Global.
Printed and bound in the United States of America on acid-free paper by IBT Global.

Library of Congress Cataloging in Publication Data

Participatory learning in the early years : research and pedagogy / edited by Donna Berthelsen, Jo Brownlee, and Eva Johansson.
    p. cm. — (Routledge research in education ; 21)
    Includes bibliographical references and index.
  1. Early childhood education—Social aspects. 2. Social learning. I. Berthelsen, Donna. II. Brownlee, Jo. III. Johansson, Eva, 1949–
    LB1139.23.P37 2009
    303.3'2—dc22
    2008030946

ISBN10: 0-415-98974-4 (hbk)
ISBN10: 0-203-88355-1 (ebk)

ISBN13: 978-0-415-98974-9 (hbk)
ISBN13: 978-0-203-88355-6 (ebk)

Contents

Figures

Tables

Preface

The development of this book, *Participatory Learning in the Early Years: Research and Pedagogy,* has been a cross-cultural project with many dimensions. First and foremost, we wanted to shed light on the experiences of the youngest participants in group care settings and their teachers across national contexts. We wanted to gather researchers and educators from different parts of the world interested in the experiences of the youngest children who take part in early childhood programs.

Many young children across national contexts now participate in group programs from a very early age. However, we know very little about how these young children 'live' their lives in their group care settings; how they experience their encounters with peers and teachers; what they learn; and under what conditions they learn. We also know little about how educators working with these young citizens perceive their goals; what their aspirations are in their work; and how they view and relate to the children. Why is there a lack of shared information? There might be many explanations for this but one is related to how young children and their teachers are valued by society. How we value children is determined by what rights we accord to them, notes the philosopher David Archard in his book, *Children, Rights and Childhood.* Our understanding is that young children and their teachers in a broad sense are given low positions in society, even if we can find that there is now greater advocacy for young children and interest in their experiences. By its core theme, this book can be viewed as one example of this interest in children's rights to participatory learning programs.

We base this book on assumptions that learning is relational, as well as culturally and contextually embedded; and that young children in group care settings, in one way or another, take part in the learning processes in those settings. The book is also based on values that young children do have a right to be involved in learning programs that afford participation as well as democratic approaches to how they are involved in their learning contexts. The issue and tension is, however, what is participatory learning and democratic approaches to practice with respect to young children across contexts? How much participation are infants and toddlers afforded and in what ways? There is of course not one answer. Participatory learning is viewed in different ways in theory and practice. However, children's participation is ultimately the responsibility of adults and society. Ultimately, this is both a question of power and of intersubjectivity. To be able to take part requires physical and mental "room" for this participation, as well as intersubjective agreements about giving and taking. To let someone take part in something also means that we (as educators) need to step back and give power to the participant (the child). This can be, from a teacher's perspective, a difficult and risky project. It presupposes both knowledge and awareness of how participation can be afforded to young children. In the book, we find several dilemmas that characterize professional practice that reflect fundamental and ongoing ethical questions about the experiences of very young children in early childhood programs.

Conditions for young children's participation are given and created by sociocultural contexts in group care settings in which teachers and children take active parts. These are concerns of the contributing authors of this book who all have different professional experiences in working, and researching with young children. The authors represent different cultural contexts and different disciplines. The common interest for all the writers is, however, a deep concern for young children and their teachers. Still, the chapters differ substantially with regard to how the experiences of very young children in group settings are explored and understood in theory and practice; as well as the assumptions about children and childhood on the important issues of participation. This diversity and community is both the advantage and the challenge in this book. Across the chapters ideas are explored about the manner in which young children's participation and learning can be understood in practice.

In the first chapter, Donna Berthelsen provides an introduction to issues around young children's participatory learning in early education. She discusses ideas about culture and how it can be understood as operating at different levels and dynamically. Four themes central to the book are explored. These themes are culture and context and young children's learning; sociocultural theorizing and learning; participation as a right; and learning as participation. In the next chapter, Helen Penn discusses the wide variations in assumptions about childhood and adult-child relationships and, consequently, the wide variations in understanding childhood across national contexts. Berenice Nyland then considers the different theories informing early childhood practice and assumptions within those theories about children's rights and participation. Her discussion is focused on the importance of a human rights perspective. Subsequent chapters by Eva Johansson, Anette Emilson, and Anne Greve present examples of research on children's learning underpinned by philosophical assumptions about children's life-worlds in the everyday interactions that they have with peers and teachers in preschool. These chapters, respectively, address how young children's morality has its own characteristics in relation to children's premises, rather than the premises of adults; the kinds of citizenship qualities that are explicit or implicit, in everyday interactions between teachers and toddlers in pedagogical practice in Sweden; and children's early learning through friendship in the course of which they learn about ethics and cooperation. The chapter by Jo Brownlee and Donna Berthelsen uses personal epistemological theory to explore the nature of beliefs about children's learning held by group leaders in toddler child care programs in Australia. Mary McMullen and Susan Dixon make a case for the importance of relationship-focused practice and how such practice form a basis for relational and participatory pedagogy. Successive chapters by Paulette Luff, Enid Elliot, and Judith Duncan report on action-oriented research in early childhood settings to support participatory learning with very young children. They illustrate the complexities and the possibilities of working with infants and toddlers and their families, across national contexts that include the United Kingdom, Canada, and New Zealand, respectively. The chapter by Artin Göncü, Barbara Abel, and Catherine Main describes features of a graduate preservice teacher education program in the United States that seeks to promote democracy in early childhood education. Embedded in this professional practice program, at another level, is a focus on how early childhood teachers' practices can support social inclusion, fairness, and participation. This book concludes with a chapter by Jo Brownlee discussing the way forward. How can the various themes in the book be connected to advance theorizing and research about young children's participatory learning?

This work focused on the important issue of *participatory learning of very young children in early childhood programs* has been an exciting challenge and we are most grateful to all the contributors who have given their knowledge and time for this project. But without all children and their educators in group care settings across the world this book would not have been realized. Thanks to all of you!

Finally, this book is now delivered to readers, researchers, and educators. Hopefully, you will be inspired to continue the discussion and the development of knowledge about infants' and toddlers' participatory learning in early childhood programs.

Donna Berthelsen, Jo Brownlee and Eva Johansson
July 2008

1 Participatory Learning
Issues for Research and Practice

Donna Berthelsen

A goal of this book is to present research about participatory learning with very young children in group care settings, as well as to understand, through that research, how participatory learning can be understood across cultures. The purpose of this particular chapter is to review key issues that inform this area of research. Across cultures, within the broad sociocultural tradition focused on children's learning, there is no clear set of theoretical principles nor a related set of methodologies associated with such research. The chapters in this book provide a range of studies informed by different theoretical perspectives in the sociocultural tradition and different research methodologies. While the chapters represent diverse standpoints, there is a common view that individuals and their contexts are intricately linked and that children's learning is a socially and culturally mediated process.

The diversity of views presented in this book indicates that, across cultures, there are different understandings about children's participatory learning and early childhood practice. While we recognize that there will be social and cultural diversity in the ideas that will inform practice with young children in group care settings, a case for cross-cultural research can also be made. Researchers and practitioners in early childhood education learn from looking across cultures to understand both the manner in which others' understand their world as well as to surface our own taken-for-granted assumptions about young children. When beliefs and practices from other cultures and national contexts are considered then one's own assumptions become more apparent.

Assumptions about how social and cultural experiences influence young children's learning have been largely ignored in the early childhood education literature until quite recently. Theory stemming from Euro-American academic research presented a view that understanding of young children's development could be generalized across societies. A shift in emphasis that has given more attention to culture and social contexts has replaced the previous reliance on normative theories. These theories described child development "as occurring in linear and universal stages" and had informed early childhood education practice for several decades (Lee & Johnson, 2007, p. 234). Sociocultural perspectives have now become prominent drawing particularly on the theories of Vygotsky (1978, 1986) and Rogoff (1990, 2003). In these theories, culture becomes the most important system in which human development occurs. Children participate within their cultural context and, from an early age, they are agents of their own learning and active makers of meaning.

In a number of chapters in this book, there is a focus on relationships as an important learning context. Children's learning is influenced by their relationships with others, both peers and adults, as well as through the relationships between adults within children's life spheres. Relationships are formed when two partners accumulate a history of interactions that bring expectancies from past experiences into their future interactions with each other. The issue for adults working with young children is to understand that these relationships are contexts for learning through which the child can be afforded agency and power. Learning is influenced by the child's interest in, and responsiveness to, the behavior and feelings of others in that context. Learning is sustained by social and affective engagement with others. Through communication and collaboration in relationships, learning occurs because activities have embedded meanings about values and traditions in that cultural context (Rogoff, 2003; Rogoff, Paradise, Arauz, Correa-Chavez, & Angelillo, 2004).

A major focus in this book is the experiences of children aged less than three years who participate in group care settings. In theory and research in early education, there has been less focus on participatory learning and democratic approaches to practice with very young children. However, many young children across national contexts now participate in group programs from a very early age. Their experiences deserve greater attention. Increasing evidence indicates the importance of this period to children's development and learning (National Scientific Council on the Developing Child, 2004). Across the chapters in this book, the experiences of very young children in group settings are explored. Those settings are variously termed, across national contexts, child care, nursery, kindergarten, or preschool. In the following sections of this chapter, four themes are explored. These sections focus on culture and context and young children's learning; sociocultural theorizing and learning; participation as a right; and learning as participation.

CULTURE, CONTEXT AND YOUNG CHILDREN'S LEARNING

Culture can be understood as the complex set of separable but related contextual factors experienced by a social group over time. Culture is not a static entity but a dynamic system that is constantly in the process of reconstruction. It is "history in the present" (Cole, 2005a, p. 3). Culture can also be understood in a more abstract way as the systems of shared meanings transmitted within and across generations through social inter-action (Miller, 1999). Culture as a concept is more complex than merely considering it as an entity with clear-cut boundaries, such as nationality and ethnicity, because essentially these are merely social addresses or iden-tity categories that underestimate the complexity in the meaning of culture (Rogoff, 2003).

Understanding the conceptual complexity in the idea of culture is a nec-essary precondition in exploring how individuals learn from a sociocul-tural perspective (Pein & Hodkinson, 2007). The manner in which culture is often discussed implies some hierarchical properties. There is a compli-cated and intertwined relationship between the culture of any specific con-text (e.g., a child care center) and the culture at large. There is the culture that prevails and is created within a child care classroom, within the child care center, and within the organization that manages that center. There is also culture in the wider sense that influences the manner in which any local, specific practice may be, in one way or another, an expression of the culture at large; although it must be recognized that this is a dialecti-cal and reciprocal process since individuals also have an influence on the expression of the wider culture. The larger idea of culture may refer to any number of dimensions. It can be the traditions in a way of life or the beliefs and practices of a group. However, it can also be used, as formerly described, to refer to institutions and to smaller units of social space within those institutions. Research that takes account of culture must inevitably address the complicated interplay between the wider cultural context and the local context of practice.

Significant cultural meanings are embedded and constructed in the everyday settings in which children participate. To understand the expe-riences of children, a close look at these contexts that are most proximal to children's lives is important. Research on children's learning is most often conducted within these proximal contexts to examine the practices that constrain or support children's agency and influence. The cultural practices within those proximal contexts, such as a child's early education program, are likely to instantiate cultural themes from both the insti-tutional culture in which the program may be embedded as well as the wider culture. Thus, local practices within the social and physical space of the program are likely to be characterized by common themes and values from the broader cultural context expressed in a variety of ways to children through activities and interactions. For example, children's independence may be highly valued in the wider culture and practices within a child care program may reflect that theme. Thus, the child learns valued behaviors associated with independence. In another cultural con-text, interdependence may be more strongly emphasized and practices to learn about cooperation will be embedded in the everyday experiences of the children. Children's learning is therefore framed by such themes which are valued in the wider culture and, consequently, will be expressed through adults' actions and interactions with children in a specific local context, an ecological niche (Bronfenbrenner, 1979, 1986).

Bronfenbrenner argued that every child's ecological niche is unique because each child experiences and takes part in different relationships and processes of interactions across proximal contexts, such as home and the out-of-home care setting. While the relationships and experiences within an ecological niche are influenced by values and practices within the wider culture, nevertheless, within many national contexts, there is increasingly greater social heterogeneity by social and economic circumstances and diversity of the ethnic composition in societies. There may not be common values and beliefs about children and childhood. Differences in the beliefs and values of families and in how dominant and minority views in the wider culture are represented in out-of-home care contexts remains a key issue for practice in early education. Penn (1999) drew attention to these critical issues in early childhood practice with very young children, babies, and toddlers. She emphasized the importance of recognizing the diversity and complexities in the lives of children and their families; as well as the contradictory values and expectations that children experience across family and out-of-home care settings. Teachers' own values and beliefs also infuse their practices and these may often be at odds with those of the families with whom they work. Thus, it is important to examine how wider and local cultures may have mutual influences on children's learning.

SOCIOCULTURAL THEORIZING AND CHILDREN'S LEARNING

Over the last two decades, paradigm shifts from positivist to interpretative theoretical perspectives in sociology, as well as epistemological changes in developmental psychology have occurred. There have been ontological shifts to understanding the lives of young children that embrace both sociological and interdisciplinary studies. Contemporary sociology and developmental psychology independently have constructed models of socialization based on a number of assumptions that include ideas about equal agency between adults and children, about the bi-directional nature of influence in adult-child relationships, and about interdependent power (Kuczynski, Harach, & Bernardini, 1999). Developmental psychologists have also come to see children as active, rather than passive recipients of culture, who actively construct and interpret their worlds (Corsaro, 1997). The child of contemporary developmental psychology is compatible with ideas about the child as a social actor who is currently claimed as "sociology's child" (Kuczynski et al., 1999, p. 23). The result of these new insights across disciplines in theory and research has resulted in new ways of understanding childhood that give credit to children as agents of their own learning.

Much criticism has been leveled at various tenets of the grand theories of developmental psychology to inform practice with young children in early childhood programs (e.g., Burman, 1994; Canella, 2002; Ryan & Grieshaber, 2005). However, the theories from developmental psychologists such as Vygotsky (1978) and Bronfenbrenner (1979), respectively, have provided a basis for other sociocultural and ecocultural perspectives that have been embraced in early education. These theories emphasized the developmental importance of the interactions between children and their social surrounds. While much has been made of the contribution of Vygotsky (1978, 1986) to understanding socially mediated learning, other theories have also made a contribution, including Piaget's recognition of the importance of social interactions to children's knowledge construction (DeVries, 1997); and Bandura's (1989) social learning theory about the importance of reciprocal relations in learning.

Sociocultural theory encompasses a variety of perspectives. It is a very broad interdisciplinary enterprise that takes cultural mediation as a universal feature of human cognition and learning. It is not possible to describe sociocultural theory: "as a mature scientific paradigm with generally accepted theoretical foundations, a methodology, and a well-delineated set of prescriptions for relating theory to practice" (Cole, 1995, p. 187). In its broad and somewhat eclectic tradition, cognition and learning are interdependent and cannot be meaningfully separated from cultural and historical processes nor can individuals be separated from the activities and contexts in which those activities take place (Cole, 2005a, 2005b). Individuals, actions, and meanings within contexts are jointly constituted. Research in the sociocultural tradition may, or may not, involve research across different cultures. It may involve research within a particular cultural setting to highlight particular processes of cultural mediation that support learning.

Children learn through activities and communications with others in their cultural context which is located in a particular historical time. "Sociocultural theory suggests that development, rather than unfolding in a predictable fashion from infancy to adulthood through the outward expression of innate biological structures, involves participation in social processes" (Smith, 2002, p. 77). Vygotsky (1978, 1986) proposed that any function in children's learning and development can be understood on two planes: first, on the social plane between individuals; and second, in the psychological plane as expressed by the idea of the *zone of proximal development*. This can be described as the gap between what children can accomplish on their own and what they can accomplish in collaboration with more competent others. The greater the richness of the activities and interactions in which children participate, the greater will be their understanding and knowledge (Smith, 2002). However, it is not just a one-way process from adult to child. It is a reciprocal relationship.

Through reciprocity individuals jointly construct knowledge. There are mutual contributions in the processes of learning.

PARTICIPATION AS A RIGHT

As new ideas about the social and cultural influences on young children's learning gained standing, political advocacy for children's rights also gained prominence. Thorne (1987) argued that there was a need to: " . . . bring children more fully into knowledge by clarifying ideological constructions, with attention to the diversity of children's actual lives and circumstances; by emphasizing children's agency as well as their subordination; and by challenging their conceptual privatization" (p. 85).

Since 1989, most nations have become signatories to the United Nations Convention on the Rights of the Child (CRC). This convention, together with the General Comment No. 7 on implementing child rights in early childhood (CRC, 2005), has maintained a momentum to protect the rights of young children. However, it is in Articles 12 and 13 of the CRC that focus on participation rights that has gained extensive attention in early childhood education (Alderson, 2000). Participation rights encompass issues about identity, autonomy, freedom of choice, and involvement in decision-making (Tomanovic, 2003). However, the notion of children's rights has presented a number of difficulties for policy and practice. Society demands that children are both protected and released to independence (Flekkøy & Kaufman, 1997). On an age continuum of childhood, this contradiction between protection and independence is less significant at different ends of the continuum than in the intervening years. Nevertheless, for early childhood practitioners, in exploring notions of independence and participation, issues arise about how such concepts can be realized in practice.

Endeavoring to understand the perspectives of the young child in any group care context requires understanding of the enabling and constraining effects on participation and individual agency that the context affords. Powerful normative models of development previously shaped beliefs about what children can and cannot do. While not designed to consider the participations rights of very young children, the model of how participation can be supported was presented by Shier (2001). It has implications about how researchers and practitioners can consider how participation opportunities are afforded to very young children. Shier proposed a hierarchical model. At the lower levels of this hierarchy, children are listened to; children are supported to express their views; and children's views are taken into account. Children can be active agents rather than just passively participating in activities defined by others. The extent to which children can participate depends not only on their capability but also adult perceptions of those capabilities. In an ideal world, adults would be sensitive to the child's current level of understanding and allow for a gradual shift in the balance of power so that children are allowed to take the initiative and have responsibility. The issue is not that children are granted absolute autonomy but instead what they will be treated with respect and supported in taking responsibility.

How do adults make a judgment on children's capacities for participation? It is likely that adults underestimate children capabilities because of the strength and influence of normative theories of child development that have shaped assumptions and expectations about what children can, and cannot, do at certain ages (Freeman, 1998; Mayall, 2000; Smith, 2002). It can also be challenging for adults to give up power over the learner and the learning process. To let go of this power may be experienced as unsafe and threatening. New ways of thinking are needed that acknowledge young children's agency and competencies which are not based on judgments of children's age-defined capabilities. Adults also need to be willing to truly engage in the learning process with a child.

LEARNING AS PARTICIPATION

Participation is synonymous with 'taking part.' This signals that learning is a process that is mediated through encounters with others, through interacting and negotiating with others (Bruner, 1986). There is no doubt that a new paradigm for understanding learning and development in social context has emerged (e.g., Lave, 1988; Resnick, 1991; Rogoff, 1990). The basic assumption of this sociocultural paradigm is that: " . . . mental functioning is inherently situated in social interactional, cultural, institutional, and historical context. Such a tenet contrasts with approaches that assume, implicitly or explicitly, that it is possible to examine mental processes such as thinking or memory independently of the sociocultural setting in which individuals and groups function" (Wertsch, 1991, p. 86).

How does participation relate to learning? Sfard (1998) proposed that there is a need to examine the conceptual metaphors that are currently used to understand learning:

> . . . This means digging out the metaphors that underlie both our spontaneous everyday conceptions and scientific theorizing. Indeed, metaphors are the most primitive, most elusive, and yet amazingly informative objects of analysis. Their special power stems from the fact that they often cross the borders between the spontaneous and the scientific, between the intuitive and the formal. (p. 4)

While Sfard focused on interpreting metaphors used to explain mathematical learning, her analysis can be applied to other learning domains and learning contexts, such as early childhood education. Sfard (1998) contrasted two metaphors. These metaphors are "learning as acquisition" and "learning as participation" (p. 5). Learning as acquisition is understood as the growth of understanding and knowledge through the accumulation of elements of knowledge that are gradually refined into rich cognitive structures (e.g., Piagetian theory). While learning as participation can be understood as ongoing learning activity to which there is no end point. Learning is not considered separately from the context in which that learning takes place (e.g., Rogoff, 1990, 2003). More recent theorizing in early childhood education research is dominated by the participation metaphor (A. Edwards, 2004; S. Edwards, 2003). It reflects a shift in understanding of what constitutes learning from a *knowledge* state to learning as *action* (and knowing). Learning can be understood as a process of becoming a member of community and acting according to its particular values and norms that may be negotiated and re-negotiated through ongoing and dynamic cultural processes (Cole, 2005a).

While the ideas on participation as the basis for learning has the potential to lead to more democratic practices in teaching young children, it remains a matter of interpretation, managed by the intentions and skills of those who subscribe to the participation metaphor. The relations between the acquisition metaphor and the participation metaphor are likely to be complementary (Sfard, 1998). Learning as acquisition is logically understood not as learning stripped of social context but rather learning where the social contextual factors have relatively less rather than greater presence (Salomon & Perkins, 1998). Learning as participation is represented by a sociocultural standpoint that it is a process of enculturation through discourse, practice and thinking.

CONCLUSIONS

This chapter has provided an introduction to issues around young children's participatory learning in early education. It has discussed ideas about culture and how it can be understood as intertwined and operating dynamically at different levels. Sociocultural theories of learning were also considered. In 2000, Anne Meade wrote about the dilemmas of early childhood practice that were set within the grand theories of child development which were constructed around readiness, choice, needs, play, and discovery. Such theories as a basis for practice did not permit teachers to see the socially constructed inequities that were evident in their practice when using this lens of traditional developmental theories. A paradigmatic shift to embrace a participatory view of learning in early education through sociocultural perspectives is now taking place. How has this shift impacted on early childhood practice across national and cultural contexts? The chapters in this book take up this topic in different ways and present perspectives from across national contexts. The chapters consider issues about young children's participatory learning across social, moral and cognitive domains of learning. The final chapter considers the way forward and how the various themes of the book might be interconnected and presents a model for understanding the interconnectedness of the themes.

Overall, this book presents important examples of current research on participatory learning in early childhood education across cultures. The project for the book was based on a shared faith that a collective view of theory and research on participatory learning in early childhood education could be presented. Across the chapters ideas are explored about the manner in which young children's participation and learning can be understood in practice. The chapters also present a kind of collective commentary on the dilemmas that characterize professional practice that reflect fundamental and ongoing moral and ethical questions about the experiences of very young children in early childhood programs.

REFERENCES

Alderson, P. (2000). *Young children's rights: Exploring beliefs, principles and practices*. London: Jessica Kingsley.

Bandura, A. (1989). Human agency in social cognitive theory. *American Psychologist, 44,* 1175–1184.

Bronfenbrenner, U. (1979). *The ecology of human development*. Cambridge, MA: Harvard University Press.

———. (1986). Ecology of the family in the context of human development: Research perspectives. *Developmental Psychology, 22,* 723–742.

Bruner, J. (1986). *Actual minds, possible worlds*. Cambridge, MA: Harvard University Press.

Burman, E. (1994). *Deconstructing developmental psychology*. London: Routledge.

Canella, G. S. (2002). *Deconstructing early childhood education: Social justice & revolution*. New York: Peter Lang.

Cole, M. (1995). Sociocultural settings: Design and intervention. In J. V. Wertsch, P. Del Rio, & A. Alvarez (Eds.), *Sociocultural studies of mind.* (pp. 187–214). Cambridge, UK: Cambridge University Press.

———. (2005a). Cultural-historical activity theory in the family of socio-cultural approaches. *International Society for the Study of Behavioural Development Newsletter*, Serial 47, 1–3.

———. (2005b). Culture in development. In M. H. Bornstein & M. E. Lamb (Eds.), *Developmental psychology: An advanced textbook* (5th edn.). Mahwah, NJ: Erlbaum.

Convention on the Rights of the Child (CRC) (2005). *Implementing child rights in early childhood*. General Comment No 7. New York: United Nations.

Corsaro, W. A. (1997). *The sociology of childhood*. Thousand Oaks, CA: Pine Forge Press.

DeVries, R. (1997). Piaget's social theory. *Educational Researcher, 26 (2),* 4–17.

Edwards, A. (2004). Understanding context, understanding practice in early education. *European Early Childhood Education Research Journal, 12* (1), 85–101.

Edwards, S. (2003). New directions: charting paths for the role of sociocultural theory in early childhood education and curriculum. *Contemporary Issues in Early Childhood, 4 (3),* 251–266.

Flekkøy, M. G., & Kaufman, N. H. (1997). The participation rights of the child: Rights and responsibilities in family and society. London: Jessica Kingsley.

Freeman, M. (1998). The sociology of childhood and children's rights. *International Journal of Children's Rights, 6,* 433–444.

Kuczynski, L., Harach, L., & Bernardini, S. C. (1999). Psychology's child meets sociology's child: Agency, influence and power in parent-child relationships. In C. L. Shehan (Ed.), *Through the eyes of the child: Revisioning children as active agents of family life.* Stamford, CT: JAI Press.

Lave, J. (1988). *Cognition in practice.* Cambridge, UK: Cambridge University Press.

Lee, K., & Johnson, A. S. (2007). Child development in cultural contexts: Implications of cultural psychology for early childhood teacher education. *Early Childhood Education, 35,* 233–243.

Mayall, B. (2000). The sociology of childhood in relation to children's rights. *International Journal of Children's Rights, 8,* 243–259.

Meade, A. (2000). If you sat it three times, is it true? Critical use of research in early childhood education. *International Journal of Early Years Education, 8* (1), 15–26.

Miller, J. G. (1999). Cultural psychology: Implications for basic psychological theory. *Psychological Science, 10,* 85–91.

National Scientific Council on the Developing Child (2004). *Young children develop in an environment of relationships. Working paper 1:* Boston, MA: Author. Retrieved May 10, 2008, from www.developingchild.net.

Penn, R (1999, June). *How should we care for babies and toddlers? An analysis of practice in out-of-home care for children under three.* Social Science Research Unit, Institute of Education London University.

Pein, N., & Hodkinson, P. (2007). Contexts, cultures, learning: Contemporary understandings. *Educational Review, 59* (4), 387–397.

Resnick, L.B. (1991). Shared cognition: Thinking as social practice. In L. B. Resnick, J. M. Levine, & S. D. Teasley (Eds.), *Perspectives on socially shared cognition,* (pp. 1–20). Washington, DC: American Psychological Association.

Rogoff, B. (1990) *Apprenticeship in thinking: Cognitive development in social context.* New York: Oxford University Press.

———. (2003). *The cultural nature of human development.* New York: Oxford University.

Rogoff, B., Paradise, R., Arauz, R. M., Correa-Chavez, M., & Angelillo, C. (2004). Firsthand learning through intent participation. *Annual Review of Psychology, 54,* 175–203.

Ryan, S., & Grieshaber, S. (2005). Shifting from developmental to postmodern practices in early childhood teacher education. *Journal of Teacher Education, 56,* 35–45.

Salomon, G. & Perkins, D. (1998) Individual and Social Aspects of Learning. *Review of Research in Education, 23,* 1–24.

Sfard, A. (1998). On two metaphors for learning and the dangers of choosing just one. *Educational Researcher, 27*(2), 4–13.

Shier, H. (2001). Pathways to participation: Opening, opportunities and obligations. *Children & Society, 15,* 107–117.

Smith, A. B. (2002). Interpreting and supporting participation rights: contributions from sociocultural theory. *International Journal of Children's Rights, 10,* 73–78.

Thorne, B. (1987). Re-visioning women and social change: Where are the children? *Gender and Society, 1* (1), 85–109.

Tomanovic, S. (2003). Negotiating children's participation and autonomy within families. *International Journal of Children's Rights, 11,* 51–71.

Vygotsky, L. S. (1978). *Mind in society: The development of higher psychological processes.* Cambridge, MA: Harvard University Press.

Vygotsky, L. (1986). *Thought and language.* Cambridge, MA: MIT Press.

Wertsch, J.V. (1991). A sociocultural approach to socially shared cognition. In L. B. Resnick, J. M. Levine, & S. D. Teasley (Eds.), *Perspectives on socially shared cognition*, (pp. 85–100). Washington, DC: American Psychological Association.

2 International Perspectives on Participatory Learning

Young Children's Perspectives across Rich and Poor Countries

Helen Penn

This chapter presents views about young children's learning, development, and participation across rich and poor countries.[1] The argument put forward in the chapter is that understandings of what young children need and what they can do is deeply rooted in their cultural context. However those understandings are more often implicit rather than explicit. The chapter attempts to explore and expose some of these implicit understandings about childhood in rich countries and contrasts these with interpretations of the context and situations of young children in poor countries. It highlights some of the complexities and contradictions of generalizing about the needs and rights of all young children across rich and poor countries.

The following quotation by the distinguished anthropologist Robert LeVine offers a challenging introduction to this theme. He suggests that rich countries overvalue individuality in children, and that this emphasis on individuality is in turn a reflection of the consumerism deeply embedded in the everyday upbringing of children. He is writing about American infants, but he could equally be writing about early childhood in Australia, the United Kingdom or most other rich countries.

> The American infant has numerous possessions earmarked as belonging to him alone; their number and variety increase as he gets older, permitting him to experience the boundaries of self represented in his physical environment. . . . From infancy onwards the child is encouraged to characterize himself in terms of his favorite toys and foods and those he dislikes: his tastes, aversions and consumer preferences are viewed not only as legitimate but as essential aspects of his growing individuality—and a prized quality of an independent person. (LeVine, 2003, p. 95)

The notion of a resource-rich environment permeates practice in rich countries. In the "child-centered" worlds that are created as children are institutionalized in nurseries, individuality and choice are intensified as goals. As Tobin (1995), another anthropologist, has commented, nurseries in the United States are like infant shopping malls. The children are the consumers in training continually pressured to "choose" between not very attractive, oversold goods (i.e., the displays of toys in the nursery). "Good" practitioners continually encourage and support children in making choices between these goods.

By contrast, Viruru, an Indian researcher contrasts the notion of play pedagogies and the separate, well-equipped fantasy world we expect young children to inhabit in rich countries with the everyday life most children experience; as she put it "growing up in the world rather than protected from it" (2001, 19).

Intertwined with ideas about individuality, consumerism and choice is an additional assumption in rich countries that children will or should grow up in a benign, protected, and educative environment. This protectiveness, as Viruru argues, has led to the creation of distinct and especially equipped spaces for children, and special ways to relate to them and instruct them. Children in rich countries who experience less than benign conditions—the death of a parent, unsafe living conditions etcetera, are seen as in need of special support, counseling, and protection.

Once you move out of the privileged orbit of rich countries and consider the majority of the world's children who live in Africa, Asia, or Latin America, as Viruru suggests, understandings about childhood begin to shift rapidly. In poor countries, hostile environments are unfortunately often the norm. A study commissioned by UNICEF (Gordon, Nandy, Pantazis, Pemberton, & Townsend, 2003) illustrated just how many millions of children—60% of all children experience hunger every day and lack access to water, sanitation, electricity, and a rainproof roof over their heads. Children take this in their stride, because they have to.

The recent work of Muthukrishna, Ebrahim, and Mbatha (2008) illustrates how children in poor areas in Kwa Zulu Natal in South Africa adapt and accommodate to the HIV/AIDs epidemic, and face the almost daily deaths of others—neighbors, relatives or even parents—with effortful attempts to understand and cope. In situations like these, survival itself is a prime goal. Young children in rich countries are rarely exposed to such stresses; indeed it is inconceivable that they should be. Yet the coping strategies of the many millions of children who survive in such difficult circumstances passes largely unnoticed in the early childhood literature.

A SOCIOCULTURAL APPROACH

It is obvious from this beginning that I consider childhood to be deeply and necessarily contextual. Socio-cultural theory is predicated on the idea that the adults around a child scaffold the world into which she grows but this relationship is much more than dyadic or limited to the home. My argument is that child-rearing practices are intensely culturally and contextually embedded "within an elusive, invisible network of assumptions and shared information," as Kelly (2007) puts it. Writing about childhood in Soviet Russia, she goes on to say "children's perceptions are shaped by adult direction in fundamental ways, particularly in the case of younger children: adults control the spaces that children may occupy and regulate the course of their daily routine, and children learn from adults how they ought to perceive the world" (p. 4).

Bruner (2000) makes a similar claim. He writes that "perhaps even more than with most cultural matters, child-rearing practices and beliefs reflect local conceptions of how the world is and how the child should be readied for living it" (p. xi). Bruner's quote comes from the preface of a witty and imaginative book co-edited by an anthropologist and a psychologist *"A World of Babies: Imagined Childcare for Seven Societies*. (DeLoache & Gottlieb, 2000) This offers a series of short childcare manuals of "best practice" in dealing with babies, as if each manual were written by a leading practitioner from a local community. The manuals come from communities as various as the Beng community in Cote d'Ivoire, West Africa; 17th Century Puritan America; Bali; rural Turkey; and Warlpiri aboriginal peoples. The book is compulsory reading on my courses. It would be difficult to find a better illustration of the particularity of cultural understandings and of the way in which cultural beliefs are inextricably threaded through childbearing and child-rearing.

DESCRIBING CULTURE

The concept of "culture" needs a word of caution. Culture describes a set of related beliefs and practices of a particular community. These beliefs and patterns are manifested in surface differences—diet, games, clothes, eating habits and folklore—but they also draw on implicit and embedded assumptions, the "elusive invisible network." Culture is usually thought of as belonging to a particular geographical space or country, but from a historical perspective, people are always on the move, and calamity always round the corner. Cultures are always porous, hybrid and shifting, and reflect the frequently forced interchanges of ideas and practices that take place over time.

Rapidly changing circumstances like the HIV/AIDs epidemic, or desertification and water sources drying up, and above all war and conflict, cause upheavals and shock people into thinking afresh about how they manage from day to day and how existing truths may no longer hold good for them. Many families in poor countries have migrant members and this gives rise to all kinds of cultural re/dislocations. For instance it is common for the entire active male population in some rural Latin American villages to migrate, temporarily or permanently, to the United States; or alternatively, many Filipino women of childbearing age migrate, and leave children behind, for whom they send remittances. Members of aboriginal or indigenous communities in Australia or Canada suffer continual cultural antagonism. The pressures of commercial globalization press down on the remotest families and communities, and even those who are outside the cash nexus are affected by it (Rosaldo & Xavier, 2002).

Children, above all, operate between borderlines or at the margins of conflictual cultural beliefs and practices, and must reconcile their several worlds. In rich countries cultural diversity is marginalized, and "culture" is frequently essentialized. "Other" people with rich and particular life histories are reduced to a few crude stereotypes. Refugee and migrant children who end up in rich countries must learn to tolerate, understand, and adapt to their new life, sometimes a very difficult undertaking when they are met with a hostile, indifferent or uncomprehending reception.

The process of cultural adaptivity for poor children from poor countries, whether moving to a new, rich country, or trying to live in changing circumstances in their own, has been partly documented, in autobiographical accounts as much as in the psychological or child development literature. Children may choose to reject their parents' past altogether, as many first generation migrant children do; or else enclose it and separate it entirely from their new experiences—as the writer Edward Said (1999) described in his autobiography, as he moved from Palestine to Egypt to the United States. But the kind of adaptations so many children in poor countries are required to make as they see illness and death all around them or as their families' livelihood crumples in front of them are profound.

Culture frames and pervades children's lives but culture is also almost always hybrid and impermanent; and at the margins and borderlands where so many children exist, children must make intense efforts of accommodation. The uniqueness of children's experiences and their adaptability as they come to terms with deep and often deleterious changes requires new research and new paradigms, using methods that give prominence to children's perspectives as they engage in challenging and demanding cultural journeys.

CONCEPTS OF CHILDHOOD

It is fairly well attested that conceptions of childhood vary across the world, although the rigidity or enduring nature or reach of these conceptions is open to question. So, for example, the African Charter on the Rights and Welfare of the Child (Organisation of African Unity, 1999) adopts in principle provision, protection and participation rights, but goes on to highlight "the preservation and strengthening of positive African morals, traditional values and attitudes" (Article 11—c) and "the promotion and achievements of African unity and solidarity" (Article 11- f).

What might these African morals and values and attitudes towards children encompass? I use some examples from Africa, but examples from other nations and continents would also indicate some profound differences in understandings and expectations of practices with young children. Very generally these include the prioritizing of collective obligations over personal concerns; rootedness in a particular community rather than within a nuclear family; independence within a community rather than dependency in an isolated family setting; spirituality; and issues of gender, patriarchy, and gerontocracy. These understandings are built into the very languages people speak.

These morals and values are, of course, much more complex, variable, renegotiated—and made unrecognizable by poverty, war, and colonialism—than this brief summary might suggest, but they are an indication of the very different possibilities which might exist.

Individual—Collective

The African guiding principle of *ubuntu* has been romanticized and sentimentalized, but it means something like togetherness, sharing, and mutual responsibility and reciprocity. Or as one writer has described it: "Your child is my child" (Swift, 2008). The dichotomy between individual and collective, the extent to which the self is seen as a separate bounded individual, or as gaining identity only from nests of relationships, is one of the classic insights of anthropology (Geertz, 1973). In many societies, people define themselves in terms of their relationships—as mother or father or brother or son or daughter or sister, or from a village or a community, but never as a unique and isolated individual making his or her own way in the world. Sharing is not something which must be painfully learned—as in so many pedagogic manuals—but something which is as natural and as human as talking and thinking. In early childhood guidance manuals it is frequent to come across the phrase "Every child should be treated as an individual." But a guidance manual following the principles of *ubuntu* might have as a starting point "every child should be treated as a member of the group."

Mapped on to the idea of collectivity is the notion of the inseparability of childhood from everyday life. Childhood is seen not as a special distinct period deserving of specialized adult behavior or physical resources, but as yet another aspect of the seamless richness and variety of everyday life. Perhaps the most vivid example that I can give is that of the West African filmmaker Abderrahmane Sissako whose extraordinary films "Waiting for Happiness" and "Bamako" give some idea of this fusion of family and community. Sissako says of his own childhood that in his family compound there were never less than 35 people. Children may differ from adults in many ways, but do not live separately from them in their own spaces with their own accoutrements.

Another related idea is the extent to which children are seen as contributors or non-contributors to the household. Small children have tasks to do, like everyone else. Serpell (1993) described how in his Zambian village, all children were trained to run errands from the moment they could toddle.

Children were expected to help—it was part of being a child! Paula Fass (2007) the American historian of childhood has argued that over time, one of the biggest shifts in the interpretation of childhood has been in the amount of time children are expected to work and contribute to the household, or play and be non-contributors to the household. In rich countries the notion of helpfulness and obligation is rarely seen as an integral part of childhood and child-rearing; and indeed there is a fraught debate around working children. As Fass remarks, some commentators consider it to be morally wrong to "exploit" children, whereas more nuanced approaches might value children's satisfaction and pride in being able to contribute to the economy of their household, however young, and whatever the arduous nature of their tasks.

Family—Community

As suggested above, life for many young children is intensely collective. Families are diffuse and fused into their local community. Wole Soyinka (2000), the Nobel Prize winning novelist, in his autobiography *Ake* describes his early childhood in Nigeria, and his experiences of compound life. He writes "Of all the women on whose backs I was carried, none was as comfortable as Mrs. B's"—a vignette of an utterly communal, although gendered life, where mothers and children were almost, but not quite, interchangeable. Many children slept with their mothers, sharing the bed and mattresses on the floor, some of them relatives, others children of friends or visitors who were staying for shorter or longer periods.

By contrast, childhood in rich countries takes place in small and isolated families. It is not uncommon for a mother to say she has never been separated from her child and has had a continuous responsibility for looking after him or her until nursery school offers some relief from the "burden" of parenting. Families are tiny, inward looking, and self-preoccupied; children themselves have become the individual possessions of their parents, a "lifestyle" choice. This particular dyadic and narrow model of parenting is continually re-echoed and re-emphasized in the services we provide and the way we write about them.

Independent—Dependent

These ideas of community, collectivity, and family, and the notion of the inseparability of the child from everyday life, produces an understanding of the child as physically and emotionally independent and robust, at least far more so than would be allowed in rich countries. Whereas the idea of attachment and the need for a continuous, sensitive caregiver is part of the understanding of infancy in rich countries, in African *ubuntu* the child is one amongst many; but a child of the community as well as of the family. This rather extraordinary quotation from the anthropologist Alma

Gottleib (2004) from the Beng community she studied, in the Cote d'Ivoire offers an example of such independence.

> Chantal, a feisty two year old in our compound disappeared from sight many mornings, only to emerge at noon for lunch and then around 5 pm for dinner preparations. Although she was too young to report on her day's travels, others would chronicle them for us; she regularly roved to the farthest ends of this very large village and even deep into the forest to join her older siblings and cousins working and playing in the fields. With such early independence even toddlers are expected to be alert to dangerous wildlife such as snakes and scorpions and they should be able to deal with them effectively—including locating and wielding a large machete. (p. 32)

What Chantal is doing is nearly inconceivable to childhood experts in rich countries, preoccupied as they are with physical risk and the need for protective environments (Greenman & Stonehouse, 1997). Despite her lack of language, at two years old Chantal is secure, autonomous, curious, and very capable. She has a sense of direction and a sense of time. She can use tools effectively. She and her parents are confident that if there is any kind of hazard she is sufficiently competent to deal with it, by recognizing and avoiding it or by calling upon others to help her.

Chantal however is not an exception in her community. Her behavior is more or less typical of the behavior of young children in the community to which she belongs. Gottleib (2004) goes on to say:

> Developmental psychologists have long posited that separation anxiety is a universal stage of infants from seven to twelve months of age. Beng infants occasionally exhibit this behavior at precisely the same age that their Western counterpoints do. But in Beng infants it is rare and actively disapproved of, perhaps because extended flexible caretaking environments for a given infant from day to day. Here the interaction of biological timetable and cultural practices appears delicate but critical. (p. 36)

THE WORLD OF SPIRITS

A pervasive theme of African folklore about the family is the spiritual world. Dead ancestors and animal spirits are part of the understanding of family life and community obligation. Children may inherit the spirit of departed relatives. This animist view, nature as continuous, rather than a belief in the distinctiveness and uniqueness of human life, sits alongside more traditional Christian or Muslim beliefs. This animism seems to represent the antithesis of modern scientific thought, although the contemporary ethicist and philosopher Pete Singer (2001) has also suggested that human life is over-valued as part of the spectrum of living things on earth.

GENDER, PATRIARCHY, AND GERONTOCRACY

These communal and collective households can also be rigidly patriarchal, hierarchical, and gerontocratic. Wisdom and knowledge come with age and experience, and elders of a society are usually respected—another reason for children's obedience. It would be unthinkable for a child to be rude to an older person. In addition, in many rural societies all new initiatives have to gain the approval of the local chieftain, who, whatever the national legislation also has a prerogative to adjudicate on tribal matters and exercise tribal law. Even in South Africa, the most modernized of African states, tribal law, and the patriarchy of chieftains, is endorsed by the State. Nelson Mandela, himself the son of a chieftain, described in his autobiography the sense of manhood he experienced as a young boy by virtue of having a father who was a wise leader. The obedience and honor due to the chieftain, and his role in achieving consensus as he settles disputes, are an essential part of African folklore.

Gender plays out in many different ways. Women in many places are seen as living a different life to men, and these differences are enshrined in language, in dress, in visible as well as invisible ways. "Equal opportunities" may be an improbable goal in many places, despite the insistence of international development agencies that it should become so.

LANGUAGE

The different understandings of childhood encapsulated in the notion of *ubuntu* are reflected in the very languages African people speak. For example terms of respect, deference, and gender are built into most African languages, and communication is meaningless without them. Similarly the expectations of solidarity are implicit in the language. Zulu for example has more tenses than English, which requires more subtlety in the interpretation of events; and it is more rhythmic and musical, more given to recitation and performance than to private and solitary reading.

Language structures thinking and communication. As Bloch (2007) comments, in most African countries young children are routinely multilingual, and their early learning is mainly aural. Those who come from oral traditions are acute listeners and children are routinely expected to be multilingual. Preschool and schooling experiences sometimes damage rather than enhance language learning by inappropriate methods, including a failure to appreciate the importance of oral learning, rhyme, chanting, and recitation.

Those with English as a first tongue tend to assume all second language learning is an effort. English has become the language of diplomacy, of commerce, and of academia, so English speakers are unconvinced of the necessity of learning other languages. But for non-English speakers, language learning is not necessarily a burden but a pleasure. As my grandson, who speaks an oral African language, as well as English, puts it: "Everybody wants to learn more languages. They love learning languages, basically the languages that come in handy." Or as the South American saying has it "monolingualism is curable."

IMPLICATIONS FOR PRACTICE

These differences in understanding how daily life is conducted result in different kinds of cognitive skills being valued in practice with young children. In an ethnographic study of practice in childcare centers in Kwa Zulu Natal in South Africa, Aubrey and Dahl (2008) demonstrated that within a childcare context, active participatory approaches, exploration and questioning were valued far less than listening, observing, and deductive processes. On the other hand singing, dance and music, and grasp of the principles of harmony and polyrhythms; and playing with language—knowing and recounting stories, sayings and riddles and adeptness in learning a multiplicity of languages in a natural setting were everyday practices.

Pedagogies and programs for young children in rich countries take active, self-directed learning as axiomatic, although this view is probably more preached than practiced. But other societies view learning itself as a rather different process. In many communities children are expected to be docile, rather than assertive, and consensual rather than adversarial in their relationships with adults. This doesn't mean that children are broken spirited. Far from it. They may be lively, mischievous, and enquiring, like Chantal whose example is quoted above; they may be strategic or subversive (Punch, 2001) but they are also expected to show respect to their elders. Tobin, Wu and Davidson (1989) in a classic study, compared children in nurseries in the United States, China, and Japan. The clips of the video show children in the U.S. nursery continuously refusing and challenging the decisions of the childcare worker: "Why must I put this away now?" and so on. Tobin et al. drily remark that the U.S. pedagogy seems like nothing so much as training in litigation!

Conversely the concept of "respect" in African childhood may also be problematic to Euro-American educators. Respectful children are not assertive or demanding. The question of how adults balance encouragement, explanation, reward, discouragement, and chastisement relates directly to the model of childhood they are striving to reproduce. Young children in many societies are routinely beaten. Wole Soyinke (2000) mentioned previously had, by his own account, a good childhood, full of interest and exploits, surrounded and encouraged by caring people, yet he also described his mother and father as "slap-happy." Colonialism and slavery reinforced the use of physical force as a means of control; for many years it was the norm for adults, let alone for children. It was also part of the puritan Christian tradition to "spare the rod and spoil the child." As configurations of childhood changed, and children became recipients of rather than contributors to the well-being and goodwill of their families and communities, so physical punishment has become more abhorrent in rich countries. In rich countries physical chastisement now is unacceptable. But within the context of respect for elders and community norms of behavior in many poor countries, children are more likely to be "good," but if they are not it is a more serious breach, and more liable to be punished.

IMPLICATIONS FOR PROVISION

There has been a global explosion of early education and care. Although the statistical information is often inaccurate, it is clear that in all cities all over the world, as women enter the workforce, childcare arrangements have mushroomed (UNESCO, 2007). Townships or favelas (slums) are usually unhealthy and unsafe places for children and accident rates are high when children are left alone, so the pressure to create some kind of provision is intense (Heymann, 2002). Mothers, often migrants from the countryside, work long hours in the market as hawkers or as domestic servants in the struggle to survive. The little private nurseries that have grown up to service demand can be rough places. I have seen many instances of silent rows of very young children crammed into dark shacks with very little to do. Their situation is part of a larger problem of inequality, which politicians and international donors are reluctant to address (Penn 2008). Advice, advocacy, and resources are sorely needed. But on the whole, where advice and advocacy exists, it is as a grossly impoverished version of the practice and pedagogies of early childhood in rich countries.

There has been a slew of recent international documents advocating various kinds of early years provision in poor countries (CRC, 2005; Grantham-McGregor et al., 2007; UNESCO, 2007; WHO, 2005) mostly dominated by evidence and rationales drawn from North America. The following example comes from a World Bank document, written by a consortium of early childhood international non-governmental organizations.

> Not only is the physiological basis for good health laid during these early years but the essential values that have such high pay-offs in competitive labor markets are transmitted from parents to children. These transfers include such critical assets as self-esteem, a work ethic and a sense of discipline, awareness of family traditions and of the community to which one belongs, a vision of opportunity and a thirst for knowledge. (Evans et al., 2000, foreword)

These documents have tended to be universalistic in approach, making generalizations which cover all societies, drawing heavily on positivistic health, and economic and psychological literature and ignoring anthropological, historical sociological or literary sources. The United Nations Children's Fund (UNICEF) is a particular culprit. Its support for early childhood in poor countries frequently produces advice and guidelines that are hand-me-downs from the United States. For example, the recent child-care registration guidelines drawn up by UNICEF for use in South Africa barely acknowledge the particular contexts in which they are applied. The idea of childhood as a construction rather than as a scientific fact is rarely voiced. The Education for All Global Monitoring Report (UNESCO, 2007) rehashes the advocacy arguments for early childhood development programs in poor countries, again drawn principally from the North American literature. The underpinning assumption is that the development of children is intrinsically tied up with the development of liberal market economies (Burman, 2007). Children who experience developmentally appropriate practice will become more competitive and successful individuals, better able to contribute to the future economy of their countries.

This material also assumes that the intellectual traffic is one way. Rich countries have more experience and more knowledge, more "facts" about child-rearing to impart. Poor countries need to learn more and do more about implementing these practices. The alternative views of childhood they may hold are an irrelevance. This is ironic since North American child care is not good by the standards of rich countries (OECD, 2006); and conversely, as Aubrey and Dahl (2008) have shown, in very impoverished environments, practice can nevertheless be cognitively demanding for children.

There have been attempts to develop ideas about local traditions or indigenous materials. I have written elsewhere about programs in Zimbabwe and Mongolia which have tried to do this (Penn, 2001, Penn and Demberal, 2006) but the need for close attention to and in depth understanding of local languages, contexts and cultures are not reflected in the discourses about developmentally appropriate practice put forward by most international agencies.

FIRST RIGHTS?

The participatory rights and entitlements of children are awkwardly encompassed or ignored altogether, especially in the health literature. For instance in the Grantham-McGregor Lancet series (Grantham-McGregor et al., 2006) and the World Health Organization documents (WHO, 2005) treat young children as objects for interventions, as variables to be manipulated.

When a colleague and I raised the question of children's rights on a recent study tour in South Africa, we were told over and over again that the basic rights for children were the rights of a decent existence—shelter, food security, clean water, sanitation, electricity, education. Only once those rights had been achieved—and for most of the world's children they are still a long way off—would it be possible to think about psychological or individual rights.

The 2005 update of the Convention of the Rights of the Child (CRC) does specifically address the participatory rights of very young children, and tries to contextualize them, although the dominant view is still an individualistic one, predicated on life in rich societies.

The CRC (2005) document is important because while it still draws primarily from North American sources, and underestimates the problematic nature of working cross-culturally, it also offers some understanding of alternative approaches. But, in general, the view of early childhood from rich countries is so powerful, and so pervasive that it shapes the literature of donor agencies and international bodies. The socio-cultural and anthropological approaches which contextualize *particular* childhoods are rarely discussed, and the struggle for basic survival is not reflected.

CONCLUSION

This chapter has offered a very general introduction to the idea of international perspectives, "international" meaning in this case, differences between rich countries and poor countries. Most of my examples have been drawn from Africa, since, as a grandmother of African children, this is the situation with which I am most familiar. If I were to draw on experiences of young children in ex-Soviet countries or in South Asia or Latin America then the examples would be very different, but the challenges would be similar; we would be looking at what seems to us alien practices and pedagogies. To say this does not cast aspersions on either side; it is to note that universal prescriptions are untenable and the range of possibilities is great.

Any notion of "best practice" in early childhood programs is inherently contextual. Ideas and practices in other parts of the world may be deeply inimical to the way in which childhood is understood in rich countries. Some of the ideas may be simply irreconcilable. As Cowan, Dember, and Wilson (2001) have argued, the discourses of participatory rights have to take account of subtleties and irrevocabilities of context. It must be even more necessary for the intimacies of child-rearing. What are the ground rules when practice and understandings are so different?

NOTE

1. The terminology and distinctions between developed countries (industrialized/first world/minority world/North/Euro-American) and developing countries (less industrialized/third world/majority world/South/non-European) shift continuously as these relationships are redefined. In this chapter I use the categorization "rich countries" and "poor countries" while recognizing that there are poor people in rich countries and rich people in poor countries. In general, inequality is increasing, and the poor are getting poorer, and the rich, richer, whether within or across countries. Despite being a very

broad generalization "rich countries" and "poor countries" offers a work-able framework to explain a wide range of differences and circumstances.

REFERENCES

Aubrey, C., & Dahl, S. (2008, January). *Mapping knowledge transfer in early child-hood education and care in South Africa.* Paper given at the EARLI Advanced Study Colloquium, Stellenbosch University, South Africa.

Bloch, C. (2007) Foreign language learning in South Africa early childhood edu-cation. In M. Cochran & R. S. New (Eds.), *Early childhood education: An international encyclopaedia, Volume 4* (pp. 1224–1226). Westport, CT: Green-wood.

Bruner, J. (2000). *Foreword.* In J. DeLoache & A. Gottlieb (Eds.), *A world of babies: Imagined childcare guides for seven societies.* Cambridge, MA: Cam-bridge University Press.

Burman, E. (2007). *Deconstructing developmental psychology (2nd ed.).* London: Routledge.

Convention on the Rights of the Child (CRC) (2005). *Implementing child rights in early childhood.* General Comment No 7. New York: United Nations.

Cowan, J., Dember, M. B., & Wilson, R. (Eds.) (2001). *Culture and rights: Anthro-pological perspectives.* Cambridge, MA: Cambridge University Press

DeLoache, J., & Gottlieb, A. (Eds.) (2000). *A world of babies: Imagined childcare guides for seven societies.* Cambridge, MA: Cambridge University Press.

Ebrahim, H., & Penn, H. (2008, in press). Young children's experiences of adver-sity: A cross-cultural perspective. *Children and Society.*

Evans, J., with Myers, R., & Ilfeld, E. (2000). *Early childhood counts: A program-ming guide on early childhood care for development.* Washington, D.C: World Bank Institute.

Fass, P. (2007). *Children of a new world: Society, culture and globalization.* New York: New York University Press.

Geertz, C. (1973). *The interpretation of cultures.* London: Fontana.

Gordon, D., Nandy, S., Pantazis, C., Pemberton, S., & Townsend, P. (2003) *Child poverty in the developing world.* Bristol, UK: Policy Press.

Gottlieb, A. (2004). *The afterlife is where we come from: The culture of infancy in West Africa.* Chicago: University of Chicago Press.

Grantham-McGregor, S., Cheung, B., Glewwe, P., Richter, L., Strupp, B. & the Inter-national Child Development Steering Group. (2007, January 6). Developmental potential in the first 5 years for children in developing countries. *The Lancet.* 369.

Greenman, J., & Stonehouse, A. (1997). *Prime times: A handbook for excellence in infant and toddler programs.* Sydney: Longman.

Heymann, J. (2002) *Social transformations and their implications for global demand for ECCE.* Policy Brief in Early Childhood, No. 8. Paris. UNESCO.

Kelly, C. (2007). *Children's world: Growing up in Russia 1890–1991.* New Haven, CT: Yale University Press.

Levine, R., Dixon, S., Levine, S., Richman, A., Leiderman, P., Keefer, C. & Brazle-ton, T. (1994). *Childcare and culture: Lessons from Africa.* Cambridge, MA: Cambridge University Press.

Muthukrishna, N., Ebrahim, H., & Mbatha, T. (2008, in press). Doing childhood in the context of HIV and AIDS: Young children in early schooling speak. *Jour-nal of African Psychology.*

Organization of African Unity (1999). African charter on the welfare and rights of the child. Accessed March 20, 2008, from www.africa-union.org.

Organization for Economic Development (OECD) (2006). *Starting strong II: Early childhood education and care 20 nation review*. Paris. OECD.

Penn, H. (2001). *Research in the majority world: The example of Zimbabwe*. In T. David (Ed.), *Handbook of research in early childhood (pp. 289–308). Elsevier Science*.

———. (2008, in press). Working on the impossible: Early childhood policies in Namibia. *Childhood*. V15 (3).

Penn, H., & Demberel (2006). *Nomadic Education in Mongolia*. In C. Dyer & S. Kratli (Eds.), *The education of nomadic peoples: Issues, provision and prospects (*pp. 213–211). Oxford, UK: Berghahn Books.

Punch, S. (2001). Negotiating autonomy: Childhoods in rural Bolivia. In L. Alanen & B. Mayall (Eds.), *Conceptualizing adult-child relationships* (pp. 23–36). London: Routledge.

Rosaldo, R., & Xavier, J. (Eds.) (2002). *The anthropology of globalization: A reader*. London: Blackwell.

Said, E. (1999). *Out of place*. London: Granta.

Serpell, R. (1993). *The significance of schooling: Life journeys in an African society*. Cambridge, MA: Cambridge University Press.

Singer, P. (2001). *Unsanctifying human life: Essays on ethics*. Oxford: Blackwell.

Soyinke, W. (2000). *Ake: The years of childhood*. London: Methuen.

Swift, A. (2008, in press). *My child is your child*. The Hague, Netherlands: Bernard van Leer Foundation.

Tobin, J., Wu, D., & Davidson, D. (1989) *Preschool in three cultures: Japan, China and the United States*. New Haven, CT: Yale University Press.

Tobin, J. (1995). Post-structural research in early childhood education. In A. Hatch (Ed.), *Qualitative research in early childhood settings* (pp. 223–43). Westport, CT: Praeger.

United Nations Educational and Scientific and Cultural Organisation (UNESCO) (2007) *Education for all global monitoring report: Strong Foundations*. Paris. UNESCO.

Viruru, R. (2001). *Early childhood education: Postcolonial perspectives from India*. London: Sage.

World Health Organization (WHO) (2005). *Knowledge network for early childhood development. Analytic and strategic review paper: International perspectives on early childhood development*. Geneva: Author.

3 The Guiding Principles of Participation

Infant, Toddler Groups and the United Nations Convention on the Rights of the Child

Berenice Nyland

> To say that education is a social function, securing direction and development in the immature through their participation in the life of the group which they belong, is to say in effect that education will vary with the quality of life which prevails in a group. (Dewey, 1944, p. 81)

The above quote by Dewey, from his book *Democracy and Education*, describes his view of the formation of the mind which he saw as a social process. Like Vygotsky (1978) Dewey considered that individual development was dependent on social relations and cultural context, while at the same time society gained meaning through its members. However, subjective experience was extremely important and had the potential to change the society. Education can therefore be seen as social participation and provides experiences based on the culture of the group and for infants their participation would be predicated on social images of infancy. Recent emphases on rights for the very young (Ize-Charrin, 2006) and participatory learning (Berthelsen & Brownlee, 2006) have the potential to increase our understanding of children as protagonists in their own development and to promote group care settings that respect and implement participation and reciprocity within practices and relationships.

This chapter gives an overview of participatory practices and discusses the general principles of participation using the United Nations Convention on the Rights of the Child (UNCRoC) as a frame. As a rights paradigm gains more currency in early childhood literature (Woodhead, 2006) it becomes a powerful tool especially when combined with a theoretical approach like socioculturalism (Smith, 2007) that emphasizes the diverse social and cultural worlds that children encounter. The chapter explores infant, toddler daily experiences, especially in relation to the Articles 12 and 13 of the UNCRoC. These are two of the six participation articles and are applicable in the everyday. When the UNCRoC was developed the participation element of the convention was considered to be representative of a new way of seeing young children. Previous approaches to rights had very much concentrated on children's needs; for example, the right to shelter, clothing, education, and a family. This needy child is gradually being replaced in the early childhood literature with the child that has agency; is an active player in learning and re-creating culture; and has enormous communicative competence to make this possible. The very idea that infants and toddlers have participation rights like "the right to have one's opinion taken into account" (UNCRoC, article 12) is a new proposition to many people and presents a more positive social image of very young children and this image has the potential to influence early childhood theory and practice. As more and more infants and toddlers are now in out-of-home environments for many hours per week the importance of voice becomes crucial to the idea of children growing and developing within the context of reciprocal relationships with more able members of their culture.

The chapter discusses differing theories and views of participation, how present theoretical debates impact upon the view of children as protagonists in their own development and the importance of situating a rights discussion in the context of everyday events and environments.

PREVAILING THEORIES OF CHILDREN'S DEVELOPMENT AND ISSUES OF PARTICIPATION

This section of the chapter examines a number of perspectives that can be used as a lens for viewing children's development and identifying different social and cultural images of the young child. Woodhead (2006) has identified four images of the very young child that are relevant to this discussion. His four perspectives are: a developmental viewpoint; a human capital model; a sociocultural perspective; and a human rights approach. The first three perspectives are extremely influential in countries like Australia and New Zealand and have had an impact on policy and therefore provision and practice.

It is worth noting that early childhood theory and practice has traditionally been eclectic in its approach. This eclecticism has created contradictions and difficulties in identifying and articulating differences in theory and practice. More recently the tensions between different theoretical approaches, as identified by Woodhead (2006), have led to strong rhetorical debates and the use of different labels to describe the same practices. For example, across developmental and sociocultural theoretical perspectives language is often used interchangeably although the theoretical underpinnings differ in significant ways (Brennan, 2007). Both of these theoretical perspectives have the potential for understanding differing levels of reciprocity in relationships between competent members of a culture (adults) and novices (very young children). Reciprocal relationships, in turn, determine the level of participation. However, the human rights perspective is not one that has generally been applied to understanding practice with infants and toddlers (Woodhead, 2006). It has not usually been researched at the level of interactions between individual children and other members of the culture (Nyland, 1999, 2004), although earlier work on children and power relations (Leavitt, 1994; Stephenson, 1999) provide a foundation for such an approach.

Woodhead's (2006) four perspectives can be used to analyze and understand differing styles and levels of participation and the quality of the environments, both physical and social, for young children. Except for the rights framework, these perspectives have been debated in early childhood education and care since the 1980s (Bredekamp, 1987; Wangmann, 1995; Dahlberg, Moss & Pence, 1999; Nyland 2006). For the purposes of this chapter, the developmental approach is represented by the theories of Piaget (1976), the human capital model is reflected in the work of economists like Heckman (Heckman & Masterov, 2007) and also the behavioral developmental approach represented by ideas presented by McCain and Mustard (1999). The sociocultural perspective can be represented by a Vygotskian view (Bruner, 1986; Rogoff, 2003), as well as through ideas from the new sociology of childhood (James, Jenks & Prout, 1998; Dahlberg et al., 1999). Smith (2007) has suggested that a rights approach combined with sociocultural theory provides a powerful image of the child. What must be emphasized is that these discussions are complex and contributions of the different disciplines (e.g., psychology, sociology, economics, and the neurosciences) to the debates about childhood need to be acknowledged.

The sequence of the discussion in this chapter has been organized to discuss the developmental approach, socioculturalism and the new sociology of childhood and the potential of these approaches for understanding participatory learning. While human capital theory with its basis in developmentalism and neo-liberal economics belongs to a different set of theories about human growth and well-being and is therefore commented upon separately. Ideas about participatory learning within a human rights approach are developed and extended in a later section of the chapter.

In the United States in the 1980s, a quality assurance model for early childhood services was developed based on the theories of Piaget and Erikson (Bredekamp, 1987). At the same time, the new sociology of childhood scholars were challenging assumptions of developmental psychology and the universal image of human growth it presented (James et al., 1998). Piaget's (1976) contribution to education was through his ideas on epistemology and children's development of knowledge and understanding. By understanding the stages in the growth of knowledge of the developing child, early childhood educators were able to organize their practices around a developmental framework. Piaget's ideas have been criticized for paying insufficient attention to culture as a developmental context (Edwards, 2003). His emphasis was on how the individual child constructed knowledge. Piaget's theory was a grand theory that applied to all people and cultures. Piaget did acknowledge that the child was embedded in a culture and through actions, such as learning language, the construction of meaning was made possible. Through such experience, children encounter the values and customs of their culture. Piaget also argued for creativity in the sense of novel construction, or reconstruction, of knowledge as the child discovers new meanings within actions. He supported ideas about the value of children playing in groups and, at the same time, the importance of the child as an autonomous learner. Piaget's approach was considered child-centered. He saw children as active learners from birth who would construct theories about the world when intrinsically motivated to pursue their individual interests. He considered children's thinking was qualitatively different from adults.

In contrast to developmental ideas, as represented by Piagetian theory, the new sociology of childhood (James et al., 1998; Corsaro, 1997) was concerned with issues of children's agency, competence, and participation. Children were viewed as social actors, possessing a competent voice and often suffering disenfranchisement. The concept of children as human beings in the present, instead of adults in waiting, as well as the idea that there is such a thing as children's culture, is central to this perspective on childhood. This viewpoint has had a strong influence on research that takes account of the voices of children and, as a result, research methods that use children's narratives have been widely adopted. This reflects a vision of the agentive child as well as a position that there needs to be valid ways of giving children a participatory voice in the early childhood research process (Soto & Swadener, 2005). This is a position that also finds alignment with a rights perspective on early education and care as the issues of voice and participation rights are integral to a rights approach.

From Vygotsky (1978) came an analysis of the social origins of cognitive processes. Central to Vygotsky's theories are concepts about the development of higher mental functions and the use of symbols. To understand the development of higher mental functions, such as logical memory, selective attention, decision-making and language development, Vygotsky placed an emphasis on the sociocultural, historical, political, and contextual aspects of children's lives. In other words a child will acquire language by nature of being human but the language itself and the use of language is socially mediated through the culture. Bruner (1986) refers to this as the second signal system and says this view of language stands "for nature transformed by history and culture" (p. 71). Vygotsky's ideas of language were similar to those of Dewey (see Mesthene, 1959). Vygotsky and Dewey considered language to be a tool that made possible categorization of experiences and therefore a way of interpreting the culture and developing a world view. There is a resonance of Piaget here who considered that activity, which became language, could in turn become action and be potentially transformative.

The notion of scaffolding also stemmed from Vygotskian ideas and emerged from studies of interactions that examined the exchange and sharing of meanings in a context of reciprocity and co-construction of knowledge (Wood, Bruner & Ross, 1976). Rogoff (2003) also has researched human activity across groups and queried observational interpretations that rely on the researchers' own values and cultural framework. She extended Vygotsky's views of context and social relationships by introducing the concept of guided participation which seeks to explain how children learn the skills of their culture. This perspective includes the idea that developmental goals are context and culture specific, although also open to adaptation when necessary. Others have examined daily experience using the developmental niche as a frame (Valsiner, 1987; Super & Harkness, 1986). The developmental niche refers to the cultural context of development (Cole, 1996) and places the child in a complex set of relationships, both social and physical. This model is built on the caregiver's own early childhood experiences, the image the caregiver holds for this child in the future and the caregiver's own differentiated awareness of the world (Dahlberg et al., 1999; Cole, 1996). In relation to language development and the niche, Cole (1996) says:

> Culturally organized joint activity incorporates the child into the scene as a novice participant is one necessary ingredient in language acquisition. As children in such activities struggle to understand objects and social relations in order to gain control over the environment and themselves they re-create the culture into which they have been born, even as they reinvent the language of their forebears. (p. 206)

Each of the approaches discussed have made contributions to the study and understandings of children and their worlds. Piaget has been most heavily criticized but it is, at least, partially, from Piaget that the notion of infants and toddlers as subjects of study in their own right came from which, in turn, has led to present discussions about children's competence.

The least participatory of the perspectives that were offered by Woodhead (2006) is that of human capital theory (Heckman & Masterov, 2007; Lucas, 2006) which Woodhead has categorized as economic and political. Like Woodhead, I feel it is essential to include this perspective as it has become very influential with policy makers in countries like the United Kingdom, Australia, Canada, and the United States. The action emphasized in many political and economic models is one of targeted intervention, for example, in services for children and families that emphasize efficiency and returns for investment. One rationale for targeted interventions is that such activities have the potential to alleviate some of the inequities created by disadvantage. It is widely accepted that the poorest, and those most at risk, with the least resources, gain most when presented with quality early childhood programs and this is reiterated through the longitudinal findings from the High/Scope Perry Preschool project (e.g., Parks, 2000). This assumption of the advantages of targeting those at risk has, however, been challenged (Deacon, 2005; Mkandawire, 2005). Critics claim interventionism is a deficit model based on identification of risk factors that attempts a 'cure' through the introduction of designed activities intended to improve measurable outcomes, like later academic performance at school. The issue of targeted intervention was taken up in the review of Sure Start (Sure Start, 2005) which argued for the importance of "delivering services for children and families on a *universal basis*" (p. 131). Early intervention programs, for example, the Perry Preschool study (Parks, 2000) or, more recently, Sure Start (Wilce, 2008) were traditionally presented as part of the social justice project but increasingly have been described in economic terms of developing human capital for the future (Heckman & Masterov, 2007). This is an instrumental view of the child that has been criticized by Penn (2002) as leading to the practice of supporting 'scientific' targeted interventions that fail to address structural disadvantage.

The fourth perspective on early childhood, identified by Woodhead (2006), is the concept of rights and, in this chapter, is combined with a sociocultural view (Smith, 2007) as ideas about children's rights are explored in relation to children's competence within the everyday contexts of their lives. Children already have the capability of communicating and are keen observers and listeners with their own desires and opinions. The responsibility of utilizing this capacity to develop reciprocal relationships belongs to more experienced members of the culture. How is this responsibility honored? One approach is to emphasize the influence of power relations within the care and education process. If these relationships are confronted then educational institutions can play an emancipatory and transformative role. Moss, Clark, and Kjorholt (2005) take up these ideas and explore them as a pedagogy of listening. A pedagogy relevant to both sociocultural theory and a rights approach as it has the potential to develop strategies, attitudes, and habits in order to provide spaces where all have a voice.

POTENTIAL OF A RIGHTS APPROACH: UNCROC AND PARTICIPATION RIGHTS

The United Nations Convention on the Rights of the Child was developed over a ten year period starting in 1979, which was the International Year of the Child. The UNCRoC is a valuable international instrument in that it has been ratified by all countries, except Somalia and the United States, and therefore represents a relatively global political consensus on views about children. Because the convention is based on political consensus this makes its universal nature a strength and invites discussions about differing approaches to early childhood. The theoretical perspective least in sympathy with a human rights approach is the human capital approach with its targeted interventions promoted by the economists (e.g., Heckman & Masterov, 2007) Such targeted policies have seen a change in attitudes towards social rights and responsibilities and we now witness the increasing involvement of the private and corporate sector in more and more facets of children's and families' lives. The universalism of a human rights approach can be more easily equated with ideals of citizenship, equality (Mkandawire, 2005), and the agentive child who is a capable member of the culture.

UNCRoC has 54 articles, 41 are concerned with rights and Articles 42 to 54 are to do with "implementation and entry into force" (Greenwood, 1993, p. 10). This means that Articles 42 to 54 are not articles of rights but articles to do with the implementation of the Convention. For example, article 42 states:

> States Parties undertake to make the principles and provisions of the Convention widely known, by appropriate and active means, to adults and children alike. (UNCRoC, DCI, 1995, p.20)

The first 41 articles have been divided into categories called the four Ps. The four Ps are: provision of rights, protection of rights, participation rights, and promotion of rights. Participation rights are a reminder that even the youngest of our culture are competent and the subject of rights. Participation is perhaps the most innovative part of the Convention as it is within these freedoms that the child's right to be heard and have a point of view is enshrined. The rights that have been categorized as participation rights are 12, 13, 14, 15, 16, and 17. These are: the right to have one's opinion taken into account, freedom of expression, freedom of thought, conscience and religion, freedom of association, protection of privacy, and access to appropriate information. The practical focus of this chapter is infant/toddler groups; discussion about participation and participation rights will now focus upon young children in child care centers.

PARTICIPATORY RIGHTS AND PROBLEMS OF RECOGNITION IN THE EVERYDAY CHILD CARE CONTEXT

For early childhood policy makers, researchers, trainers, providers and practitioners it is in within the area of participation that children's rights in everyday interactions can be most easily ignored. In child care, there is research evidence to suggest there is a lack of everyday individual interactions in the experiences of many children (e.g., Smith, 1999). There are also questions about the quality of interactions that take place in child care. In early childhood group settings, many interactions are based around routines. Children have little freedom during the day but are constantly organized through daily schedules. The quality of interactions within routines and the ability of children to express an opinion are dependent on how group interactions are arranged. How UNCRoC Article 12 (have one's opinion taken into account) and Article 13 (freedom of expression) are respected in everyday practice will vary, depending on the age of the child, the philosophical beliefs about children and childhood held by the practitioners, and the constraints within the physical, social, and regulatory environment. Children may have no choice (voice) about their basic daily experiences, as whether to play inside or outside, when they will have snacks or meals, what they will eat, when they will rest, or whether they will sit in a group for songs and stories. How these considerations are taken into account in daily practices with children will impact on, how we, as practitioners, work with children.

Articles 12 and 13 challenge practitioners to ask: Can infants and toddlers have opinions about everyday experiences? How do we listen to them? The following observations are examples of daily experience from child care settings. In each observation preverbal children are expressing an opinion about their present circumstances and, in each case, they fail to have their voices heard. Two of the observations are drawn from the published early childhood literature. The national context for the first observation is New Zealand and the second observation is from North America, while a third is taken from my own research in Australia.

OBSERVATION 1

A study in New Zealand (Stephenson, 1999) that explored the interrelationship between inside and outside environments for toddlers found the play of a group of one-year-old children interesting. These very young children displayed a much stronger motivation to be outside than the researcher had expected. Stephenson observed young children and noted how they made their preferences clear. She wrote of Leo who, at fourteen months, expressed his desire to go outside by shouting, pulling on his gumboots, positioning himself by the door of the center, watching the outdoors, finding a woolly hat and trying to slip out when an adult opened the door. Leo had an opinion of where he wanted to be and had given at least six clear messages to the adults present of his preference for the outdoors. On this occasion staff had decided it was still too cold for the younger children to be outside.

Comment

Leo could not go outside initially as it was a very cold morning. Staff were concerned about the children's health and well-being. This was a center that tried to give access to inside and outside as much as practicable. Staff did not constrain the children when they were outdoors and Stephenson (1999) observed how the outdoors was "a particularly empowering environment" (p. 12) for the group of one-year-olds she was observing. Staff therefore expressed the opinion that they were acting in the best interests of the child (Article 3) and considered the cold weather to be a health risk. This was a protective voice and very difficult to argue against. Can the decision be questioned? Is Leo being seen in the light of the child of development theory who has needs and needs must take precedence over desires? There is also the issue of how cultural is our attitude to nature and cold weather? Staff and parents in the Forest Schools of Norway (Borge, Nordhagen & Lie, 2003) might have considered Leo's desires in a different light.

OBSERVATION 2

In a research study from the United States, Leavitt (1995) explored the emotional culture of infant/toddler child care. She used composites of observations to provide a portrait of familiar situations she had seen over the years.

> Kara (4 months) was crying. She lifted her arms up to me, her eyes brimming with tears. As I reached down to her, the caregiver said to me, "Don't pick her up. She does that to everyone at first. We don't need to spoil her." Kara continued to cry. I hugged her briefly and then tried to interest her in a toy. She continued to cry. The caregivers ignored her (Leavitt, 1995, p.12).

Comment

For Kara there are different considerations in relation to Leo's predicament. In Leo's case there was a benevolent protective action on the part of the staff. For Kara there are social constraints in the image of young children that is held by the caregivers. Ideas of responding to infants, the notion that holding a child can lead to "spoiling" are very much culturally constructed and practiced in western child care centers is still influenced by concepts about spoiling. Leavitt (1995) included the observation of Kara in her writing as a composite of a situation she had seen many times. This is often reflected in the practitioner literature. In a recent article Balaban (2006) comments:

> If attachment is misunderstood as dependence, it may be wrongly discouraged. I saw an example of this recently. A director admonished a teacher for holding a two year old on her lap several times during the morning because "you are spoiling and babying the child" (pp. 1–2).

Beliefs about spoiling are strong in some cultures and raise the issue of what knowledge is most relied upon by staff when they make intuitive decisions. Beliefs about the importance of touch and the significance of positive interactions are highlighted in the early childhood literature. Vygoyskian theory emphasized the importance of relationships and reciprocity within relationships. This begs the question as to where the director in Balaban's observation derives her knowledge for practice.

Balaban (2006) identifies the importance of cultural context when observing children in group settings, as they separate from parents. She cites a number of small research studies that have attempted to identify differences in thinking and beliefs of parents about their children and separation. Data was collected from a number of different ethnic groups in America including Anglo-Celtic, Korean, and Puerto Rican mothers. Differences in expectations of child reactions to the separation situation were identified across the groups with the Anglo-Celtic group being least sympathetic to what was labeled "clinginess" (2006, p. 6). In a book on parent's cultural belief systems that explored parental values, beliefs, perceptions of infants and toddlers, Harkness and Super (1996) identified the relationship between culture and ingrained thinking. Such thinking was influential on the beliefs expressed by the caregiver in the observation of Kara and the beliefs of the director observed by Balaban.

OBSERVATION 3

In my own research in Australia I have observed children in child care centers and recorded their joint attentional experiences on video and transcribed these as communicative acts in order to try to interpret the child's view of their experiences. In one study, two children were observed over a period of eighteen months and, in both cases, joint attention was minimal, even though both children were effective meaning makers, capable of expressing desires and displeasure. The following is an example observation of a familiar incident in an Australian child care center. The observation involves an infant in a high chair watching while older and more active toddlers are attended to. This is a commonplace situation that has been identified in other research. During a study of quality in a number of child care centers, Ebbeck and Winter (2003) used the category "waiting" to describe babies left in high chairs which they found was a common occurrence.

Angela is fourteen months old and is sitting in a high chair. She has a lidded cup in front of her. There are two empty high chairs next to her and then another high chair with a baby in it. The room is noisy and there are two tables with eight toddlers having morning tea. Two caregivers move around the room serving the children and assisting them. Angela leans towards the video camera and smiles. She leans twice and then vocalizes. She redirects her gaze towards the caregivers, looks back at the camera and points to the person holding the camera. She repeats the pointing gesture emphatically a number of times and then leans back in her chair and squirms. She has a look of displeasure on her face now. Angela tries to undo the buckle of the high chair strap and then tries to pull the strap down over her shoulder. She leans towards the photographer, holding out her arms. Angela puts the index and middle finger of her right hand in her mouth and looks across the room to the tables and the toddlers. She does this for almost a full minute. She then turns back to the photographer, smiles, points to the other baby and says "Bubba." The toddlers are now leaving the room and as Angela observes this departure she point outside and vocalizes. She arches herself in her chair and then sits back. A caregiver comes over and asks, "Are you finished?" and then wipes Angela's face before she has time to respond to the question. Angela is lifted to the ground and follows the other children outside.

Comment

In this third example of everyday experience, Angela has been placed in a high chair and is actively expressing a desire to be lifted out. She uses vocalization, facial expression, smiling, eye contact, body movement, gestures, and pointing to no avail. When the adult does approach Angela she has her face cleaned and is placed on the floor with no recognition that she has a point of view. In this case, there were structural restraints as the adults in the room were attending to the larger, highly mobile group of older toddlers. The decision to leave Angela and "bubba" in the chairs was probably one of necessity. However, one change that could have been made would have been a verbal acknowledgement that she had expressed a wish to get out of the high chair and she had waited. Without such an acknowledgement she can be seen as lacking the power to be heard within this context. As young children are experiencing and interpreting cultural practices such experiences potentially can have an intergenerational effect.

DISCUSSION

In the three observations presented young children actively voiced desires and preferences. What each wanted was neither harmful nor unusual and yet the children made themselves heard but were not able to achieve their aims. On each occasion staff had made a decision not to listen. What were the factors leading to the children's lack of success in gaining: 1) access to the outdoors; 2) a cuddle; and 3) removal from the high chair? Some of the factors were probably to do with the structural nature of child care as an institution and staff actions were presumably heavily influenced by child/ staff ratios and the routines and schedules of daily life within the centers and cultural beliefs about children. These were three situations where staff were well-meaning but were acting within the structural constraints of child care that impacted on decisions about child choice, and what Valsiner calls the "Zone of Free Movement" (Valsiner, 1987, 97), as well as process constraints that involve the caregiver's theories of childhood and cultural constructs about child competence (Super & Harkness, 1986).

If a rights approach is to be embraced in formal early childhood settings then there is an identified need for early childhood policy-makers, practitioners, and researchers to understand the content and spirit of the concept of children's rights as part of their advocacy for children. Smith (2007) pointed out that in countries, like Australia and New Zealand, discussion about children's rights has received little attention. As most countries in the world have signed the UNCRoC, she argues there is an international awareness of the need to recognize children's rights and assist them to be aware of the rights of others. Recognition of rights, promoting appropriate levels of participation, and providing the opportunity to learn about rights and the rights of others are all part of our responsibilities under the Convention. Smith (2007) argued that a 'rights' perspective is strengthened when sociocultural theory is also used. The social nature of learning, the role of culture, the importance of relationships and an acknowledgement of the significant influence history has on the everyday experiences of children provides a framework for developing respectful and democratic practices in child care settings. Within this process, Smith (2007) emphasizes the importance of the child's voice: "Social interaction and participation with others in cultural activities with skilled partners leads to the internalization of the tools for thinking, enhancing children's competence (p. 4).

Potential of a Rights Approach

As children grow, their understanding and awareness of the world expands as does their capacity for co-constructing reality in the context of relationships. All children participate within their culture. However, the concept of participation rights goes beyond the act of participation and must include the quality of the environment itself and the relationships in which the child is engaged. The observations, about young children's everyday experiences, described in this chapter have been presented as examples of how our images of children, and our theories of children, can impact on practice and influence children's levels of freedom and their rights of participation. To argue for a 'rights' approach to early childhood education and care and that these rights should be manifest in everyday interactions, is to suggest that the meanings we take from the theories that inform practice may need to be revisited. There are also philosophical issues that need to be reconciled with current ideas on diversity, the importance of culture, and that children are part of our human capital. Rights are considered to be for all, to be universal, and in laying claim to rights we are also acknowledging that others share the same rights. Participation rights are the rights that can be most difficult to express but are most significant when the context is everyday interactions with young children.

Using rights as a basis for practical decision making Lansdown (1996) suggests there are a number of issues to be taken into account and these must be seen in a context of collaboration, support, and awareness of the rights of others. Lansdown identified three areas to be considered when adults are responding to children's right to make choices about their daily lives. These categories are applicable to all children including the very young. The first is that when the child makes a reasonable choice then adults have a duty to help the child develop the capacity for effective decision making. In other words, adults respond to a reasonable choice by helping it happen. The second category involves a choice that imposes obligations on others. In this case, the child is entitled to an explanation of why this can happen now or why it cannot happen. The third category concerns choices that might impact upon the rights of others. In this case, it should be acknowledged that all parties have rights and therefore a legitimate view. Conflicts should then be resolved by negotiation. Such a framework could have transformed the possible meanings derived from the three observations recounted in this chapter. Leo and Angela's situations might not have changed but they could have participated in the reasons the situations existed. Kara's situation was, and is, a more invidious scenario that would need to be challenged through professional education. However, by taking a rights approach the adults in the context and culture of child care would be called upon to articulate and justify decisions made for others.

A human rights perspective has the potential to reframe the image of the child that practice is based upon. By acknowledging participation rights, then ideas of choice, voice, and power within relationships, within the immediate environment, become more reciprocal. The concept of reciprocity fits well with a sociocultural view of humans growing and learning in relationships. Within the notion of reciprocity there are different styles of exchange that reflect the most benevolent view of the child and reflect the give and take that exists within non-market cultural and social exchange systems (Levi Strauss, 1967). Children are engaged with many relationships within their cultural worlds and one direction suggested by a rights approach is asking children about their own views of their experience. The children in the observations could all express a view and if these views were taken into account then the relationships within the context and hence, the image of the child might change. A child seen as having communicative competence and the right to an opinion could very well change the nature of the relationships and the practices in child care.

Guiding Principles of a Rights Approach

Within this discussion of UNCRoC and infant and toddler participation in their own learning, within the experience of formal group care, I now suggest some specific guiding principles for participation, based on rights, for infant and toddler programs. These principles are broad enough to be embraced by a range of constructivist theories about early childhood. Guiding principles underlie goals and strategies and will help determine policy and practice. Principles represent philosophical underpinnings and are the values that signify what is desirable and positive. A number of principles, based on the belief that children are active learners who construct their knowledge of the world in the social milieu of their culture, can be identified. Children have a right to high quality learning environments that foster reciprocal relationships and offer opportunities for exploration and experimentation with both the natural world and cultural artifacts like expressive languages.

Guiding principles of a rights approach to participatory learning for infants and toddlers in group care are:

1. *The right to participate*: The right to participate for the young child means the right to make meaningful choices. This in turn suggests adults must listen to children and take their opinions into account when designing learning environments, daily schedules, routine practices, and relationships. The early childhood literature frequently mentions the value of child-choice but this is frequently limited to short periods of the day and does not involve significant decisions about nurture and care arrangements.

2. *Rights must be a "living thing" if they are to have meaning in the life of the child*: Although all human beings are considered to be the subject of rights, for very young children this can be a problematic idea. The Convention clearly states that all children have rights but how these are exercised obviously differs across culture and context. In a socially constructed environment, like a child care center, staff are encouraged to be reflective in their practices and educated in their decision making. Daily decisions about freedom of movement and promoted activity should take into account children's expressed interests and desires. Children will then experience rights in action and will actively learn about the concept of participatory rights.

3. *Participatory rights exist in the everyday context*: Young children are vulnerable to context meaning that they often have little choice about the context they find themselves in and have little physical control over events. If they are to participate actively in their own learning then this participation must be situated in the here and now. Children need to discover the world through direct experience with people, other children, objects, events, and ideas. The connection between experience and learning gives children a sense of purpose.

4. *Participatory learning is promoted in environments that encourage reciprocal relationships*: The foundation of the educational project lies in the relationship between the child and other members of the

culture. The child learns by being in the culture and the interpretation of what is learned is based on relationships. Children can confidently build knowledge and take an active role in their own learning when there is a shared experience based on trust, respect, and interest.

5. *Participatory learning means active learning*: Active learning is predicated on adults who will scaffold and extend a child's understanding of the world through participating in the child's explorations and providing stimulating environments and artifacts. Communicating about experiences and taking note of verbal and non-verbal language are an important part of active learning. Children who have the freedom to follow their own interests will become self-regulated learners.

6. *Participation encourages growth, well-being, and imagination*: Children who experience opportunities for exploration and problem solving from birth should become informed and curious about their world and the people in it. As children enjoy positive relationships and enjoy experiential learning they develop the ability to: be able to reason, to develop logic, and to engage in a reflective process. These aspects of development form a sound basis for future creativity and the ability to analyze, predict, and formulate new thoughts and ideas (Babbington, 2006, unpaged).

CONCLUSION

In conclusion, I return to the categories of Woodhead (2006) that reflected differing perceptions of children. There was the child of developmental theory, the political and economic child, a sociocultural perspective, and a rights approach. These latter two viewpoints, I have argued, can be complementary as a sociocultural perspective has space for the child to assume citizenship rights within the group and the emphasis on relationships has the potential to give children a reciprocal voice in their own experiences. The only image of children that does not fit with the concept of participation rights in the everyday is the view of children as human capital. As Woodhead (2006) states:

> So, framing policy for ECCE services from a rights perspective is not about charity towards the young, needy and dependent. Children are no longer envisaged merely as the recipients of services, beneficiaries of protective measures, or subjects of social experiments. Nor should early childhood be seen as an investment opportunity, about exploiting human capital. (p. 33)

Rights belong to a universal paradigm and theories and images of children that best support ideals of participation are those belonging to theoretical approaches where children are perceived as strong communicators and reciprocal members of the culture from birth. Choice, freedom to act, and opportunities to act and negotiate with others is necessary if children are to be accorded participation rights. If we design environments around ideas of competence in the here-and-now, respecting children's opinions, and listening to children then children themselves might have a great influence on deliberately constructed environments, like child care.

REFERENCES

Babbington, S. (2006). Emma's story: A case study of a toddler's problem solving development. *ACE Papers*. Issues 17. Auckland, New Zealand.

Balaban, N. (2006). Easing the separation process for infants, toddlers and families. *Young Children*, 61 (6), 14–18.

Berthelsen, D., & Brownlee, J. (2006). Respecting children's agency for learning and rights to participation in child care programs. *International Journal of early Childhood*, 38 (1), 49–61.

Borge, A., Nordhagen, R., & Lie, K., (2003). Children in the environment: Forest day-care centers—Modern day care with historical antecedents. *The History of the Family*, 8 (4), 605–618.

Bredekamp, S. (Ed.) (1987). *Developmentally appropriate practice in early childhood programs serving children from birth through age 8*. Washington, DC: National Association for the Education of Young Children (NAEYC).

Brennan, M. (2007). Beyond child care—how else could we do this? Sociocultural reflections on the structure and cultural arrangements of contemporary Western Child care. *Australian Journal of Early Childhood*, 32 (1). 1–10.

Bruner, J. (1986). *Actual minds, possible worlds*. Boston, MA: Harvard University Press.

Cole, M. (1996). Cultural psychology: A once and future discipline. Boston, MA: Harvard University Press.

Corsaro, W. (1997). *The sociology of childhood*. London: Sage.

Dahlberg, G., Moss, P., & Pence, A. (1999). *Beyond quality in early childhood education and care: postmodern perspectives*. London: Falmer Press.

Deacon, B. (2005). From 'Safety Nets' back to 'Universal Social Provision': Is the global tide turning? *Global Social Policy*, 5 (1), 19–28.

Defense for Children International (DCI) (1995). *United Nations Convention on the Rights of the Child*. Geneva: DCI International Secretariat.

Dewey, J. (1944). *Democracy and education*. New York: The Free Press.

Ebbeck, M., & Winter, P. (2003, February). *An evaluation of a curriculum framework for 0–3 aged children in South Australia*. Paper presented as the Australian Institute of Family Studies Conference. Melbourne.

Edwards, S. (2003). New directions: charting the paths for the role of sociocultural theory in early childhood education and curriculum. *Contemporary Issues in Early Childhood*, 4 (3), 251–266.

Greenwood, A. (1993). Children's rights: The United Nations Convention on the Rights of the Child. *Research in Practice*. Canberra, ACT: Early Childhood Australia.

Harkness, S., & Super, C. (Eds.) (1996). *Parent's cultural belief systems: Their origins, expressions and consequences*. New York: Guilford Press.

Heckman, J., & Masterov, D. (2007). The productivity argument for investing in young children. *Review of Agricultural Economics*, 29 (3), 446–493.

Ize-Charrin, M. (2006). Even the youngest children have rights. *UNICEF, A guide to general comment 7: Implementing child rights in early childhood* (pp. 10–11). The Hague, The Netherlands: Bernard van Leer Foundation.

James, A., Jenks, C., & Prout, A. (1998). *Theorizing childhood*. Cambridge, United Kingdome: Polity Press.

Lansdown, G. (1996). Respecting the right of children to be heard. In Pugh, G. (Ed.) *Contemporary issues in the early years* (pp. 68–82). London: Paul Chapman.

Leavitt, R. (1994). *Power and emotion in infant-toddler day care*. New York: State University of New York Press.

———. (1995). The emotional culture of infant-toddler day care. In Hatch, J. (Ed.) *Qualitative research in early childhood settings*. Westport, CT: Praeger Press.

Levi Strauss, C. (1967). *Structural anthropology*. New York: Doubleday.

Lucas, K. (2006). *Investing in infants and toddlers: The economics of early childhood development programs*. Washington, DC: National Centre for Infants, Toddlers and Families.

McCain, M., & Mustard, F. (1999). *Reversing the real brain drain: Early years study—Final report*. Toronto, Ontario: Ontario Children's Secretariat.

Mesthene, E. (1959). The role of language in the philosophy of John Dewey. *Philosophy and Phenomenological Research, 19* (4), 511–517.

Mkandawire, T. (2005, March). *Targeting and universalism in developing countries*. Paper presented at the Department of Economic and Social Affairs (DESA). Forum on "Integrating Economic and Social Policies to achieve the United Nations Development Agenda. Geneva, Switzerland.

Moss, P., Clark, A., & Kjorholt, A. (2005). Introduction. In Clark, A., Kjorholt, A. & Moss, P. (Eds.) *Beyond listening* (pp. 1–17). London: Policy Press.

Nyland, B. (1999). The United Nations Convention on the Rights of the Child: Using a concept of rights as a basis for practice. *Australian Journal of Early Childhood, 24*(1), 9–15.

———. (2004). Infants, context and participation rights: An Australian image. *The first years Nga Tau Tautahi, New Zealand Journal of Infant and Toddler Education, 6* (1), 19–23.

———. (2006, January). *In search of quality: local and global perspectives*. Paper presented at the Australian Research in Early Childhood Education Conference. Melbourne.

Parks, G. (2000, October). The High/Scope Perry Preschool project. *Juvenile Justice Bulletin*. Washington, DC: Office of Juvenile Justice and Delinquency Prevention.

Penn, H. (2002). The World Bank's view of early childhood. *Childhood, 9* (1), 118–132.

Piaget, J. (1976). *The child's construction of reality*. London: Routledge and Kegan Paul.

Rogoff, B. (2003). *The cultural nature of human development*. New York: Oxford University Press.

Rubtsov, V. (2007). Making shared learning work. *Children in Europe: Special Vygotsky Issue* (pp. 12–14). Edinburgh, Scotland.

Smith, A. (1999). Joint attention: learning to "know other minds." *Early Childhood Folio 4*. Wellington, New Zealand: New Zealand Council for Educational Research.

———. (2007). Children's rights and early childhood education: Links to theory and advocacy. *Australian Journal of Early Childhood. 33* (3), 1–8.

Soto, L., & Swadener, B. (2005). *Power and voice in research with children*. New York: Peter Lang.

Stephenson, A. (1999). Images of empowerment: the outdoor experiences of one-year-old children. *Early childhood folio 4*. (pp. 8–13). Wellington: New Zealand Council for Educational Research.

Super, C., & Harkness, S. (1986). The developmental niche: A conceptualization at the interface of child and culture. *International Journal of Behavioural Development, 9*, 545–569.

Sure Start (2005). *National evaluation report. Implementing Sure Start local programmes: An integrated overview of the first four years (Report 10).* National Evaluation of Sure Start (NESS) Team. London: University of London.

UNICEF. (2006). *A guide to general comment 7: Implementing child rights in early childhood.* The Hague, The Netherlands: Bernard van Leer Foundation.

Valsiner, J. (1987). *Culture and the development of children's actions.* New York: John Wiley and Sons.

Vygotsky, L. (1978). *Mind in society: the development of higher psychological processes.* Boston, MA: Harvard University Press.

Wangmann, J. (1995). *Towards integration and quality assurance in children's services.* Melbourne: Australian Institute of Family Studies.

Wilce, H. (2008). How the government's plans to end child poverty were botched. *The Independent.* Retrieved May 19, 2008, from http://www.independent.co.uk/news/education.

Wood, D., Bruner, J., & Ross, G. (1976). The role of tutoring in problem solving. *Journal of Child Psychology and Psychiatry, 17* (2), 89–100.

Woodhead, M. (2006). *Changing perspectives on early childhood: theory, research and policy:* Background paper prepared for Education for all: Global Monitoring Report 2007, Strong foundations: Early Childhood Care and Education. Paris: United Nations Educational, Scientific and Cultural Organization.

4 'Doing the Right Thing'

A Moral Concern from the Perspectives of Young Preschool Children

Eva Johansson

This chapter deals with morality from the child's perspective. The base for the discussion is two investigations of morality among children (aged one to three years) in different day care contexts in Sweden and Australia (Johansson, 1999, manuscript). The aim was to create knowledge about the children's lived experiences of values and norms concerning treatment of, and behavior toward, each other in their every day life-world of day care. The results indicate that children defend and value their own and others rights and care for others' well-being. The children also gave power a moral value, for instance: the power to assert their own rights and the rights of others. In the Australian study, the initial analyses of the data of children's interactions revealed a value of 'doing the right thing' (Johansson, manuscript) as a specific moral concern among the children. This value had not been evident in the Swedish investigation of toddler's morality (Johansson, 1999). However, on re-analysis for this chapter this value came into view. Thus, through a process of mirroring the different studies towards each other new insights on young children's morality were gained.

This discussion refers to conventions and 'doing the right thing' as a specific moral concern among the children. Whether conventions have a moral relevance or not is an unsolved issue in moral philosophy and in empirical research. Some researchers separate conventions from morality (Killen & Smetana, 2006) whereas others view conventional and moral issues as intertwined (Shweder, Much, Mahapatra, & Park, 1997). Shweder, Mahapatra, & Miller (1987) argued that the distinction between morality and convention is culture specific. Events from one cultural perspective could be interpreted as a conventional transgression but from another cultural perspective similar events might be viewed as a moral transgression. Therefore to separate moral and conventional dimensions in children's social life can be a problem when analyzing and understanding children's interactions across cultures.

Conventions refer to shared behaviors such as uniformities and rules whose meanings are defined by the social system in which they are embedded. The conventional rules are related to context and may vary by socially constructed meanings. In this text, conventions are viewed as part of the moral life in preschool and are discussed as the children's concern for the rules and also as concerns for their teachers and friends. Yet, the children's experiences of conventions may also pertain to the children's specific life-worlds in their different cultures of preschools.

In this chapter, the theoretical bases for the investigations will be initially outlined followed by a discussion on previous research on children's morality. The analysis of the value of 'doing the right thing' is then described focusing how this value can impact on children's interactions. The following questions will be addressed: How is the value of 'doing the right thing' constituted from the point of view of the children in these two groups of toddlers in Sweden and Australia? What moral meanings from a child's perspective arise from this kind of moral value and, in what way, can teachers relate to this kind of moral understanding among the children?

In general terms, Australia and Sweden can be described as oriented towards an individualistic morality (Shweder, Jensen, & Goldsterin, 1995) with certain commonalities with regards to values and norms. On the other hand, the countries are part of and carry very different sociocultural histories, which most likely leads to some different understandings of childhood and children, of knowledge and values, and children's interactions have to be interpreted in the light of such understandings. Moss (2001) points to the risk of losing sight of the child in cross-national studies and also to the idea that there is a universal child who is knowable irrespective of time or place, context or perspective. Instead, the idea of many possible childhoods constructed within particular social and historical contexts has emerged. It is therefore important to note that a cross-national comparison is not the focus of interest in this discussion. The purpose here is rather to mirror the content of 'doing the right thing' to the structure of relevance (Schütz, 1972) in the different preschool groups and viewing these as aspects of the children's different sociocultural life-worlds (Merleau-Ponty, 1962; see also Moss et al., 2003). The analyses indicate that the value of 'doing the right thing' can be interpreted as both a moral obligation and a moral responsibility. This value seems to be a question of obeying preschool rules but it is also about trust and showing concern for adults and friends.

PERSPECTIVES OF CHILDREN'S MORALITY

Research within sociocultural traditions represents various perspectives that emphasize both social learning and social constructivism as the basis for morality.[1] Common to these various positions is the assumption that the origins of morality are related to significances that are shared and communicated by members situated in a specific culture, related to a specific practice, located at a certain time, or having a specific history. Children's moral discoveries reflect not only their personal history, but also the values, expectations, and forms embedded in the culture. Morality is not related to some single factor in development, neither is it a product of a sudden shift in cognitive level. It is a continuous and overlapping process of children's developing functions, their experiences and meanings (cf. Nelson, 2003).

MORALITY—A RESULT OF INTERSUBJECTIVITY

Morality is here understood as children's *lived* experiences of their relations with peers, expressed as values and norms for how to behave towards each other in everyday life in the context of preschool (Johansson, 1999). The word *lived* emphasizes that morality is not primarily a question of critical reflection or rationality. Furthermore, children's morality is not supposed to become liberated from the context, from their own subjectivity or from the influence of adults and peers.

Morality grows out of inseparable relationships between subjects rather than being the result of an autonomous subject's logical reasoning (Johansson, 1999, 2001, 2005). The theoretical foundation for the studies is phenomenology and the theory of life-world, mainly as the French philosopher Maurice Merleau-Ponty (1962) discusses it. The ontological basis of the life-world is related to the child as a perceiving subject who is inseparable from, and in interaction with, the world. Merleau-Ponty (1962) sees human life as intersubjective and enmeshed in relations with other people, with culture, history, and society. We are related to others and we are dependent on each other. There is also an intertwined relationship of subject and body; furthermore, the body is central for all our being in the world. The child's body is not only an object; it is a union of senses, thoughts, emotions, language, and motor actions. The child is in communication with the world and with other people. The child creates meaning and is able to understand other people by their bodily existence in the world.

Thus we can understand that even the very young child experiences and expresses morality through his or her body. At the same time meanings are conveyed to the child; things and people make references to the use and purpose of various phenomena in the world. Power is always present in human relations. According to the theory of ethics proposed by Løgstrup (1994), we are given to each other. We are always locked in this relation of dependence and responsibility for the other. But the relation is not built upon rationality and logic. It is a concrete intersubjective relationship out of which moral values and norms of behavior emerge.

THE STRUCTURE OF RELEVANCE

Let us shortly consider the concept of relevance structure such as it has been developed by the sociologist Alfred Schütz (1972). The individual's everyday knowledge of the world is a system of typified constructions, writes Schütz (1972). As human beings we are not only situated in a physical world, we are situated in a sociocultural situation of history.

This sociocultural situation is a result of layers of intersubjective human experiences, of knowledge and interpretations, organized as the individuals taken for granted knowledge. Yet, the sociocultural situation is also defined and interpreted by the individual and is in one sense the individual's disposable property. The sociocultural situation inhabits and structures future practical and theoretical actions. This structure of relevance decides and gives meaning to both individual and collective activities, knowledge and interpretations (Schütz, 1972).

To conclude, morality does not simply involve autonomous logical thinking, but is part of children's life-worlds. In the context of preschool, meanings and interactions are intertwined with the structure of relevance. The structure of relevance embraces historical, cultural, and societal understandings of the goals and intentions with preschool, including knowledge of children and childhood but also the teachers and the children's interpretations of "what is going on" in everyday interaction. This means that certain interpretations, activities and knowledge affiliated with values such as 'doing the right thing' in the daily life of preschool are relevant while others may be not. Of particular importance is the idea that our body is lived and, as such, central for all our being in the world. Because of toddlers' limited verbal ability, their moral experiences must be viewed as a totality, where tacit bodily experiences and expressions are of importance (Johansson, 1999, 2001). This idea places stresses upon the intertwined relationship between the physical and psychological—which occurs before experiences and knowledge can be described in words.

TODDLER'S MORALITY—A PART OF THEIR LIFE-WORLD

Previous research (see Johansson, 2006 and Killen & Smetana, 2006, for overviews) has provided a view of the moral capacity of young children. Very young children appear to be aware of their social knowledge and they use this in their relationships with others. The child's moral development emerges in interaction with others, and the child is an active part in this process (Dunn, 2006). Moral understanding emanates from the child's self-interest in others' actions. The child is driven by a desire to participate in and to understand others' experiences, rules for interaction, and how to influence others. Emotions, motivation, and affective experiences are crucial dimensions in this process.

Morality is part of children's lives from the time of their first relationships (Damon, 1990). Indeed, morality emanates from children's various social experiences with parents and peers in which they are part of from the beginning of life. Children have access to the cultural values and belief system as soon as they start to communicate and can make inferences about their social interaction. This begins in infancy. With regard to Ivar Frønes (1995), communicative competence is central to the child's moral learning. Norms, for instance, must be justified and questioned through critical argumentation. Communicative competence emerges from the child's experiences of interaction with others, especially with peers. Discernment for complex social situations requires a capacity to communicate and be open to various social perspectives.

Moral issues have been found to be an important part of the children's life-worlds (Johansson, 1999, 2007a). Previous investigations of young children's experiences of moral values and norms in everyday life within the context of preschools in Sweden show how children defend and value their own and other's rights and care for each others' well-being. The children also gave power a moral value, for instance: the power to maintain rights and shared worlds. Moreover, power came from the assertion of rights and from the unity of sharing worlds. Children in powerful positions were also highly esteemed by the other children. Positions of power were related to age as well as physical and psychological strength. The findings uncovered that conflicts of rights as well as acts that threaten one's own and others' well-being held potential for children's moral learning. A child can learn about morality under certain important conditions. These include the other's reactions, what the implications and consequences of the acts might be, personal closeness to the other, and whether or not the child is the recipient or 'victim' of the acts.

Smetana (1993), along with Turiel, Killen and Helwig (1987), and Smetana, Killen, and Turiel (1991), studied children's understanding of social rules. These researchers wanted to find out if and how children discriminate between the moral, the conventional, and the personal domain. The children, between two and five years of age, were presented with a series of social acts or infringements in accordance with the distinctions of the domains. The researchers found that even three-year-old toddlers discriminated between conventional and moral rules even if the distinctions between the moral and social conventions became more consistent by about the ages of four or five. The children were deeply concerned with transgressions of moral rules, but seemed to be somewhat uninvolved with conventional transgressions. The children assessed harming others more to the consequences of acts than conventional transgressions, which in contrast were related to rules. Children, by the end of their third year, judged moral infringements independently from the influence of authorities such as their teachers.

CHILDREN'S MORALITY AND THEIR RELATIONS TO TEACHERS

Before we turn to the analyses let me briefly touch upon positions held by researchers regarding children's relations with adults and teachers. On the one hand, researchers claim that children's morality is subordinated to adult authority (Piaget, 1960), on the other hand, it has been stated that children evaluate and question the legitimacy of social rules and authority (Crane & Tisak, 1995). According to Piaget (1960) there exist in the child two separate moralities. One concerns duty and is related to the moral constraint imposed by the adult. The other is connected to autonomy and mutual cooperation. The young child's capability to be moral is related to the concept of egocentrism; that is the child's confusion of the ego and the external world. When a child's thinking is freed from the immediate context, from the child's own subjectivity, and from the influence of grown-ups and older peers, the child is able to be moral. Piaget argues that the egocentric child is subject to external constraint but has little capacity for cooperation and objective justice. In order to cooperate, one must be conscious of one's own ego. The subject has to liberate him- or herself from the thoughts and wills of others.

Piaget's thesis that young children are governed by grown-ups and thus not capable of a self-guided morality has been questioned on empirical grounds. Indeed, many studies have shown that even toddlers, children between one and three years of age, defend moral values; discern and value moral transgressions differently from conventional ones; are aware of moral standards; and seem to make moral decisions. There is empirical evidence that children both evaluate and question the legitimacy of social rules and authority (cf. Crane & Tisak, 1995; Damon, 1990; Dunn, 2006; Eisenberg, Spinrad & Sadovsky, 2006; Johansson 1999, 2007a; Smetana, 2006).

ANALYSES

Let us now study some examples of the interaction between the children and how the value of 'doing the right thing' manifests itself in the children's experiences of morality. The presented examples have been selected from two studies of children's morality (Johansson, 1999, Johansson, manuscript). They serve as illustrative examples of how the children relate to the value of 'doing the right thing.' One of the investigations took place in a Swedish day care center (Johansson, 1999). Nineteen children in a toddler group, ten boys and nine girls, aged from one year to three years of age, participated in the study. The daily interaction of the children was video recorded across a period of seven months. The other investigation took place in two day care groups in Queensland, Australia (Johansson, manuscript). This study involved 19 children, eight boys and eleven girls, two to three years of age. The daily interaction of these children was video recorded across a period of three months.

The overall aim of these investigations was to create knowledge about children's lived experiences of values and norms concerning treatment of, and behavior towards, each other in everyday life in the context of preschool. The children's interactions were analyzed with a focus on two main questions: What moral values do children experience and express through their interaction? What norms do the children express and value?

In this chapter, the focus is on analyses of the data dealing with morality as 'doing the right thing.' Initial analyses from the Australian study revealed a value of 'doing the right thing' (Johansson, manuscript) as a specific moral concern among the children. This value did not occur at first in the Swedish investigation of toddler's morality (Johansson, 1999). However, as mentioned in the introduction, when re-analyzing some of the data from the Swedish study, aspects of this value came into view. The analyses in this chapter aim to interpret and describe the meanings of this particular value from the children's perspective. How is the value of 'doing the right thing' constituted from the point of view of the children? How are questions linked to conventions for behavior manifested in children's inter-subjective agreements with friends and teachers?[2] A cross-national comparison is, as already stated, not of interest in this discussion. The analyses is rather directed towards differences and similarities of 'doing the right thing' in relation to the structure of relevance in the different preschool groups as parts of children's different sociocultural life-worlds. This means that certain interpretations, activities and knowledge, affiliated with doing the right thing in the everyday life of preschool are relevant for the teachers and the children while others may be not.

DOING THE RIGHT THING—A VALUE OF OBLIGATION AND A MORAL RESPONSIBILITY

The results from the initial analyses imply that the children irrespective of different cultural life-worlds uphold the value of 'doing the right thing.' At the same time, there are occasionally some differences in the children's moral expressions, in their strategies and the moral contracts that they draw up in relation to this value. These differences may pertain to the children's specific life-worlds, to the culture of preschool, and the structure of relevance.

In the following text, some examples from the studies are outlined. They serve as illustrative examples of how the children relate to the values of 'doing the right thing' and how they approach transgressions of rules in relation to teachers but also with reference to friends. Rules for behavior seem important for all the children. The children showed in different and often subtle ways that they were concerned with the adults' reactions to their behavior. They often looked for the teachers in situations of conflicts and when rules were transgressed. They sometimes could escape from such a situation. The children could inform the teachers when a friend has broken the rules or they could act as a 'help teacher' and encourage their friends to follow rules. Occasionally, the children also defended the position of their teachers.

Inform Teachers of the Transgressions

In the following example, we meet some of the Swedish toddlers (Johansson, 1999). The structure of relevance in this toddler group can be described with words such as 'motherliness,' individuality, negotiations, and acceptance. Embedded in interactions are often issues of the children's development, their play, and routine care issues. The focal point of communication between the teachers and children is less upon explicit rules and more on children's well-being and play activities, their developmental progress, and issues of inclusion in the children's interactions. The atmosphere is calm, open, and tolerant. Teachers often observe children's interactions; they pay little attention to (small) breaking of rules; and they seem to be amused (in a positive way) by the children's different personalities and behaviors. The safety and care of the children seem to be in the forefront of these teachers' intentions. Rules are more or less an implicit part of the everyday life, yet the children are aware of their own, and others', breaking of the rules.

> The children are on their way out to play. Some children are gathered in the hall waiting. Björn (2:1)[3] goes to the door. "Out, out," he says eagerly. He tries to reach the handle. He stretches his body, stands tiptoe and tries to open the heavy door. "No, locked," he complains. He quickly glances at the teacher in the room next to the hall. Olle (2:0) stands nearby watching Björn. With a lot of effort Björn slowly succeeds in opening the door a little bit. "So, so," he says. He turns around, looking at the teacher, and then he quickly slips out through the narrow opening. "So, so," he repeats. Olle runs forward but the door closes in front of him. Olle gazes through the small window and laughs happily at his friend outside. Now Karl (2:0) comes. He clings to the handle trying to open the door but with no success. Again Olle looks through the window laughing at Björn outside. Then Olle goes to the teachers. He points at Björn outside the window and says in a loud and excited tone of a voice: "Björn out! Björn out!"

The excitement in this interaction seems to concern transgressions and the possible boundaries of the rules. The boys seem aware of the meaning of 'doing the right thing' in this situation: the door is not to be opened and the children are not allowed to go out alone. Björn glanced hastily at the teacher while he continued trying to open the door and again before he slipped out. Olle is enjoying the situation; he looks and laughs at Björn's efforts to open the door. Also Karl is motivated to try to open the door but fails.

It looks like Björn is expecting or searching for some kind of reaction from the teachers but this does not prevent him from wanting to open the door. Björn's breaking of the rules makes Olle excited but eventually he finds it necessary to inform the adults about the situation. We cannot know the reasons for Olle's behavior but there are different interpretations: maybe Olle wants to share his delight with the teachers (his whole body expresses glee and excitement); maybe he wants to point to a notable and risky situation where Björn is outside alone; maybe he wants to show teachers that his friend is breaking the rules. A possible interpretation is that he wants to present himself in a positive way to the teachers. However, it may also be a question of trusting the teachers to know what is going on. Yet, Olle still takes a level of responsibility for his friend.

In this situation the sharing of joy seems to be important. From the point of view of the children, there seem to be no or little fear of exposing the transgressions to the adults; rather there is a spontaneous sharing of the excitement with the teachers.

Defend Teachers' Positions

Doing the right thing also involves upholding the order of the children's and the teachers' positions and rights. In the following situation, from the perspective of the children certain rules seem to be important. To follow the rules about where to sit can be important for different reasons. From this situation we can learn how one of the girls is concerned with defending the teacher's position and trying to deter a friend from sitting in a specific spot where it is intended that the teachers will sit.

> It is circle-time. The children gather in the circle which has designated places indicated by pictures pasted on the floor. Each picture is designated for a particular child and two pictures indicate where the teachers are to sit. Björn (1:9) crawls to a teacher's spot but Malin (2:1) covers the spot with her hands and prevents him from sitting on the spot. "No, no," says Björn angrily while pressing his head close to Malin's body trying to bite her. She moves backwards. Now Björn makes himself comfortable by sitting on the adult's spot. Malin points at Björn's own spot (a sun) and says: "Un, un [sun, sun]". "Nooo, un," she repeats firmly and pulls Björn's shirt. Björn remains still. He looks at her. He is quiet. Malin continues pulling his shirt. Now Björn falls over. He hits Malin's hand. Malin turns around looking at me, the observer, and says impatiently: "Look him, look him!" Again she pulls Björn's shirt.

'Doing the right thing' in this situation, according to Malin, is for the children not to sit on the teacher's spot, rather to sit on their own. Malin defends the rules for circle-time but she also protects the teacher's position trying to impede Björn in his efforts to sit on the teacher's spot. It is interesting to note that she takes the position of a 'help-teacher,' carrying the teachers' role of guiding the children. Malin takes responsibility not only for the order of the circle-time situation but also for the teachers' right to the spot. In this way, Malin shows concern for the teacher.

The rule for where to sit is well established among the children and the teachers in this group. The circle-time normally starts when everyone (children and adults) is seated on the correct spot. Sometimes a child can sit on a teacher's lap, but the expectation is that the children should sit on their designated spot. This rule seems to be valued by the children. Björn knows that the spot with the picture of the sun belongs to him and he probably is aware of the rule but today he wants to sit on the teacher's spot. We don't know the reasons for these efforts. One interpretation is that the teacher's spot is surrounded with special meanings. Sitting on the teacher's spot might be considered a privilege, with an implicit message of closeness to the teacher. This can be a powerful position. To sit on the teachers' spot can also be an adventure, just as a breaking of rules can be an adventure as we saw in the previous example.

Finally Malin turns to me, the observer, for help. She wants me to know about the transgression and to intervene. This outreach can be interpreted as a question of trust. She trusts me to help her since her friend is breaking the rule of doing the right thing.

Guiding Your Friends

As we have seen, the children take responsibility for the order and the rules in preschool. They show their friends right and wrong and look after each other in multiple ways. Let us now see what happens in the continuing interaction above:

> Karin (2:6) and Niklas (3:3) are sitting on their spots in the circle gazing at Björn and Malin. Karin whispers something to Niklas. Now Björn grabs Malin's hand and tries to bite her but she quickly pulls her hand away from him. She hits him. With a serious look Karin turns to the children: "Be kind, be kind! Don't do," she admonishes them: "He [will be] sad," she continues.

Karin intervenes when the conflict escalates. She addresses both of the children telling them to stop. She also refers to the consequences of the act and to Björn's future feelings of distress. In this situation, she directs her friends to follow rules and she explains her statements. The moral issue from Karin's perspective appears to be an obligation that it is important to be kind because otherwise someone might get hurt. She shows concern for her friends but she also judges their behavior and holds them responsible for not being kind. Her facial expression and her tone of voice are serious and she leans forward them. Her whole being implies the gravity of the situation. She does not touch upon the content of the conflict and what position she might support in this situation. This seems not important or relevant to Karin. At the forefront of her intentions is the care of the other. Different values are confronted in the interaction—obligations to follow rules and the value of others' well-being.

Let us now consider an example from the Australian study (Johansson, manuscript). One part of the relevance structure in this group is a particular concern for manners. Embedded in the interactions are often issues about behavior and focal points of communication are frequently around rules. The teachers, the parents, and the children in this group often raise issues about rules in their communications. The atmosphere often shifts from being intensive and controlling, on one hand, to a calmer and more friendly emotional tone, on the other. The value of 'doing the right thing' is strongly expressed sometimes in a demanding manner. In contrast, teachers also often approach the children with a caring attitude, encouraging and supporting positive interactions among them. In the next example one of the boys is involved in teaching values. He corrects his friend and indicates his dislike of his comrade's behavior.

> Aron (2:7) sits on a chair outside on the terrace. Charlie (2:10) comes along and he says something to Aron. "No," shouts Aron. His voice is loud. "Don't say no to me. Don't say no to me," objects Charley. He looks at Aron who kicks his feet towards Charlie. "Don't hit me! No hitting," says Charlie with a strong and determined tone of voice. "No kicking Aron," says the teacher nearby. Some minutes later, Charlie approaches Aron again. "I don't like your behavior. You have a naughty behavior." Charlie admonishes his friend. The teacher then addresses Aron: "Are you listening to him? He says it's not a good behavior to kick." Then she turns to Charlie: "That was very good words. I am impressed," says the teacher. Now Aron runs away into the garden. Charlie runs after him. The teacher calls Charlie back. "He is running away! He is running away," Charlie says excitedly. "Don't bother. I will deal with that," the teacher says. Later she tells her colleagues about the incident. She is impressed by the fact that Charlie supervised his friend without any interference from herself.

Different values are involved in this situation. The moral issue from the perspective of Charlie concerned the well-being of others (not to kick or hit); his own and others' integrity ("Don't say no to me."); and manners ("I don't like your behavior"). Charlie makes references to absolute norms, that he dislikes Aron's behavior and that he finds Aron naughty. Charlie seems offended by Aron's behavior. The moral issues from Aron's perspective are harder to interpret. Maybe Charlie said something to Aron that upset him in the first place. Maybe Aron is then defending his own integrity by shouting, "No" and then kicking. From Aron's perspective this situation seems both uncomfortable and threatening. Eventually he escapes out into the garden.

Similar to Karin, the girl in the previous situation, Charlie takes responsibility for order in the toddler group. He acts as a 'help teacher,' he corrects his friend and he supports the teacher in her guidance. He shows concern for his teacher. It is however interesting to note that the children in the two examples are concerned with different aspects in guiding others. Karin, in the previous interaction, provides instruction. She tells the children to be kind. She refers to the other's emotions, to Björn's sadness. Charlie refers to his own distress, his dislike of the behavior, and to naughty manners. He tries to ensure that Aron returns by making the teacher aware that Aron is running away. In this way, he maintains the value of 'doing the right thing,' protecting the common rules and defending the teacher's position.

It is worth noting how well Charlie has understood the discourse for communicating not 'doing the right thing' within this group. Despite his young age, he uses the words "behavior" and "naughty behavior." This kind of communication is relevant for Charlie since it is part of a general structure of values, expectations, and communicative forms of this pre-school culture. The teacher shows her approval of Charlie's expressions. She is impressed and she praises him and encourages Aron to listen. She tells her colleagues of Charlie's initiative. It is interesting to note that the words used by Charlie hold potential for an encounter where "the other" is objectified rather than "the other" being met in an intersubjective relation. Of course, this is not what is in the mind of this young child but it is the way in which discursive patterns has an impact by mediating both the language, the messages conveyed, and subsequently behavior. This is the communicative form that underpins interactions about rules that also become part of the children's life-worlds. Through this lived communication, the structure of relevance is built, confirmed, and sustained by both children and teachers.

Show Your Good Manners to the Teachers

Another strategy found in the data is to expose your good manners to others. The children emphasize their good manners in interaction with friends and teachers. The following example is gathered from one of the Australian day care centers. The structure of relevance in this toddler group can be described with words such as motherliness, authority, and obedience. Some rules are central and are often on the agenda in the interactions between teachers and children. Teachers lay down a lot of effort and energy in making children understand and follow rules for behavior. A story about Max can illustrate this kind of relevance structure. The teachers have shaped the story and they have also created a big doll called Max. Max is a model for the children, showing clearly how to behave when 'doing the right thing.' Whatever Max is doing he uses his gentle hands and his gentle voice.

The children are out in the big yard playing.

John (3:7), Adam (3:6), Ron (2:9), and Charlie (2:10) are playing on the slide. They climb on the slide, slide down, and climb up again. They laugh while climbing. Sara (3:4) comes along and climbs up. The boys protest loudly, they want Sara to go away: "It's only boys. Go!" they shout in chorus. They reiterate their message several times. "It's only boys. Go away!" Charlie continues to shout at Sara with his face is close to hers: "Go!" His tone of voice is accusing: "No," says Sara firmly and remain sitting on the top of the slide. Suddenly Charlie changes his attitude. He stretches his hand towards her face and gently he caresses her cheek: "I am using gentle hands. I am using gentle hands," he says softly. Then, he climbs down, goes up to me the observer, and says: "I am using gentle hands. I am using gentle hands." He sounds satisfied and climbs up the slide again. Meanwhile Sara has left the slide.

Together the four boys had made a moral agreement: the slide is only for boys. They defend their right to play on the slide and decide on the conditions for playing. They insist that Sara should leave and the motive for their decision is the fact that she is a girl. Sara does not accept the rules stated by the boys. She takes it for granted that she also can play on the slide.

Let us now consider Charlie in this interaction. His intention is to make Sara leave the slide. He uses different strategies. At first he shouts at her, but he fails to achieve his intention. Sara remains on the slide. Then he suddenly changes his approach. Charlie's voice becomes soft, he caresses her cheek, and he explains his good manners to her. He shows his good intentions with his whole body. Indeed he also wants to make me aware of his positive behavior, since he climbs down and informs me of his efforts in 'doing the right thing.' From Charlie's point of view 'doing the right thing' in this situation seems to be about being gentle to Sara but also to make friends and adults aware of his good actions. Maybe Charlie is happy with himself remembering how to behave. He seems pleased when he tells me of his gentle behavior. Maybe he also wants to please me as a concern for adults. He is eager to follow the teacher's rules. Both an obligation and a concern for others may be the grounds for his interaction.

CONVENTIONS—DEPENDENCE AND TRUST

In this chapter, we have discussed the value of 'doing the right thing.' The analyses intend to show that this value is a question of obeying preschool rules implemented by adults but also to show concern towards others, adults, and friends. The value of 'doing the right thing' seems to be closely intertwined with the intersubjective life of preschool and the relations built up between children and adults.

Regardless of these young children's different sociocultural life-worlds in Sweden and Australia, the value is similar. However, the lived expressions of the value seem to differ with respect to the preschool culture and to the structure of relevance that may follow (Schütz, 1972). In this respect, some differences in the children's moral expressions and in their strategies and nature of their moral interactions seem to occur. Of importance in this process is, on one hand, adults' and friends' reactions to transgressions of rules and, on the other hand, how the children want to present themselves to the teachers and friends. The structure of relevance seems to influence very much the value of 'doing the right thing.' It is a question of how and to what extent the value of 'doing the right thing' is lived out in the life-world of preschool. When the structure of relevance and the focal point of communications are focused around rules, these impact on children's morality and the meanings given to this value. According to Piaget (1960), the child believes not only in the adult's omniscience, the child also unquestionably believes in the absolute value of the imperatives he or she receives from the adults or other authorities. This proposition is partly supported in this investigation. However, it is important to notice that this dependence on authority becomes visible when the value of 'doing the right thing' is strongly supported in a distinct and sometimes demanding manner. This points to the missing element in Piaget's analyses namely that the different meanings that can be embedded the life-worlds of the children and in the children's moral discoveries.

This part of children's morality refers to duty and respecting issues of importance for the social life in preschool. Duty is about an obligation to 'do the right thing' and to follow the rules in preschool. The teachers implement these rules. Therefore, they are mainly related to the authority of the adults. The children do not seem to question the rules rather they are taken for granted. This is in contrast to values about rights and others' well-being which often are revealed as a result of the children's own experiences of care or humiliations (see also Johansson, 1999, 2007a, 2007b). Yet, we have also learned from this presentation that children's morality is intertwined with the structure of relevance in preschool. If the focal point of everyday interactions is to uphold rules, then the relevant and possible ways for behavior for children (and teachers) is to rely on and follow these imperatives. Duty will be a strong moral concern. However if the structure of relevance is gathered round a diversity of moral issues and if the rules are more implicit than explicit, then the meanings of rules may differ as well as the possible ways of acting in the situation. 'Doing the right thing' does not necessarily mean that children follow the rules without reflection. Indeed they sometimes relate to and choose to transgress the rules. The children seem to take from the rules what they regard as valuable and possible in different situations. Teachers and friends are important to the children and the children follow rules because they care for their teachers and friends. This way of reasoning widens our understanding and gives other dimensions to the children's purposes for following rules than those offered by Piaget (1960).

Conventions also involve other dimensions than obligations—dimensions of both trust and dependence. These values do not only evolve from the children's lived sense of duty but also from a concern for the adults and their relations with the teachers. The teachers are important to the children since they are part of children's life-worlds in preschool. The children show that they want to build good relations with their teachers while, at the same time, they seem aware of the fact that the teachers decide the rules and the consequences that might follow from transgressions of the rules. The moral dimension is here to be good, to act and behave well as a concern for the adults. The children want to present themselves in the best possible light and show the teachers their good intentions and their good manners. It is however important to notice that a mixture of wanting the adults to see them in the best light and to avoid being blamed for certain actions is involved in the children's behavior (cf. Hoffman, 2000).

From this discussion we have learned that conventions can be the basis for how children value their own and others' behavior. In this way, conventions are of importance in children's moral life as are their preferences about how to interact with others. The position in this chapter nuances the propositions of a borderline between conventional and moral issues (cf. Killen & Smetana, 2006). On the one hand, we have seen that differences between moral and conventional issues may not always be distinct in children's (and teachers') worlds. Breaking common agreements and rules can be experienced as humiliating and unjust. Children's (and teachers') engagement can, however, differ with respect to situations and to individual children's interpretations. Indeed these young children show a deep involvement in moral issues and they participate with emphasis in each other's moral learning.

Understanding children's morality from a broad sociocultural perspective means to discern and interpret meanings in preschool, as situated in a specific culture, in a specific preschool practice, in a certain time and with a specific history. Children's moral discoveries reflect not only their personal history, but also the values, expectations, and forms embedded in the culture (Nelson, 2003). Indeed, it is important to notice that rules are vital in helping us to organize everyday life. Rules can be more or less implicit. However, the children still seem to be aware of their own and others' rule-breaking. We have also learned from this study how young children learn and carry out discourses about rules. The communicative form that underpins the interactions for rules is confirmed and sustained by both children and teachers. The proposition here is that communicative competence is important for children's moral discoveries. Discernment in complex social situations requires a capacity to communicate and be open to various social perspectives (Frønes, 1995). This requires a structure of relevance that can be described with words such as negotiations, acceptance and diversity, rather than obligations to follow authorities and imperative rules.

NOTES

1. The relation between these various perspectives is however complex and deserves a more developed discussion which is not possible to give in this chapter.

2. In this text all persons working in the studied groups are called teachers or adults regardless of their professional education.
3. The child's age is stated in years and months in brackets.

REFERENCES

Crane, D., & Tisak, M. S. (1995). Does day-care experience affect preschool children's judgments of home and school rules? *Early Education and Development*, 6(1), 25–37.

Damon, W. (1990). *The moral child: Nurturing children's natural moral growth.* New York: The Free Press.

Dunn, J. (2006). Moral development in early childhood and social interaction in the family. In M. Killen & J. Smetana (Eds.), *Handbook of moral development* (pp. 331–350). Mahwah, NJ: Lawrence Erlbaum.

Eisenberg, N., Spinrad, T., & Sadovsky, A. (2006). Empathy-related responding in children. In M. Killen & J. Smetana (Eds.), *Handbook of moral development* (pp. 517–549). Mahwah, NJ: Lawrence Erlbaum.

Frønes, I. (1995). *Among peers: On the meaning of peers in the process of socialization.* Oslo, Norway: Universitetsforlaget AS.

Hoffman, M. L. (2000). *Empathy and moral development: Implications for caring and justice.* Cambridge, MA: Cambridge University Press.

Johansson, E. (1999). *Etik i små barns värld: Om värden och normer bland de yngsta barnen i förskolan* [Ethics in small children's worlds. Values and norms among the youngest children in preschool]. Göteborg Studies in Educational Sciences, 141. Göteborg, Sweden: Acta Universitatis Gothoburgensis.

———. (2001). Morality in children's worlds: Rationality of thought or values emanating from relations? *Studies in Philosophy and Education. An International Quarterly, 20,* 345–358.

———. (2005). Children's integrity—a marginalised right. *International Journal of Early Childhood, 3*(36), 109–124.

———. (2006). Children's morality—Perspectives and Research. In B. Spodek & O. N. Saracho (Eds.), *Handbook of research on the education of young children* (pp. 55–83). Mahwah, NJ: Lawrence Erlbaum.

———. (2007a). *Etiska överenskommelser i förskolebarns världar* [Moral agreements in preschool-children's worlds]. Göteborg Studies in Educational Sciences, 251. Göteborg, Sweden: Acta Universitatis Gothoburgensis

———. (2007b). Morality and Gender—Preschool Children's Moral Contracts. In O. N. Saracho & B. Spodek (Eds.), *Contemporary perspectives on socialization and social development in early childhood education,* (pp. 267–300). Vol. 7. Charlotte, NC: Information Age Publishing.

———. (manuscript). *Morality in toddler' s different life-worlds. A cross-cultural study.* Göteborg, Sweden: Göteborg University and Queensland University of Technology.

Killen, M., & Smetana, J. S. (Eds.) (2006). *Handbook of moral development.* Mahwah, NJ: Lawrence Erlbaum.

Løgstrup, K. E. (1994). *Det etiska kravet* [The ethical demand]. Göteborg, Sweden: Daidalos.

Merleau-Ponty, M. (1962). *Phenomenology of perception.* New York: Routledge.

Moss, P. (2001, June). *Beyond Early Childhood Education and Care.* Keynote address at the Early Child Education and Care Conference: Stockholm.

Moss, P., Petrie, P., Cameron, C., Candappa, M., McQuail, S., & Mooney, A. (2003.) *Early years and childcare international evidence project.* Thomas Coram Research Unit, Institute of Education, University of London.

Nelson, K. (2003). Narrative and self, myth and memory: Emergence of the cultural self. In R. Fivush, & C. Haden (Eds.) *Autobiographical memory and the construction of a narrative self: Developmental and cultural perspectives* (pp.3–28). Mahwah, NJ: Lawrence Erlbaum.

Piaget, J. (1960). *The moral judgment of the child.* London: Routledge and Kegan Paul.

Schütz, A. (1972). *The phenomenology of the social world.* Evanston, Ill: Northwestern University Press.

Shweder, R. A., Jensen, L. A., & Goldsterin, W. M. (1995). Who sleeps with whom revisited: A method for extracting the moral goods implicit in practice. In J. Goodnow, P. J. Miller & F. Kessel (Eds.), *Cultural practices as contexts for development: New directions for child development* (pp. 21–39). San Francisco: Jossey-Bass.

Shweder, R. A., Mahapatra, M., & Miller, J. G. (1987). Culture and moral development. In J. Kagan & S. Lamb (Eds.), *The emergence of morality in young children* (pp. 1–83). Chicago: University of Chicago Press.

Shweder, R. A., Much, N. C., Mahapatra, M., & Park, L. (1997). The "Big Three" of morality (autonomy, community, divinity) and the "Big Three" explanations of suffering. In A. M. Brant & P. Rozin (Eds.), *Morality and health* (pp. 119–169). New York: Routledge.

Smetana, J. G. (1993). Understanding of social rules. In M. Bennet (Ed.), *The child as psychologist: An introduction to the development of social cognition* (pp. 111–141). London: Harvester Wheatsheaf.

———. (2006). Social-cognitive domain theory: Consistencies and variations in children's moral and social judgments. In M. Killen & J. Smetana (Eds.), *Handbook of moral development* (pp. 119–153). Mahwah, NJ: Lawrence Erlbaum.

Smetana, J. G., Killen, M., & Turiel, E. (1991). Children's reasoning about interpersonal and moral conflicts. *Child Development, 62,* 629–644.

Turiel, E., Killen, M., & Helwig, C. (1987). Morality: Its structure, functions, and vagaries. In J. Kagan & S. Lamb (Eds.), *The emergence of morality in young children* (pp. 155–243). Chicago: University of Chicago Press.

5 The Desirable Toddler in Preschool

Values Communicated in Teacher and Child Interactions

Anette Emilson and Eva Johansson

This chapter explores how values are fostered by teachers and expressed through the everyday interactions between teachers and children in the context of Swedish preschools. The specific aim of this chapter is to examine observational data concerned with the values that teachers explicitly or implicitly encourage and how these values are communicated to children. Values of interest are those concerned with how to treat others and the virtues that children are expected to develop in early childhood education programs. An assumption is that values that are encouraged say much about the picture of the desirable child in preschool and about what kind of child the preschool seeks to constitute. According to the curricula, a teachers' role is to consciously mediate and convey fundamental democratic values of the Swedish society to children (Ministry of Education and Science, 1998). However, the meaning of these values can, within a pluralistic society, be interpreted in various ways. It is not certain that society's interests and needs coincide with those of individual teachers, thus, a critical discussion about how and what values are fostered is important.

Ontologically, the study is inspired by the way Jürgen Habermas (1995) views society from both a life-world and a system perspective. From a life-world perspective, educational processes are directed towards individuals' understanding and meaning-making through communicative action while the system directs the same processes towards goals and successes for the overall society through strategic action. A communicative action is a cooperative action, between individuals oriented towards mutual understandings which enable dialogue in a subject-subject relationship. Strategic action, on the other hand, aims at gaining the goals of one party—which makes the other the object of the action—rather than creating a dialogue based on intersubjectivity. Therefore strategic action leads to an objectification of fellow beings since people are used instrumentally to protect personal interests. In this study, these concepts have been used when analyzing the communication of values.

FOSTERING VALUES IN PRESCHOOL

Previous research on fostering values in preschool provides three themes of relevance for this study. These themes are related to fostering values about *social order, care,* and *democracy.*

Fostering *social order* in preschool has, in several studies, been described in terms of a faceless discipline through actions that regulate and direct through routines (Ehn, 1983; Henckel, 1990; Nordin-Hultman, 2004). However, the expression of this value to foster social order has changed over time from more open authoritarian forms of exercising power to more invisible means of exercising power which are directed towards children's self-regulation. Implicit forms of fostering social order may be embedded in the impersonal rules and routines of the preschool and not necessarily through the use of explicit power used by an authoritarian adult (Nordin-Hultman, 2004). According to Berthelsen (2005) early childhood teachers emphasize the importance of conformity and adherence to rules and routines. Governing children by encouraging them to follow norms, take personal responsibility, and to self-regulate their own behavior has also been conceptualized by Bartholdsson (2007) as benevolent government. Play is another disciplinary technique in governing the child found by Tullgren (2003).

Fostering *values of caring* is also evident in educational practice and is based on ideas about nurturing and motherhood (Florin, 1987). Most teachers are women who are most likely to base their work on an ethic of solicitude and an ideal of caring in their educational practices in the early years (Gannerud, 1999). According to Thronton and Goldstein (2006) early childhood teachers take the position of caregivers by protecting children, offering children affiliation and comfort, and by emphasizing children's individual accomplishments. Markström (2005) found that, while caring is important in teachers' perspectives, their overarching goal is that the child should become independent and competent in caring for him or herself. Johansson (2002) identified that teachers encourage children to learn to share and respect others' belongings, care for others, develop an understanding for others' experiences and to show compassion. Teachers' strategies in fostering caring values were related to teachers' different ideas about how children learn moral values. Such ideas can exist side by side and are related to the specific context in which the value was communicated but also to the character of the actualized value (Johansson, 2002; Johansson & Johansson, 2003).

Fostering *values of democracy* in preschool has been explored in terms of children's participation and opportunities to influence pedagogical practice (e.g., Berthelsen & Brownlee, 2005; Cowell & Howes, 2001; Emilson, 2007; Emilson & Folkesson, 2006; Sheridan & Pramling Samuelsson, 2001). These studies have identified that children's influence is limited; often as a result of teachers´ attitudes, rules and their use of power. Emilson and Folkesson (2006) found that teacher control frames the everyday interactions in preschool. Strong teacher control restricts children's participation while weak teacher control can enhance children's participation on their own terms. Essential for children's participation is a teacher who creates meaningful contexts while being emotionally present, supportive, and responsive. Emilson (2007) also found that children's influence increases when teachers' control over the 'what' and 'how' aspects of communication is weak. To stimulate children's influence, control can be exhibited by adopting a playful manner that requires sensitive responsiveness by the teacher that endeavors to come close to the child's perspective and the child's life-world. Eriksen Ødegaard (2007) has discussed children's participation as a matter of negotiation. She found a shift in the locus of power between teachers and toddlers could occur through a child's engagement in a popular story. One of the boys in the toddler group introduced the story by repeatedly enacting it in play which led to the teachers' pedagogical practices changing from ignoring this play to capitalizing on this engagement with the story and the play that included the child's voice.

Values of democracy also refer to children's experiences of rights. According to Helwig (2006) experiences that allow children to exercise and develop their understanding of rights involve issues about how the child is allowed autonomy and given choices, as well as by involving children in complex social situations that require them to make decisions. Johansson (1999, 2007) found that the everyday activities in preschool, to a large extent, involve a variety of negotiations between teachers and children on rights—such as children's right to particular things; to share their worlds with friends; and to raise their voices. In this respect, teachers and children may differ in their assessments for children gaining rights. For instance, rights in the context of preschool seemed very restricted in the perspective of the children; however, the teachers meant that they assigned children rights in preschool. While the teachers highlighted the children's right to speak, the children referred to their obligation to be quiet.

To summarize, the research overview indicates that fostering of social order in preschool may have changed from more open authoritarian forms to more invisible means of exercising power. Moreover, while caring seems of high importance in teachers' perspectives, values of democracy in preschool seem to have less priority. Research has identified that children's influence is limited often as a result of teachers' attitudes, rules, and their use of power. However, none of the investigations reviewed were concerned with the totality of these value orientations, how they are interrelated and how they are communicated to children. This is the focus of interest in this study.

METHOD

The data reported in this chapter is drawn from video observations of everyday interactions between teachers and children in preschool. The fieldwork took place with three different groups of toddlers in Swedish preschools. Forty-six children (aged one to three years) participated, as

well as their ten teachers who were all women with several years of professional experience in early childhood teaching. The data consisted of 777
minutes of video observations including 115 teacher and child interactions
of different character and length. The first step in the analyses was to focus
on *what* kind of values teachers explicitly or implicitly communicated to
the children in all of the 115 observed interactions. Both verbal and non-
verbal communication, such as emotional expressions, glances, gestures,
and attitudes were taken into account in the analyses. Next, all situations
were summarized and written down and sorted out into different values.
The norms and the competencies that the teachers appeared to encourage
in their behavior or that they appeared to hinder in their interactions with
the children have been interpreted as values. These analyses resulted in
the identification of ten values. These values were analyzed in combination with theoretical inspirations from the work of Habermas concerned
with *how* the teachers communicated the values when they interacted
with the children. The key concepts of interest were the communicative
and strategic action (Habermas, 1995). While a communicative action
is oriented towards mutual understandings, which enable dialogue in a
subject-subject relationship, a strategic action, aims at gaining the goals
of one party, thereby the other (i.e., the child) becomes the object of the
action. The dialogue results in a subject-object relationship.

The next step was the analysis of all situations representative of every
value in order to choose situations that appeared to be typical and to select
one representative for each value. To facilitate a deeper analysis, these chosen situations were then transcribed in full. The transcriptions focused
mainly on the characteristics of the value evident, but also how these values
were communicated. Later, the nature of the ten values was reviewed in
order to conceptualize the relationships between the values. Three overall
value dimensions were found which appeared to have two different social
orientations.

Below the results are summarized. They are empirically exemplified by
four chosen situations.[1] These situations are chosen because they represent
the three value dimensions as well as different communication forms.

RESULTS

The analyses resulted in ten specific values embedded in value dimensions
of: caring, democratic and discipline. These, in turn, can be differentiated
into two social orientations—collective and individualistic. In Figure 5.1.,
the model identifying the values and their organizational relationship to
each other is represented.

The figure shows the ten values that were frequently encouraged by
the teachers when they interacted with the children. These values may be
viewed to have either collective or individual orientations. They encompass

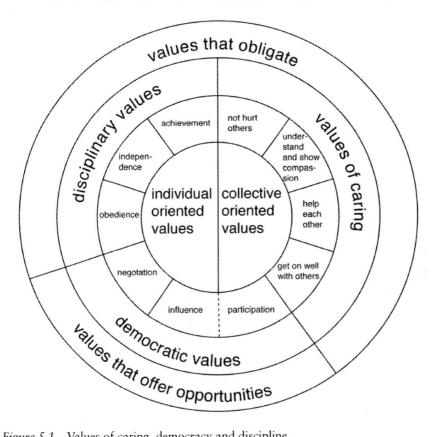

Figure 5.1 Values of caring, democracy and discipline.

value dimensions of caring, democracy, and discipline. The collective orientation encompasses value dimensions of care for others and democracy that accentuates participation in the preschool community. The individual orientation encompasses the value dimension of discipline, as well as democracy that was a value dimension also evident in the collective orientation. The care and discipline value dimensions reflect values and behaviors that obligate while the democratic value dimension reflects values and behaviors that provide offers for participation to children and that afford opportunities for participatory behaviors in the preschool classroom.

When the teachers explicitly or implicitly encourage children to develop particular values, they use different communication forms, here interpreted as either communicative or strategic. However, a strategic action was more common when values in the disciplinary dimension were in the forefront of the teachers' intentions, while the democratic dimension seems to presuppose a communicative action. A strategic action was more common when discipline was communicated, while a communicative action seems to be needed to mediate values within the democratic dimension.

Values connected to the disciplinary dimension, on the one hand, often take shape through demanding imperatives and thereby making the child an object of the action, whereas values related to the democratic dimension, on the other hand, seem to diminish and give rise to another value if they are expressed through strategic action. The values within the dimension of caring are also communicated strategically, although a communicative action appears as well. Interactions related to caring values come about both as subject-subject dialogues between teachers and children but also as acts for gaining the goals of one party (the teacher), and the child thereby becomes the object of the action.

The Dimension of Caring Values

In the dimension of caring, the values have a collective social orientation that supports the child's integration into the preschool community. These values obligate the child to get on well with others, help each other, understand and show compassion, and not hurt others (See Figure 5.1.). The analyses show that values within the caring dimension can be communicated differently, strategically as well as communicatively. In this session two situations are chosen representative of this caring value dimension (i.e., 'not hurt others' and 'understand and show compassion'). Moreover these situations represent both forms of communication and, from the example, we can learn how these different forms of communication impose on the content of the value.

Children should not hurt others.

In the interactions the teachers strongly emphasized that the children should not hurt each other.

> Steven (2:3) and Patrick (2:8) are playing with bricks in a corner of the play-room. Suddenly Steven throws a brick at Patrick's head and Patrick starts to cry. The teacher looks up and exclaims: "Steven!" She walks towards the boys and grasps Steven's arms and says with an angry voice: "Look here! What have you done to Patrick?" Steven tries to get free from the teacher's grasp but she doesn't release him. "Look at me! Don't do that. Look how sad Patrick is," she says resolutely while trying to gain eye contact with Steven. Patrick cries. Steven looks quickly at Patrick. The teacher holds Steven's arms and still tries to achieve eye-contact. She exhorts Steven to give Patrick a pat on the cheek, but Steven looks like he doesn't want to. He looks down at the floor. "And you . . . now you look at me," the teacher continues. "You are not allowed to have these things if you are going to fight over them.

You must not do so again. Don't do such things again," the teacher says with an angry voice. "No-o," says Steven.

The teacher communicates that it is not allowed to fight in preschool. This is strongly marked by the teacher's serious attitude. She also communicates that hurting others should be punished. Steven is presented with an ultimatum, namely if he fights with the bricks he won't be allowed to use them. Furthermore, it is communicated that a transgression towards others' well-being should be recompensed which is why Steven also is exhorted to give Patrick a pat on the cheek. This value can be interpreted as about not hurting others and includes an emphasis that there is a need to control the body, personal needs, and feelings.

The teacher's action is to be viewed as *strategic* whereby Steven becomes an object for the teachers' goals for fostering values. In the teacher's immediate interpretation of Steven's behavior she decides how she is going to act irrespective of what might have caused Steven to throw the brick. While holding Steven's arms the teacher exhorts him to look at her. She seems angry and she uses scolding and threats in order to correct his behavior. Steven's way of acting is disqualified and he appears as guilty. One interpretation is that Steven offers a form of resistance to the teacher's reprimands. He doesn't look at her and he tries to break free from her grasp. Nevertheless, there is an asymmetrical relationship which makes his objections and attempts to escape ineffective. He surrenders to the order by finally saying what the teacher seems to be waiting for, namely agreement with her interpretation of the situation that he will not throw bricks at others any more.

Children should understand and show compassion.

The teachers do not just seem to encourage the children not to hurt each other but they consider it desirable that the children are able to understand other children's perspectives.

Patrick (2:8), Steven (2:6) and one of the teachers play with water. The children sit next to a big bath-tub with just napkins on. Both children splash and pour the water. While Patrick laughs happily Steven seems to dislike when the water splashes. Patrick takes a big plastic crocodile to splash around. The crocodile hits Steven's hand and Steven starts to cry. Patrick looks at the teacher who turns to Steven and says with compassion in her voice: "Ow, ow, ow! What did the crocodile do?" Steven cries and Patrick looks at the teacher. The teacher continues with a playful voice: "Ohh, what a crocodile! Did he bite you? Shame on the crocodile!" Steven becomes silent and looks wondering at the crocodile. Patrick returns to the play and splashes close to Steven. Steven tries to avoid the sprinkling water. "Ohhhh," he says. His voice is whining. The teacher asks calmly if it is too much splashing now: "Ye-es, too

much," Steven answers. His voice is low. He holds his hands in front
of his face when Patrick continues to splash: "Patrick you should not
splash any more with that [the crocodile]. Steven doesn't like it when
the water splashes," says the teacher calmly and with an appealing
voice: "That crocodile has to swim a little bit more carefully."

As in the previous example, this situation is also basically about not hurting others, but more specifically the teacher in this situation communicates
the importance of understanding others and showing compassion. This value
here seems to contain both an emotional and a cognitive aspect where the
emotional appears most explicitly by emphasizing the experience of the other.
A cognitive dimension is also discerned when the teacher tries to explain why
Patrick can't splash the water any more which also implicitly communicates
that Patrick is seen as capable of understanding the meaning of this value.

The teacher's action is interpreted as communicative when she takes up
an intersubjective attitude and encounters the children in a dialogue where
mutual understanding seems to be essential. The teacher is alternating
between tuning in to each child and being playful. Neither of the children
is held responsible for what happened which was the case in the previous
example. In this situation, the guilty one is the crocodile. Patrick continues
to splash close to Steven and the teacher asks Steven twice if it is too much
splashing. She then appeals to Patrick to stop splashing the water and she
directs his attention towards Steven's experience. It seems as though the
teacher tries to encourage understanding and feeling for others by each boy
when she indicates respect for both Steven's and Patrick's point of views.

The Dimension of Democratic Values

Values referring to democracy can be both collectively and individually
oriented. The value dimension of democracy when it is collectively oriented
is about *participation*, while individually oriented values emerge as opportunities for the children, partly to *influence* pedagogical practice and partly
to make themselves heard through a form of *negotiation* (See Figure 5.1.).
Democratic values seem to be based on a communicative action and a strategic action was not found within this category. If teachers try to mediate
democracy strategically a different value will arise. Below we will analyze
how influence can be communicated to toddlers in preschool. This value
has been selected because it illustrates an individually oriented value that
presupposes some kind of participation that is collectively oriented.

Children are offered opportunity to influence.

According to the data related to this dimension, children are provided
opportunities to influence pedagogical practice by making choices, taking
initiatives, expressing their will, and protecting their own integrity.

The children are on their way out and most of them are putting their outdoor clothes on. Cleo (2:11) and Morgan (3:2) are still in the bathroom. Morgan stands on a stool in front of the wash-basin and runs the water. With a washcloth he starts to scrub the wash-basin. The teacher comes and says: "How elegant, Morgan. It's nice of you to tidy up." Cleo, who stands beside Morgan, looks at the teacher. Then she turns towards Morgan and watches what he is doing. Morgan puts liquid soap on the washcloth. Cleo also fetches a washcloth. The teacher walks away and the children are allowed to continue. Morgan turns the water on and off several times. Cleo laughs. Then he starts to scrub again. He takes more soap. "Not too much," Cleo says, but Morgan takes even more. The teacher comes back and asks the children if they are ready yet. They are not, so she leaves. Also Cleo takes a place on the stool and the children scrub together. After a while the teacher returns. She places herself close to the children and watches. Cleo steps down and the teacher asks Morgan: "Are there still some stains left?" Morgan scrubs at the stains. "It slides away." Morgan says and tries to catch the stain, which slides down outside the wash-basin. "Yes it slides," confirms the teacher. "Does it slide down? Where does it go?" asks the teacher. Morgan follows the stain. "It slid away," says the teacher again. There is a small stain left. "Are you going to tidy up that one too?" The teacher points at a stain in the wash-basin. Morgan scrubs. "Now it is elegant," says the teacher. She takes the washcloth and puts it on the wash-basin and tells Morgan that he can continue later. When Morgan continues to scrub the teacher says: "Stop." At first, Morgan ignores the instruction but when she says, "Stop," once again he stops without objections.

Besides the value of influence including opportunities to make choices and to take initiatives the interaction seems to convey trust and respect. Morgan and Cleo are allowed to make their own choices and take initiatives and each one seems to have control over the activity, even if the premises differ. It is Morgan who mainly directs the activity, since it was his initiative from the beginning. Therefore, he seems to have the right to the activity. It is obvious that the children influence the situation, which the teacher makes possible by her support. This situation points at individuality in which the child's own needs and interests are in focus. The emphasis is rather on the individual than on the collective and the public good.

Also here the teacher's action is to be viewed as *communicative*, when concordance and mutuality seem to be guiding the actions. It appears that she treats the children as communication partners. She asks open questions, like when she wonders where the stain has gone. It seems like she tries to encounter the children symmetrically by meeting them respectfully, with trust, and by coming close to the children's perspectives. She gives them more time to engage in the activity when they do not seem to be ready. However, it is the teacher who finally decides when the activity must cease. It might be interpreted as the teacher having the overall control but it also shows that communicative action isn't without direction. The teacher says, "Stop," which is ignored at first by Morgan but when she marks one more time that the activity must be ended, he stops without objections. Partly, this can be interpreted as that he simply obeys an authority, partly that the activity is broken off in some form of agreement. For the moment, both parties seem to be agreed, perhaps because the teacher expresses that Morgan can continue later which she marks by showing him where she has put his washcloth.

The Dimension of Disciplinary Values

Disciplinary values are individually oriented and deal with *obedience, independence* and *achievements* (see Figure 5.1.). These values lay claim to specific behaviors and are interpreted as values that obligate children to behave in certain ways. Discipline is almost always communicated strategically by the teachers and below we will look closer at how such communication can emerge. This example is selected because it illustrates how the goal of the teacher is in the forefront of the communication. Through explicit authoritarian forms of communication the teacher tries to reach a certain purpose and there is no room for the child either to question or to negotiate.

Children should show obedience.

In several situations the teachers indicate that children shall do as they are told.

> It's circle time. The children sit on the benches and on the carpet that frame the circle time corner. In front of the children, the teacher sits on a low chair. Before starting the circle time the teacher tries to induce everyone to sit on the benches. Sofie (2:8) doesn't want to sit on the bench and looks at the teacher and says: "Carpet." "Yes you sit on the carpet," the teacher answers. "Sit here," says Robin who is also sitting on the carpet. "Yes but you shall not sit on the carpet. You shall sit on the bench," says the teacher. "Where is the bench?" she asks the children. "There," says Sofie and points at the bench behind her back. "Yes, go and take a seat then," says the teacher. Sofie doesn't move. "I sit," says Sonny (2:4) and sits down on the carpet next to Sofie. Sofie and Sonny look at the teacher. "Well, the teddy bear and the rabbit won't come until you sit on the bench. They are waiting for you," the teacher says. Sonny sits close to Sofie. She protests and looks at the teacher who says with an irritated voice: "Yes, but go and take a seat at the bench then." Sofie mumbles something about that Sonny must not shove and the teacher once again tells Sofie to take a seat on the bench. "Well, then the teddy bear and the rabbit won't come.

When you sit on the bench the teddy and the rabbit will come," says the teacher. The children stay on the carpet and the teacher continues. "Then I'll wait until you take your seats on the bench." Sonny crawls on all four towards the bench and immediately he is confirmed by the teacher who happily says: "Good Sonny." Another teacher enters the room and says: "What . . . you should sit here . . . come on." She drums with her fingers at free seats on the bench. Sofie mumbles: "Sit here." "No on the bench," the teacher answers still drumming at the bench. "Sit there . . . I sit there," says Robin and points at the carpet. "Robin, when there are lots of children, then you are allowed to sit on the carpet. But today we sit on the bench," says the teacher who recently entered the room. She goes towards Robin and lifts him up and puts him on the bench. Thereafter, she does the same to Sofie. Now the teddy bear comes and the circle time starts.

The teacher communicated to the children that they should do as they are told without questioning or negotiating. What is to be understood from the situation is that the children usually are allowed to sit on the carpet during circle time when there is not enough room for them all on the benches. The demand to sit on the bench in this case might be interpreted as an adult decision formulated for the time being. It is neither motivated nor explained to the children. This seems to be confusing to them and they meet the demand with resistance by not taking seats on the bench. Finally this leads to the teacher simply lifting them up. The value of obedience comes from the teacher's perspective in this situation and might be used to maintain control. This position is about the *adapted and formed* child who is capable of taking instructions and is to do what she/he is told.

The teacher's actions are to be viewed as *strategic* when her orientation seems to be directed towards success. It looks like her intention is to reach a certain purpose and to get the children to do as she says and this maintains order in the preschool. The way to obedience seems to be by control, threats, and dominance. The teacher uses an authoritarian voice and remarks that the circle time will not start until the children have taken their seats on the bench. When the children don't do as they are told she uses another strategy, namely threats. Dominance is shown as asymmetry between the teacher and the child. There is no room for negotiation and objections are ineffective.

DISCUSSION

The aim of this chapter was to study the values that teachers explicitly or implicitly demonstrated and encouraged in their interaction with children, as well as how these values were communicated. In this section, the values identified and discussed in this chapter are reviewed. Thereafter, the findings are discussed ontologically from the points of view of this study: a life-world perspective and a system perspective.

Caring, Democratic, and Disciplinary Values

In this research, three value dimensions were identified as caring values, democratic values, and disciplinary values. One conclusion that can be drawn from the findings is that the desirable child in preschool is caring, democratic and disciplined. The caring child shouldn't hurt others; instead he or she should understand and feel for others, help others and get on well with others. These values obligate the child to act in certain ways. The democratic child, on the other hand, steps forward and influences everyday life in preschool. However, influence is not just taken; it is also given by the teachers. Partly the democratic child contributes to the public good by participating and engaging in the educational practice, partly he or she contributes to his/her own good by influencing and negotiating which sometimes leads to the child's own voice being heard. Democratic values appeared as more or less explicit offers to the children. This means that these values emerge neither as obligations nor as a necessity. The disciplinary value dimension referred to a child who should adapt to the prevailing order by obeying adults, being independent, as well as being able to take instructions and do what is expected. In other words, the values of caring and discipline require specific actions (i.e., the child is obligated to act in accord with these values) while the democratic value dimension offers opportunities for specific actions but the child is not required to behave in accordance with these values and can be engaged on his/her own terms.

Moving between Collectively and Individually Oriented Values

The values identified in this study are directed either towards collective or the individual orientations, thus teachers' actions towards children seems to alternate between sociability on the one hand; to support inclusion; and individuality on the other hand, to promote children as autonomous persons. Alternating between these approaches might be seen as ambivalence between containing a child who, on the one hand, should be adaptable and who does not question or negotiate and, on the other hand, should be able to step forward as a communicative subject who is expected to have something to say. We can also see similar alternation in the teachers' actions. On the one hand, teachers try to regulate the child's behavior and, on the other hand, they try to be responsive to the child's perspective by listening to, and interpreting, the child's intentions and expressions of meaning.

Strategic and Communicative Action

Values are communicated differently. When teachers act strategically they are communicating to the children from their ideas about what a child is and should be. The tone of the communication can be formal or sharp, and sanctions as well as threats may be presented. Such normalizing techniques are discussed by Tullgren (2003) who argues that these aim at homogeneity: to get children to follow norms, take responsibility, behave themselves, and make good choices. Johansson (2002, 2004) has shown that threats and punishment might occur when values of importance to the teachers are threatened. Therefore, there is a risk that teachers act in a way that creates distance from children's life-worlds and meaning-making. Similarly, claims for absolute obedience were sometimes expressed in this study, for example, in the circle time situation.

When the teachers are striving to be responsive to the child's perspective there is room for communication *with* the child instead of *to* the child. These actions can be described as *communicative*, which means that the child is ascribed their own way to both understand and be active in the world. The findings also give support to previous research by Emilson (2007) and Johansson (2003, 2004) regarding teacher and child interactions in preschool. Both argue that a teacher's ability to come close to children's perspectives is an important issue for children's learning and participation. Closeness to children's perspectives presumes bodily as well as mental presence, playfulness, and a kind of shared meaning-making.

However, communicative and strategic actions do not exclude each other. Instead educational practice holds both types of actions. Hence, dichotomy thinking should be avoided. According to Habermas (1995) it is of importance to understand that the forms of communication are rational in different ways and lead to different consequences that must be professionally considered. In the next section, such consequences for upbringing in the context of preschool will be discussed. These two types of actions will be put into a wider context and the communication forms will be linked to the concepts of the system and the life-word.

Fostering of Values in Preschool from the Perspective of the System and the Life-World

Values within the care and discipline dimensions seem to be deeply rooted in preschool traditions. This was established by Gannerud (1999) who suggested that preschool develops a fostering discourse in which caring is given priority. Several other researchers argue that discipline values and discourses are also more, or less, taken for granted (Markström 2005; Nordin Hultman, 2004). It is within these care and discipline dimensions we can find one important aspect of cultural reproduction in how the preschool fosters values. This specific reproduction is probably established in both societal systems as well as the every day life in preschool. This reproduction maintains the values that together constitute the picture of the desirable child. From a system perspective, the reproduction might be understood as an effective 'forming' or shaping of the child in a given direction. This direction might be taken for granted in preschool culture but is also a direction formulated in terms of goals that are found in the curriculum (Ministry of Education and Science in Sweden, 1998). These goals express, for example, that each child should develop openness, respect, solidarity, responsibility, consideration, helpfulness, and an understanding of equality. The goals are formulated within the system to guarantee a particular fostering and maintaining of order in the name of society. In this way, teachers represent society's interests and their commission is to mediate these specific values.

From a system perspective, teachers act in accordance with a goal-oriented rationality. This means to act in a manner in which the prescribed goals can be reached effectively. When such a goal orientation is prevalent, there is a risk that teachers act strategically with an objectification of the child as a consequence. This is evident in the data of this study. However, the curriculum goals do not advocate a reproduction of the culture of order and obedience; rather these goals imply that children are active competent co-constructionists. Hence, it is reasonable to suggest that the system can contribute to new experiences that can reconstruct ideas concerning values. This appears in data when the teachers act communicatively and when they take a starting-point in children's perspectives. It is shown in the data that a communicative action is not without direction. Teachers can both allow room for children's initiatives and choices and, at the same time, direct their attention towards a goal. This was shown in the example where the children were cleaning the washbasin.

From a life-world perspective, the reproduction of values changes focus, moving from a goal orientation towards an orientation of understanding in which the child's own perspective becomes a central issue. Hence the reproduction seems to be more flexible and dynamic when the child becomes an actor in their own integration in preschool. This is exemplified in the situation that communicates the value of participation in which Cleo and Morgan both were engaged in a meaningful activity. The conditions for the children's participation related to the teacher's orientation towards understanding and being able to do this from the children's point of view. However, this is not enough. Another condition is that the teacher must believe that children both are, and can be, active subjects, providing them with opportunities and offers to be active.

Intersubjectivity—Mutuality and Playfulness

When a teacher's actions take their starting-point in children's perspectives some essential qualities in the communication of values emerge. What is most striking is the playfulness that seems to permeate these situations. A characteristic feature is that the participants are laughing and joking. It looks like fostering contains an intersubjective dimension here, in which the teacher acknowledges the child as a dialogue partner. Such communication creates an encounter in which both the teacher and the child become subjects, and the relationship seems to rest on a mutual curiosity of the perspective of each other. From a life-world perspective, the reproduction might be widened so a production of values within the democratic dimension might be included. Above curiosity, the communication needs to be directed towards a specific content—a democratic value to obtain mutual understanding about the focus of attention.

Mutuality and Power—a Problematic Relationship

Questions of democracy have been stressed by educational thinkers for many years and are highlighted in the curriculum. According to Lindahl (2005) a child's right to a democratic upbringing is still a new focus in the everyday life in preschool. In such upbringing communicative action with the aim to obtain cooperation and mutual understanding is of importance (Habermas, 1995). Sometimes such mutuality occurs in teacher-child interactions but still the concept remains somewhat problematic.

The question is whether the relations between teachers and preschool children admit mutuality. In contrast to children, adults possess power, responsibility, and a completely different opportunity to survey situations and actions. Symmetry in these relations is almost impossible. In several examples it is difficult to say whether there is an agreement between teachers and children or whether children just are adapting to the adult's viewpoint, even if it appears that teachers and children are agreed. Does Morgan for example agree with the teacher when he, after the teacher's explanations and commands, finally stops his activity with the wash-cloth? Of course we can't say why he acts as he does but he looks satisfied and he does not protest any longer. Perhaps his actions are grounded both in a feeling of an agreement (he is promised to be allowed to continue later) and an adaptation to the teacher's authority.

One can ask if values of democracy are a form of implicit control; a way for teachers to maintain power. What appear to be values of democracy in some of the interactions presented could also be expressions of a new and more implicit control of children that is described by Nordin-Hultman (2004). Allowing children to express themselves and involving them in decisions is not necessarily just an expression of democracy. It might be a goal-directed strategy whereby protests and conflicts are avoided with the purpose of controlling children or encouraging obedience. Johansson (2007) has questioned the rhetoric of democracy in preschool pedagogy since reflections on the power relations between teachers and children are often missing. Preschool children do not have real influence over their own situation or over their preschool activities. Instead, they are always dependent on an adult's good will, which might mean that rights can be given to them but also easily taken away from them. Thus, adults have the responsibility to both defend and work for children's rights in early childhood education (Johansson, 2005).

In summary, we have found that the desirable preschool child is caring, democratic and disciplined. We have also found that these values can be communicated differently and that the 'what' aspect of the communication (the value) is interrelated with the 'how' aspect of the communication. In other words, how teachers communicate influences and sometimes change the communicated value. If the intention, for example, is to communicate democracy, a communicative action seems to be needed, otherwise another value arises. Intersubjectivity, including playfulness and curiosity, is found to be a central aspect in the teacher's communicative actions. However, one conclusion is that the different communication forms generate different values. On the other hand, if certain values are essential to the teachers this sometimes leads to strategic action. The dilemma that occurs is that the values communicated can counteract the values that the teachers want to emphasize. Therefore, it is important to be aware of the consequences that follow from the two types of action. It then becomes possible for teachers to more consciously decide how to act and when an action might be rational. The values discussed in this chapter can all be seen as more or less important. In the Swedish curriculum, however, democratic values are explicitly expressed and emphasized as well as values of care. To promote these values, this research has shown that a communicative action is needed. However, the point is not to reduce the communication to either communicative or strategic, but rather to realize when the different types of actions are justified.

NOTE

1. The entire result of this investigation is presented elsewhere (cf. Emilson, manuscript).

REFERENCES

Bartholdsson, Å. (2007). *Med facit i hand: Normalitet, elevskap och vänlig maktutövning i två svenska skolor* [Having the correct answer: Normality, pupils and benevolent government in two Swedish schools]. Stockholm: HLS förlag.

Berthelsen, D. (2005). Organizational morality and children's engagement in early childhood programs. In J. Mason & T. Fattore (Eds.), *Children Taken Seriously: In theory policy and practice* (pp. 317–339). London: Jessica Kingsley Publications.

Berthelsen, D., & Brownlee, J. (2005). Respecting children's agency for learning and rights to participation in Child care programs. *International Journal of Early Childhood*, 3(36), 49–60.

Cowell, K., & Howes, B. (2001). Moral education through the 3 Rs: Rights, Respect, and Responsibility. *Journal of Moral Education*, 30(1), 29–41.

Ehn, B. (1983). *Ska vi leka tiger?* [Shall we play tiger?]. Lund, Sweden: Liber förlag.

Emilson, A., & Folkesson, A-M. (2006). Children's participation and Teacher control. *Early Child Development and Care*, 3–4(176), 219–238.

Emilson, A. (2007). Young Children's Influence in Preschool. *International Journal of Early Childhood*, 1(39), 11–38.

Eriksen Ødegaard, E. (2007). *Meningsskaping i barnehagen. Inhold og bruk av barns og voksnes samtalefortellinger* [Narrative meaning-making in preschool]. Göteborg, Sweden: ACTA Universitatis Gothoburgensis.

Florin, C. (1987). *Kampen om katedern, feminiserings- och professionaliseringsprocessen inom svenska folkskolans lärarkår 1860–1906* [The fight for the teacher's desk]. Stockholm: Almquist & Wiksell International.

Gannerud, E. (1999). *Genusperspektiv på lärargärning: om kvinnliga klasslärares liv och arbete* [Gender perspectives on teaching: female teachers' life and work]. (Göteborg Studies in Educational Sciences, 137). Göteborg, Sweden: Acta Universitatis Gothoburgensis.

Habermas, J. (1995). *Kommunikativt handlande, Texter om språk, rationalitet och samhälle* [Communicative action. Texts about language, rationality and society]. Göteborg, Sweden: Daidalos.

Helwig, C. C. (2006). Rights, civil liberties, and democracy across cultures. In M. Killen & J. S. Smetana (Eds.), *Handbook of Moral Development* (pp. 185–210). Mahwah, NJ: Lawrence Erlbaum.

Henckel, B. (1990). *Förskollärare i tanke och handling: en studie kring begreppen arbete, lek och inlärning.*[Pre-school teachers in thought and actions]. Umeå, Sweden: Umeå universitet, Pedagogiska institutionen.

Johansson, E. (1999). *Etik i små barns värld: Om värden och normer bland de yngsta barnen i förskolan* [Ethics in small children's worlds. Values and norms among the youngest children in preschool]. Göteborg Studies in Educational Sciences, 141. Göteborg, Sweden: Acta Universitatis Gothoburgensis.

———. (2002). Morality in preschool interaction: Teachers' strategies for working with children's morality. *Early Child Development and Care, 172, 203–221.*

———. (2003). *Möten för lärande. Pedagogisk verksamhet för de yngsta barnen i förskolan* [Encounters for learning—Quality aspects of early childhood education for toddlers]. Swedish National Agency for Education, Forskning i fokus no 6. Stockholm: Fritzes.

———. (2004). Learning encounters in preschool—interaction between atmosphere, view of children and of learning. *International Journal of Early Childhood, 1*(36), 9–26.

———. (2005). Children's integrity—a marginalised right. *International Journal of Early Childhood, 3*(36), 109–124.

———. (2007). *Etiska överenskommelser i förskolebarns världar* [Moral agreements in preschool-children's worlds]. Göteborg Studies in Educational Sciences, 251. Göteborg, Sweden: Acta Universitatis Gothoburgensis.

Johansson, E., & Johansson, B. (2003). *Etiska möten i skolan* [Moral encounters in school: Values in interaction between young children and their teachers]. Stockholm: Liber förlag.

Lindahl, M. (2005). Children's right to democratic upbringings. *International Journal of Early Childhood, 3*(36), 33–48.

Markström, A-M. (2005). *Förskolan som normaliseringspraktik. En etnografisk studie* [Preschool as a normalizing practice—an ethnographic study]. Linköping, Sweden: Linköpings Universtitet, Department of Educational Sciences.

Ministry of Education and Science in Sweden. (1998). *Curriculum for preschool, Lpfö-98.* Stockholm: Fritzes.

Nordin Hultman, E. (2004). *Pedagogiska miljöer och barns subjektsskapande* [Educational contexts and children's identities and subjectivity]. Stockholm: Liber.

Sheridan, S., & Pramling Samuelsson, I. (2001). Children's conceptions of participation and influence in preschool: A perspective on pedagogical quality. *Contemporary Issues in Early Childhood, 2*(2), 169–194.

Thronton, C. D., & Goldstein, L. (2006). Feminist issues in early childhood scholarship. In B. Spodek & O. N. Saracho (Eds.), *Handbook of Research on the Education of Young Children* (pp. 515–531). Mahwah, NJ: Lawrence Erlbaum.

Tullgren, C. (2003). *Den välreglerade friheten. Att konstruera det lekande barnet* [The well-regulated freedom. To construct the playing child]. Malmö, Sweden: Malmö högskola, Lärarutbildningen.

6   Friendships and Participation among Young Children in a Norwegian Kindergarten

Anne Greve

The aim of this chapter is to develop knowledge about the nature of young children's friendships in a Norwegian kindergarten (*barnehage*) and to examine what children learn from participation in these friendships. According to a sociocultural theory, learning is first and foremost a process that takes place through relationships with others (Greve, 2007; Williams et al., 2001). What very young children learn from their peers is different from what they can learn from adults and older children (Frønes, 1994). In the research which is reported in this chapter, Norwegian toddlers were videoed in their kindergarten activities across a ten month period (Greve, 2007). The analyses presented are based upon observations from two groups of toddlers but also includes comment on analyses from a current study of friendship among one-year-old toddlers. In both studies, observations of groups aged from one to three years of age have been made. In the first study, I found that the friendships of toddlers, as with friendships of older children, are about closeness and connection. Through participation in friendships, children learn about ethics, cooperation, and intersubjectivity.

In this chapter, I will describe different relationships between children that were observed in these studies (Greve, 2007). Each friendship is unique and different in style. I will focus, in particular, on Ivar who participated in several different relationships with peers and present analyses of these friendships. I will examine the meaning of participation. Finally, I will discuss what toddlers learn through participation in these friendships.

THE SOCIAL CHILD

In understanding that children are social actors who create social order through their interactions with other children, we can come to understand the everyday life of children through children's perspectives (Ivarsson, 2003). In this chapter, I wish to challenge the viewpoint that very young children do not benefit from social interaction with peers. Traditional theories of socialization consider development as merely the individual child's internalization of adult abilities and knowledge. These theories attach particular importance to individual outcomes. Such individually-focused approaches ignore the complexity of social structure, culture, and communicative processes in young children's interactions. Socialization is not only a matter of adaptation and internalization but also a process of appropriation, reinvention, and reproduction (Corsaro, 2005). Within modern pedagogy, the child's lived worlds and the child's experiences are more in focus, reflecting a so-called paradigm shift in psychology and pedagogy in how the child is viewed (Sommer, 2003b). Instead of considering the child as a *tabula rasa*, the child is now considered as a social person able to communicate and understand from an early age (Sommer, 2003a; Stern, 1985; Trevarthen, 1993).

A LIFE-WORLD PHENOMENOLOGY

One central aspect of the life-world phenomenology is that humans are situated in the world as a body subjects (Merleau-Ponty, 1945). Young children are able to express their thoughts and feelings even though they do not always express themselves verbally. Considering children as body-subjects within the tradition of a life-world phenomenology, it is possible to understand that toddlers express meanings with their bodies, with their voices, and with their whole appearance (Bengtsson, 2005; Greve, 2007; Johansson, 1999; Løkken, 2000; Merleau-Ponty, 1945). This is a starting point if we want to understand what toddlers intend to tell us and, thus, how we can come to understand and respect toddlers' ways of participating and contributing in their daily lives. According to the United Nation's Convention on the Rights of the Child, Article 12 (1989), children have a right to express themselves, participate and contribute. This implies a right to choose and have friends.

While many studies within sociocultural traditions consider friendship as a way of developing social competence (Frønes, 1994), or crucial to the children's culture (Corsaro, 1985, 1997, 2005; Corsaro & Eder, 1990; Ivarsson, 2003; Michélsen, 2004), I propose that friendship is a phenomenon with intrinsic value and will discuss in detail the characteristics and expression of friendship between very young children.

DIFFERENT STYLES OF FRIENDSHIP

Every friendship has its own history. This history is developed through everyday meetings between children. These meetings may lead to the experience of the mutual "we", as children learn how "just the two of us" are together. Schutz (1972) used the metaphor "growing older together" (p. 103). Every friendship is unique and distinct (Blum, 1994). It is possible to acknowledge the unique friendships of every child, without separating out the cognitive and the emotional dimensions and without focusing on a linear development from the immature to the mature.

Definitions of friendship between young children have hitherto been quite narrow. Almost all research on friendship claims that reciprocity is a requisite criterion of such relationships (Bliding, 2004; Damon, 1977; Dunn, 2004; Gottman, 1986; Howes, 1987; Whaley & Rubenstein, 1994). However, my research findings indicate that a more nuanced definition of friendship between young children is possible. While reciprocity may be an important condition for friendship, it does not always have to be present consistently in the relationship in order for the relationship to be defined as a friendship. Sometimes one person in a friendship may indicate that he or she does not want to be with the other person. This does not necessarily destroy the feeling of a mutual "we," as long as there is reciprocity in the relationship at other times. This represents the complexity which characterizes the dialectics of our existence (Merleau-Ponty, 1967).

THE MANY DIMENSIONS OF FRIENDSHIP

Friendship can have different dimensions, for example, one person can enter into different friendships that have unique and distinct characteristics. In my research, I found four dyads and two triads of friendship within one group of children (Greve, 2007). Each relationship had a different style that had developed through a mutually lived history that the children had experienced. The children had experienced what it is like to be together with their specific friend. Through different meetings, the children have built up a store of mutual experiences. Schutz (1972) uses the concept "stock of knowledge" to describe the grounding of experiences that each individual possesses as a basis for interpretation and action in the world (p. 169).

Ivar and Kari—A Relation of Rules and Care

Ivar and Kari, for example, have a style that focused on being fair, on politeness, and on rules. They had rules in their relationships, such as: one shall share toys; one shall ask before taking a toy; one shall respect a negative answer; one shall help the other; one shall say, "thank you." Kari and Ivar often talked to each other in an intimate way. Since Ivar and Kari played together almost every day, they had a store of mutual experiences and they knew immediately how to behave within their friendship. Thus, when Kari says, "Hi, cat—where are you?" Ivar knows exactly what to do. He knows how it is to be a cat when he plays with Kari. During the year, the friendship between Kari and Ivar became somewhat weaker in character. One reason for this might be that Kari took on a parenting role with Ivar. She made sure that Ivar ate his food and that he wore his cap when he was going outside. Ivar did not seem to appreciate being "nannied" by Kari. They remained friends across the whole year, even though Ivar also sought other friends, Fredrik and Nils.

Ivar and Fredrik—A Relation of Humor and Danger

When Ivar was with his other friend, Fredrik, there was much more humor than in his relationship with Kari, combined with a way of being dangerous. Ivar and Fredrik were frightening the other children. They were chasing monsters and huge dinosaurs. They pretended to be dangerous pirates so that they could destroy things. When they were together, they talked with deep voices and walked in a special bouncing way. None of the other children walked like this. This was Ivar's and Fredrik's way of being in the world together. At the same time, the two boys expressed a lot of humor and joy. They looked at each other with twinkles in their eyes; they laughed and had lots of fun together. Ivar and Fredrik defended their friendship against others. By refusing other children's admittance, they protected their own relationship. However, this was not any absolute rule in their relationship. Sometimes Ivar and Fredrik opened up for other children to join them in play.

Ivar and Nils—A Relation of Bodily Togetherness

When Ivar was with his friend Nils, they focused on bodily activities. They had lots of fun climbing on mattresses, jumping from the sofa, chasing each other, etcetera. This relationship was mostly based on bodily communication and not so much on verbal language. Nevertheless, there were some words like cast, nod, look, boo, which contributed to feelings of solidarity and mutual humor. Like the other friendships in the kindergarten group, this friendship grew up as a result of the everyday experiences. Ivar was a popular boy with whom many of the other children wanted to play. Nils was less stable in his physical movements and also verbally, than many of the other children in the group. It was not always easy for him to be included in Ivar's play. Ivar would often choose to play with other children. At the beginning of the year, Ivar and Nils played together more often when they used small play areas such as the cloakroom or the bathroom. For example, play in the cloakroom involved playing peek-a-boo behind the coats.

During the year, Ivar and Nils built up a mutual store of experiences as a foundation for their relationship, thus, it became easier for them to play together, both indoors and outdoors. Sometimes it seemed that they knew exactly what each other was thinking and a simple word from one or the other was enough to enable an understanding of what was required in the play. Sometimes the friendship between Ivar and Nils was characterized by Nils' one-sided desire to be with Ivar. Nils really cheered up when he observed Ivar come into the room. It often seemed that he missed Ivar and he would show real joy when the two of them met—stretching his arms towards Ivar and calling his name. Ivar did not always show the same feelings in return. If we were to describe friendship as dependent on reciprocal relations which demands mutuality, then it would not be possible to talk about friendship between these children. It is possible that Nils' desire to be with Ivar also had an effect on Ivar. In his admiration, Nils confirmed Ivar. This suggests that it might be necessary to accept that friendships between young children have several dimensions. In those situations where Ivar, in return, wanted to be with Nils, the two children expressed their experience as a mutual "we." Additionally, sometimes their interactions were quite limited in time. In any event, these meetings and the sequences of interaction contributed to build a friendship between the two boys with special and unique ways of being together in the world.

Ivar, Kari, and Fredrik—A Relation of Negotiation

Ivar also took part in other two triads in the kindergarten group. One was with Kari and Fredrik, the other was with Nils and Fredrik. The first triad was characterized by negotiation. In the beginning, Fredrik did not play a prominent part in the relationship. He would imitate Kari or Ivar and he took a more passive role in their mutual play. Nevertheless, his participation in the group of three contributed to a mutual friendship between these children. Together they built a store of mutual experiences. Over time, Fredrik played a more active role in the friendship group and, thus, the element of negotiation was stronger. It seems like both Kari and Fredrik wanted to be with Ivar and there were often negotiations about who was to be included in their play. By the end of the year, Kari seemed to have established a secondary position in the triad. As previously noted the relationship between Kari and Ivar also changed in its character across the year. Ivar choose to play more frequently with children other than Kari who initially had been his first choice at the beginning of the year.

Ivar, Nils, and Fredrik

In the other triad of Ivar, Nils, and Fredrik, there were elements of competition. It seemed like the relationship was more dependent than the other relationships on participation from an adult[1] or that Ivar had a role as the connecting link between Nils and Fredrik. Without participation from an adult or Ivar's willingness to act as a connecting link, this triad fell apart. Still, these three children expressed feelings of mutuality in their relationship and, therefore, it was defined as friendship. In this triad, Ivar and Fredrik were the leaders. Nils followed the other two children in their activities. For example, once Ivar asked Fredrik if they should be dangerous animals. Nils did not ask any questions but would just follow into their play. Nils wanted to be with Ivar and Ivar did not deny him this. Ivar provided the connection between Fredrik and Nils. When these three children were together, there was not so much verbal interaction but rather close bodily contact. There was a lot of laughter when they were together. They communicated and showed their mutuality through imitation and through waiting for turns in play activities.

These findings point to the complexities of friendship among young children and emphasized the unique features in each friendship. Within the friendships described, one child could not be replaced by any other child. The relationships between these young children described constituted unique and special friendships.

THE MEANING OF PARTICIPATING

Friendship is about participation. Children want to participate and share their lived worlds with their peers (Corsaro, 1997; Johansson, 1999). From my initial research on understanding toddlers' friendships, I became increasingly interested in what it means to participate in a relationship. Are there different levels and features of participation in young children's friendships?

From an early age, children are astute observers of other children. A child has to observe what is going on within any play in order to be able to join the activity. Corsaro (1997) maintained that children carefully observe what other children are doing as an access strategy. According to Corsaro (1997), gaining access is often more successful if observation precedes initiation to join an activity rather than to ask "Can I play with you?" Such direct questions call for a direct answer and the answer will often be negative because children want to protect their ongoing activity from others and fear that the activity may be disrupted by the entry of another child. While observing, a child gathers information about the play and can then join in the play by producing a variant to the ongoing activity. For example, from the research with the group that involved Ivar and Fredrik, Ivar was seen to observe Fredrik as he pretended to saw a basket with a plastic knife. After watching a while, Ivar took a plastic fish and started to saw in the same way. However, Fredrik did not approve of Ivar's tool for sawing and told him repeatedly that it was wrong, until Ivar finally found a plastic fork to use as the sawing tool. He was then accepted into the play but with the variant of using a fork instead of using a knife. Ivar was actually quite active in his initiation to join the activity with Fredrik. However, if a child is just observing, is this considered participation? Traditionally, such "onlooker behavior" is seen as an indicator of timidity or immature social skills (Corsaro, 1997, p. 125). My research confirms the proposition that observation may be a way of gaining access to other children's play and that it can be a form of participation.

Participating and Contributing

During my career as a teacher in early childhood education, I have observed many different ways in which children participated in the play of others. On one occasion, a six-year-old boy was with other children in a group whom he did not know. The children were playing outside while the boy sat and watched them. When one of the teachers asked the boy if he wanted to play with the other children, the boy looked at her, astonished and indignant and said: "I do play with the others. I am the audience." He had a clear understanding of participating in the other children's play and he was participating by observing. The other children might not have noticed his participation in their play. In fact, they might not have realized his presence at all. On the other hand, the other children might have been well aware of the audience and, thus, been inspired and encouraged in their play. It may be necessary to make a distinction between participating and contributing.

As an observer, the child does not necessarily contribute to the ongoing play but through observation of others the child may still have a sense of participation in any ongoing activity. With very young children, this is more obvious. They may not always have the necessary skills to contribute to the play but through observing they have some form of participation. I once observed three one-year-old children who were playing together. Two of the children were more skilled in running and walking than the third child. The three children were in a line with their backs against a closed door. Suddenly the two more skilled walkers ran out to make a tour around the room. The third child remained by the door. Her eyes were very wide; she had a big smile and her whole body was trembling. She watched the two running children intensively. When they came back to the wall, she was pleased and lined up again with them against the closed door. This sequence of activity was repeated several times. These three children participated in the same activity according to their capacities and skills. The girl who stood against the wall participated with her whole body. It was only her feet that were not running. If I could have asked her, but she had no verbal language skills, I am sure that she would have answered me in the same way as the six-year-old boy who had pretended to be the audience: "I play with the others." In this way, these children build up a store of mutual experiences. Even though they were not friends yet, their participation and sharing of their experiences in their lived worlds may be substantial for a development of friendship.

Participation through Communication

Communication is a central aspect of participating. Many of the young children in my research (Greve, 2007) do not have well-developed verbal language. Nevertheless they communicate with body language and movements in addition to any spoken words. Hence, children's feelings and intentions are expressed. We learn to understand each other's being-in-the-world through the body and through facial expressions, that is, through body language as well as through spoken words (Merleau-Ponty, 1945). In this way, communication occurs in an immediate way between two body subjects.

Moreover imitation is also indicated as a part of the children's friendship. The American psychologists, Meltzoff and Moore (2002) observed that even newborn children had capacities to imitate facial expressions. Imitation is much more than a mechanical reproduction of acting or a movement. It is a form of communication. Stern used the term "affect attunement" to represent a wider meaning for the role of imitation in communication (Stern, 1985, p. 140f; 2004, p. 84). Imitation is evident through actions and body language while affect attunement refers to the feelings that lie behind imitative actions. According to Stern, affect attunement is a phenomenon in dyadic interactions between an adult caregiver and a child. However, affect attunement could also describe the mutuality that is evident in the imitative actions in which children engage that express their feelings toward each other.

The experience of engaging in the same actions as others seems to have a special attraction to young friends. In my research, friends often wanted to do the same things. If one of the children slides down a slide backwards, the other wants to do this as well. If one child crawled like a cat, the other child also wanted to be a cat. During mealtime, if one child ate a sandwich with cheese, the other child wanted cheese, too. In the cloakroom, I saw one child putting his shoes on his hands and another child immediately imitated these actions. The friends confirmed each other's being and showed this mutuality through imitation. Doing the same things became a way of sharing in the world. By performing the same actions as another child, especially a friend, the child is expressing a desire to be like the other, as if the child was saying: "We are doing the same thing, we are alike."

Young children are also fascinated by repetition. The Danish philosopher, Søren Kierkegaard, (1872) noted that repetition makes man happy. Young children never tire of playing peek-a-boo. Over and over again, they may climb up the steps of the slide, just to slide down again. The children in my research (Greve, 2007) frequently climbed on a sofa in the playroom and then jumped down over and over again. Children also love to look at the same pictures in a book or sing the same songs several times. Even the youngest children enjoy when they recognize the tune of a familiar song. Such repetitions are also a form of imitation of previous experiences that can constitute reciprocal interaction between friends. If the repetition involves several children, this repetition provides an acknowledgment of the others and recognition of relationship between the children.

Both imitating and being imitated are signs of social interest. According to the Norwegian pedagogue Nina Johannesen (2002), through imitation of others an interest in, and recognition of, the other person is made. The child, who is imitated, often understands this and replies in a way so that joint actions become meaningful. It is an experience of the mutual "we" in the relationship. It is as if the children were thinking: "We do something special together." Trevarthen, Kokkinaki, and Fiamenghi (1999) noted that the one who imitates and the one who is imitated often change roles and this indicates the reciprocity in the relationship.

Both imitation and observation are different ways of participating in friendships. It is important to recognize what participation may mean in children's worlds.

HOW CAN TODDLERS PARTICIPATE IN LEARNING THROUGH THEIR FRIENDSHIPS?

It is problematic to state in a categorical way that children learn specific things through their friendships which they would not learn without these friendships. However, friendships differ from other relationships, for example, in the way that there is a strong and mostly mutual desire to be together. This allows for unique learning. Through friendships, there are mainly three domains in which learning can occur: the ethical domain, which include learning about care and respect, an interactional domain, which include an experience of a mutual "we," and learning about the nature of friendship itself.

Learning about Care and Respect

There are several dimensions of ethics in young children's worlds. One important aspect of ethics relates to the rights of other people (Johansson, 1999). Through friendship children learn to show respect for others' rights and wishes. An important dimension of ethics evident between young children is their right to possess things (Johansson, 1999). In my research, children often start their conversation with the words: "It's mine. This is yours." In this way, children learn through their participation how to distribute toys and they learn that friends share with each other. However, it is questionable if this notion of the right of possession has been clearly understood. Johansson (1999) found that the right to possess a toy is understood according to who had the toy first. My research supported this proposition. When disagreement occurred over possession, the question, "Who had it first?" was often asked, both by the children and by the adults. Other ethical aspects of such a situation like, "Who needs it most?" or "Who wants it most?" are usually not discussed.

A second ethical issue relates to care for others. Friends care about each other. Through participation in friendships, children learn how to be considerate towards others and how to receive care from others. Both aspects can be a challenge for very young children. Young children are concerned about the well-being of their friends. Children want to comfort someone who is sad (Greve, 2007; Johansson, 1999). An example from my research (Greve, 2007) to illustrate this ethical behavior occurred in a group situation when the children were gathered together for singing. One of the adults turned the lights off to set the mood for the singing session. Ivar told his friend Fredrik that he was afraid. Fredrik patted Ivar's chin and sat closer to his friend and said that he would look after Ivar. Later the lights are turned on and everything is right.

Children might also comfort others as a form of apology for their own actions if they have hurt another child. During mealtime, Ingeborg (18 months old) scratched the girl who was sitting beside her. This girl started to cry and the adults comforted her. While the adults were occupied in cleaning the wound, Ingeborg stroked the back of the girl's head. The adults didn't notice Ingeborg's little gesture.

The Complexity of Friendships

The complexity of friendships makes it possible for children to deal with more challenging situations of social relationships. Friendship is not just good, harmonious, and perfect idyll. Friendship might also be unpleasant, deceitful, unfaithful, and troubled with conflicts. A friendship is not necessarily a stable relationship that will last forever. On the contrary, friendship is a result of continuous negotiations and affirmations through mutual interactions. Kari and Fredrik once played together in the kitchen, a play that ended up with a conflict because the two friends had different agendas. Kari was most concerned with educative rules about how things *should* be: She stirred the stew pan like her parents used to do, she looked after Fredrik so he didn't burn himself—while Fredrik on the other hand was more interested in his own way of doing things. They didn't manage to sort things out together, and Fredrik at last grabbed a pot lid from Kari claiming it was his. Kari started to cry very loud, thus calling on an adult. The interesting point in this example is that even though the children turned out to disagree more and more with each other, they continued to stay together. As friends, they wanted to be together.

As body-subjects, children meet both physically and mentally in their relationships. Thus, a lived experience of a mutual "we" arises. The lifeworlds of children in the kindergarten consist of play and interactions with others. Because friendships are established and confirmed through children's mutual history, a particular friendship relation is not necessarily threatened by a single conflict.

Learning about Togetherness

Friends want to be together and therefore through friendships, young children can learn how to cooperate. They learn about rules for interactions. Interacting implies acting together. A considerable part of such mutual engagement by young children consists of different forms of physical movements like jumping on mattresses, jumping from the sofa to mattresses, running together, or rocking together on a rocking horse. When toddlers are moving like this together, they learn about their own body's potential for movement and also how bodies can be together. In my research, these physical interactions were characterized by different emotions like excitement and joy, as well as confidence and trust in the other person. In one research example, two toddlers were visiting another class with older children. Being left alone among unfamiliar children and adults, the toddlers kept together. In this situation they learned how a relationship can provide a safe basis in an uncertain context. To take care of this dimension of the friendship, children need teachers who can observe and acknowledge the children's need of being together without being disturbed by others.

One condition in being able to act together is to learn how to make one's intentions clear. A child must learn how to communicate in a way that the other child understands. In addition, it is necessary to learn how to interpret the other's intentions. An example from my research concerns Ivar and Nils who, at the time, were both two years old. They were able to act together almost without verbal utterances. They were sending cars to each other on a bench. Although they did not speak verbally, they understood each other's intentions and managed to interact in a meaningful way. It was interesting to notice that an adult who was passing by did not take the children's perspectives in this situation. The adult observed that Nils actually had two cars while Ivar had none. She asked Nils to give one of his cars to Ivar. She was not aware that the boys were sending the cars to each other. From their point of view, it was meaningless to have one car each. Neither Ivar nor Nils reacted to the teacher's request. It seemed that they just waited for her to go away. When the teacher left, the two boys continued to play. The children had learned that it was not always necessary to pay attention to the adult's commands. As a preschool teacher, I recognize this situation quite well. Adults are often on their way to do something else and only observe children in passing. Sometimes teachers intervene without knowing exactly what is going on. In these situations, there is a risk that the children learn something other then what the teacher intended.

Toddlers' interactions are characterized by turn-taking. They learn this rule of interaction. Turn-taking is important in sharing of meaning (Storm-Mathisen, 1995). Turn-taking is also important in communication. Friendships give children many opportunities to learn turn-taking. In my research, the children explicitly indicated "my turn" and "your turn" while they were playing. Even when they did not express it verbally, children demonstrated it in games of peek-a-boo or in the way they took turns in running games.

FRIENDSHIP—A MULTIDIMENSIONAL PHENOMENA IN TODDLERS' WORLDS

Through participating in friendships, children learn about different aspects in *being* a friend, *becoming* a friend, *having* a friend and also *losing* a friend. Through these experiences, toddlers learn about intersubjectivity. In this context, intersubjectivity is understood in the way that we, as body subjects, are directed towards other people in our lived worlds. As human beings, we are born into a social world; a world that we share with other people (Merleau-Ponty, 1962). I am situated in the world with my body together with other people who also are situated in the world with their bodies. Together we are melded in the world with others in an inseparable mixture (*Nous sommes mêlés au monde et aux autres dans une confusion inextricable)* (Merleau-Ponty, 1945, p. 518).

Foremost, children from a young age learn that friendship has an important value. Sometimes children can experience that a friend supports you in a conflict. For example, once Fredrik and Nils were fighting. Fredrik pushed Nils several times, hit him and bit him. After a while, Nils bit Fredrik back. Fredrik started to scream very loudly. Ivar, who had been watching the whole episode, told the adult that Nils bit Fredrik. He didn't say anything about what Fredrik had done to Nils initially. In this way he supports his friend Fredrik.

Through friendships, children can learn that they can have different types of relationships with different people. In my research, children had quite unique friendships with different children. Through friendship, children learn that about having different feelings for different people. I observed that when children met their friends, they cheered up. Friends also learn different mannerisms for how they will interact. When Ivar and Fredrik were together, they often acted being gloomy. They talked with dark voices and walked with heavy steps, breathing through their mouths. Although they did not always act like this when they were together, they had developed a mutual understanding about how to act together in this gloomy way if they so chose.

Joy and humor are important dimensions of children's intersubjectivity and construction of friendships. I observed a lot of laughter between children in my research. Through laughter, and what one may call exaggerated laughter, children expressed feelings toward each other like: "We are having fun" or "Now, we want to have fun" (Løkken, 2004, p. 116). In my research, children's intentions about having fun *together* were particularly evident.

When friends got to know each other well, they developed a subtle competence in interpreting each other's behaviors. For example, Ivar and Fredrik were playing together with a ball. They were both trying to catch the ball. Ivar managed to take the ball before Fredrik. Fredrik shouted out, "I won. I won." Ivar, instead of getting upset because of this unfair statement, seemed to understand that his friend was joking. As another example, the children were throwing snow at each other in the playground outside. The whole body was used to take part in such action. At the same time, children shouted: "Throw" and "Ow," pretending that it hurt when they were hit by the snow. The children learned to interpret each other's intentions but also they learned to follow each other in subtle ways. In this situation, the teacher did not seem to understand that the implicit message through this play was: "We are just playing." She tried several times to stop the children's play with the snow. Ivar, one of the boys, answered the teacher by calling her "stupid" and tried to escape when the teacher caught him. At the same time, Nils continued to throw snow on the ground, while laughing. He tried to tell the teacher that it was just for fun but the teacher kept telling the boys to stop. She finally succeeded and so the interaction between Nils and Ivar was brought to an end.

Thorough friendships children learn about more complex aspects of life, like sorrow, conflict, loss, and disappointment. The friendship between Kari and Ivar, as described previously, became weaker in character during the year. When Ivar chose to play with one of the other children, like Fredrik or Nils, Kari sometimes expressed a sort of a sorrow, it seemed to me that she was afraid of loosing Ivar permanently. She could, for example, start to cry if Nils or Fredrik sat down beside Ivar. Several times the adults did not understand why Kari was so upset and told her that she should find herself another place to sit. Young children will have more difficulties than adults in verbalizing contradictory feelings which are a part of the more complex aspects of friendships. Kari does not manage to explain to the teachers why she is so sorry. One the one hand, she wants to be with Ivar, on the other hand, it makes her sad to see Ivar playing with other children. As a pedagogical consequence, it is important for teachers to be in tune with the children's feelings, observing them, and trying to understand and respect their feelings and experiences.

CONCLUSION

This chapter is based upon observations of children up to three years of age in a Norwegian kindergarten, with the aim to develop knowledge about the nature of young children's friendships as well as to examine what children learn from participation in these friendships. Within the tradition of a sociocultural theory and a life-world phenomenology, this chapter has described different styles of friendship that occurred in these observations. The study shows that one child can enter into different friendships, and that each friendship has unique and distinct characteristics.

Children want to participate and share their lived worlds with their friends. Children participate through observation, imitation, and communication. Through friendships and participation, there are mainly three domains in which learning can occur: the ethical domain, an interactional domain, and learning about the nature of friendship itself. One important implication of this research is that friendship is both a multidimensional and a complex phenomenon in toddlers' worlds. With a deeper knowledge about how children express preferences towards and friendship with other children, teachers in preschools can help the children to understand the code of interaction. More knowledge about peer relationships and friendships among toddlers could clarify this issue.

NOTE

1. In Norwegian kindergartens, there are usually one early childhood educated teacher and two assistants without any formal education. In this article I use the terms *caregiver*, *teacher* and *adult* interchangeably to refer to all the staff in the kindergarten without regard to their education.

REFERENCES

Bengtsson, J. (2005). Med livsvärlden som grund: Bidrag til utvecklandet av en *livsvärldsfenomenologisk ansats i pedagogisk forskning.* Lund, Sweden: Studentlitteratur.

Bliding, M. (2004). Inneslutandets och uteslutandets praktikk: En studie av barns relationsarbete i skolan. Göteborg, Sweden: Acta Universitatis Gothoburgensis.

Blum, L. A. (1994). *Moral perception and particularity.* Cambridge, UK: Cambridge University Press.

Corsaro, W. A. (1985). Friendship and peer culture in the early years. Norwood, NJ: Ablex.

———. (1997). *The sociology of childhood.* Thousand Oaks, CA: Pine Forge Press.

———. (2005). *The sociology of childhood (2. ed.).* Thousand Oaks, CA: Pine Forge Press.

Corsaro, W. A., & Eder, D. (1990). Children's peer cultures. *Annual Review of Sociology, 16,* 197–220.

Damon, W. (1977). *The social world of the child.* San Francisco: Jossey-Bass.

Dunn, J. (2004). Children's friendships: The beginnings of intimacy. Oxford: Blackwell.

Frønes, I. (1994). *De likeverdige: Om sosialisering og de jevnaldrendes betydning.* Oslo, Norway: Universitetsforlaget.

Gottman, J. M. (1986). The world of coordinated play. Same and cross-sex friendships. In J. M Gottman & J. G. Parker, J.G. (Eds.) *Conversations of friends, speculations on affective development.* Cambridge, UK: Cambridge University Press.

Greve, A. (2007). *Vennskap mellom små barn.* (PhD-theses) Oslo, Norway: Universitetet i Oslo, institutt for spesialpedagogikk.

Howes, C. (1987). Social competency with peers: Contributions from child care. *Early Childhood Research Quarterly, 2,* 155–167.

Ivarsson, P. (2003). *Barns gemenskap i förskolan.* (PhD theses). Uppsala, Sweden: Acta Universitalis Upsaliensis.

Johannesen, N. (2002). *Det glemte språket: Hvordan de minste barna i barnehagen bruker imitasjon i kommunikasjonen seg imellom* (Master theses). Høgskolen i Oslo, Avdeling for lærerutdanning.

Johansson, E. (1999). *Etik i små barns värld: Om värden och normer bland de yngsta barnen i förskolan.* (PhD theses).Göteborg, Sweden: Acta Universitatis Gothoburgensis.

Kierkegaard, S. (1872). *Gjentagelsen: Et forsøg i den experimenterende psychologi* (2nd ed.) København, Denmark: C.A. Reitzels Forlag.

Løkken, G. (2000). *Toddler peer culture: The social style of one and two year old bodysubjects in everyday interaction.* (PhD theses). Trondheim, Norway: Pedagogisk institutt. Fakultet for samfunnsvitenskap og teknologi. NTNU.

———. (2004). *Toddlerkultur om ett- og toåringers sosiale omgang i barnehagen.* Oslo, Norway: Cappelen Akademisk.

Meltoff, A. N., & Moore, M.K. (2002). Imitation, memory, and the representation of persons. *Infant Behavior and Development, 25*(1), 39–61.

Merleau-Ponty, M. (1945). *Phénomenologie de la perception.* Paris: Gallimard.

———. (1962). *Phenomenology of perception* (C. Smith, Trans.). London: Routledge. (Original work published 1945).

———. (1967). *Signes.* Paris: Gallimard.

Michélsen, E. (2004). *Kamratsamspel på småbarnsavdelingar* (PhD theses). Stockholm: Pedagogiska institutionen, Stockholm Universitet.

Schutz, A. (1972). *The phenomenology of the social world.* London: Heinemann.

Sommer, D. (2003a) *Barndomspsykologi : Udvikling i en forandret verden* (Psychology of Childhood: development in a changing world). København, Denmark: Hans Reitzel.

———. (2003b) Børnesyn i udviklingspsykologien. Er et børneperspektiv mulig? (Is a child's perspectives possible?), *Pedagogisk Forskning i Sverige, 8* (1–2), 85–100.

Stern, D. (1985). *The interpersonal world of the infant. A view from psychoanalysis and developmental psychology.* New York: Norton.

———. (2004). *The present moment in psychotherapy and everyday life.* New York: W.W. Norton.

Storm-Mathisen, A. (1995). *Walkers, non-talkers. A sociological study on peer interaction among toddlers* (Master theses). Oslo, Norway: Institutt for sosiologi, universitetet i Oslo.

Trevarthen, C. (1993). The self born in intersubjectivity: An infant communication. In: U. Neisser (Ed.). *The perceived self: Ecological and interpersonal knowledge of the self* Cambridge, UK: Cambridge University Press.

Trevarthen, C., Kokkinaki, T., & Fiamenghi, G. A. (1999). What infants' imitations communicate: with mothers, with fathers and with peers. In: Nadel & Butterworth (Eds.), *Imitation in infancy* (pp. 127–185). Cambridge, UK: Cambridge University Press.

U.N. Convention on the Rights of the Child (1989). UN General Assembly Document A/RES/44/25. Retrieved April 20, 2008, from http://www.cirp.org/library/ethics/UN-convention/

Whaley, K., & Rubenstein, T. S. (1994). How toddlers 'do' friendship: A descriptive analysis of naturally occurring friendships in a group child care settings. *Journal of Social and Personal Relationships,* (11), 383–400.

Williams, P.; Sheridan, S., & Samuelsson, I. P. (2001). *Barns samlärande: En forskningsöversikt.* Stockholm: Skolverket.

7 Beliefs About Toddlers' Learning in Child Care Programs in Australia

Jo Brownlee and Donna Berthelsen

There is increasing interest in the beliefs child care teachers hold about the nature of learning and teaching and the influence of such beliefs on adult-child interactions (e.g., see Vartuli, 2005) and, consequently, children's learning. The research reported in this chapter was focused on finding out what child care teachers believed about toddlers' learning and how they interacted with toddlers in their practice. Specifically, we investigated the nature of child care teachers' epistemological beliefs (beliefs about the nature of knowing and learning). There is some evidence to suggest that such beliefs may play a role in how adults interact with children in participatory learning (Berthelsen, Brownlee, & Boulton-Lewis, 2002; Brownlee & Berthelsen, 2004). Participatory learning, in the context of this study, refers to learning in which toddlers create their own understanding and are active in the processing of information.

Sociocultural theory typically views learning as embedded within the culture, leading to culture specific beliefs about what learning is and what learning processes are to be valued (Rogoff, 1990, 2003). According to Edwards (2003), this is a transformative perspective of sociocultural theory. It is not concerned with the cognitive processes that accompany knowledge and is critical of individual knowledge construction. Rather, the transformative perspective foregrounds historical and cultural aspects in which language constitutes reality and is a pre-condition for thought and a form of social action (Young & Collin, 2004). Essentially, the transformative perspective of sociocultural theory foregrounds the significance of cultural experiences for learning.

Another lens with which to view sociocultural theory involves using social constructivist theory (Edwards, 2003). From a social constructivist perspective, the individual as a knowledge constructor is foregrounded. The individual is a distinct entity that exists separately from, but interacts with, the social and cultural contexts. For example, a teacher operating in a child care setting individually constructs his/her own beliefs, knowledge, and understandings relevant to professional practice but this individual knowledge is influenced by social and cultural contexts. It is possible for child care teachers with strong participatory beliefs about children's learning to experience adult-oriented, behaviorist teaching practices within their centers, and subsequently find themselves enacting more transmissive beliefs in order to "fit in" with the culture of that center. This means that beliefs are a social construction because they influenced by social and cultural contexts.

CHILD CARE QUALITY AND TEACHER PRACTICES

Increasingly, there is an important focus on providing quality programs for children less than three years of age (Cost, Quality and Child Outcomes in Child Care Centers Study Team, 1995). A growing body of literature demonstrates that quality child care is linked to child outcomes in a range of developmental areas (Shonkoff & Phillips, 2000). We view quality programs as promoting well-being including learning and development.

Quality indicators of group size and staff-child ratio are important because these structural aspects of quality impact on the process aspects related to relationships between children and staff (e.g., sensitivity of interactions and high involvement by staff with children). Good quality care has as a core component, a focus on interactions (Rolfe, Nyland, & Morda, 2002). A significant body of research indicates a link between responsive, sensitive, stimulating interactions with children and levels of qualifications and training (Karp, 2006; Phillips, Mekos, Scarr, McCartney, & Abbott-Shim, 2001). This suggests that a significant way to improve quality is through professional preparation of the early childhood workforce (Pianta, 2006). Why is this so? Is it because of the increased specialized knowledge base acquired through such professional preparation? Or is it more to do with the learning and knowing processes that develop through further educational experiences—"the how"? There is some evidence to suggest that further and higher educational experience influences the nature and sophistication of beliefs about learning and knowing (Berthelsen, Brownlee and Boulton-Lewis, 2002); Brownlee & Berthelsen, 2008) and that these beliefs are related to the quality of interactions with children (Brownlee, Boulton-Lewis, Berthelsen, & Dunbar, in press; Brownlee & Berthlesen, 2004). Nyland (2003) also advocates for a focus on "beliefs that theory and practice are based on and [to] study how these beliefs are manifest in the context of childcare" (p. 4).

BELIEFS ABOUT PRACTICE IN CHILD CARE

Over the last three decades a growing body of research has described a range of beliefs about the nature of knowing and knowledge and how this is linked to qualifications. In Perry's (1970) seminal research he noticed that liberal arts students changed the way they viewed the nature of knowledge and knowing over the course of their studies. To begin with, these students described dualistic beliefs where knowledge was viewed as simple, absolute, and transmitted by authorities. These black and white views soon developed into what was described as multiplistic beliefs where knowledge can not be known with any certainty and so personal opinions are all that can be relied upon. Such beliefs led to a valuing of personal opinion, irrespective of whether or not there was evidence to support it. In the next position, relativism, individuals started to view personal opinions as needing to be based on critique, evidence, and a range of perspectives. This involved an understanding that knowledge is a personal, reasoned interpretation and that it is complex, tentative, and uncertain. Since the 1970s, many researchers have described a similar range of epistemological beliefs. For example, Kuhn and Weinstock (2002) described a continuum from absolutist beliefs (reality is replicated—similar to dualism) to subjectivist (similar to multiplism) and finally evaluativist beliefs (similar to relativism). This body of research reflects a strong psychological perspective of knowing and learning.

In the past, most research into early childhood teachers' beliefs has centered on the differentiation between child-centered and teacher-centered beliefs (Vartuli, 1999), stressing the importance of child centered learning (McMullen & Alat, 2002), rather than epistemological beliefs. Much of this research is focused on how developmentally appropriate beliefs link to high quality practice. For example, Kowalski, Brown, and Pretti-Frontczak (2005) in researching the effect of education on early childhood teachers' beliefs and classroom quality, concentrated on the effects of changing teachers' knowledge of developmentally appropriate practices and high quality classrooms. Daniels and Shumow (2003) reviewed research related to how an understanding of child development contributed to teachers' beliefs and practices and emphasized the importance of that knowledge to a relationship between understanding of children's learning, teacher qualities, and classroom practice. However, very little research describing child care teachers' beliefs about knowing and learning exists.

Epistemological beliefs have been shown to influence teaching practices although little research has taken place specifically in the context of early childhood teaching practice. Chan and Elliott (2004) showed that epistemological beliefs were related to the decisions teachers made about what knowledge was important in particular learning situations. These core beliefs influence what knowledge a teacher will actually process and retain thus influencing how they go about teaching and promoting learning. For example, a teacher who holds evaluativist epistemological beliefs is likely to view teaching (the meaning of teaching and the roles of teachers) as a process of supporting construction of meaning, while a teacher with an objectivist framework is more likely to think that the role of the teacher is to provide knowledge (Chan & Elliott, 2004).

Beliefs about children's learning can be described in broad terms along a continuum from instructivist to constructivist beliefs (Katz, 2002; McQuail, Mooney, Cameron, Candappa, Moss, & Petrie, 2002). Instructivist beliefs reflect an objectivist epistemology and teachers with such views are more likely to see their role as one in which they must transmit information to children. This refers to an adult-centered view of how children learn. For example, when teachers view knowing and learning as absolute, then interactions with children are more likely to be adult-focused with teachers transmitting information and children observing and modeling (Brownlee,

Berthelsen, & Boulton-Lewis, 2008). Constructivist beliefs are character-ized by a focus on the child, their agency, and competency as well the pro-cess of co-construction of knowledge. Such constructivist or participatory views of learning reflect a more evaluativist epistemological stance. Teach-ers who hold more evaluativistic epistemological beliefs view learning and knowing as a process of analysis, critique, and making meaning. They are more likely to be child-focused in their interactions with children because they see learning as participatory (Brownlee et al., 2008).

Berthelsen and Brownlee (2005) described four categories of children's learning espoused by long day care providers. In the first category, children learn as observers and listeners. From this perspective children merely watch and listen and the focus is on what the adult does. In the second category children learn through engagement. Children are active in learning and so the movement is towards a child centered approach although adults play a large role. The third category involves a view that children learn as collabo-rators. Children collaborate with teachers and peers in order to learn and so learning is more child-centered, as is the case for the final category where children learn as agents of their own learning in a participatory learning process. Here children initiate their own learning experiences. These four categories reflect beliefs related to instructivist through to more construc-tivist dimensions of children's agency in the learning process.

It is important to focus on child care teachers' epistemological beliefs in regard to toddlers' learning because these will influence effective professional practice. Indeed evaluativistic beliefs about knowing and constructivist beliefs about children's learning have been linked to child-centered pedagogy (Arre-dondo & Rucinski, 1996; Berthelsen, Brownlee and Boulton-Lewis, 2002). This study does not focus on the content of professional beliefs (e.g., the nature of developmentally appropriate practice). It investigates beliefs about learning and knowing for child care teachers who interact with toddlers in long day care programs.

THE RESEARCH STUDY

The aim of this research was to find out what child care teachers believed about toddlers' learning in the context of their interactions with toddlers. The findings from this study form part of a larger study that focused on the nature of epistemological beliefs of child care teachers and the quality of child care practice (Berthelsen, Irving, Brownlee, & Boulton-Lewis, 2002).[1]

We chose the centers in this study by randomly selecting them from a list of long day care centers in a metropolitan area in Australia. The directors of these centers were sent letters which outlined the nature of the project and then followed up with a phone call to determine the center's interest in participating in the study. If the directors were interested, they were asked to invite the child care teachers in their toddler programs to participate. It was stressed that participation by the child care teacher needed to be voluntary.

When preliminary agreement was obtained, detailed information was forwarded to the child care teacher about the specific processes involved in the project and formal consent was obtained. Parental consent was also obtained for children who were in the programs because a video of the program was made as a part of the larger research process.

The data discussed in this chapter focus on 12 child care teachers for whom complete data was available (i.e., from the interview, video of practice, and demographic information). Table 7.1. provides a summary of background information about each of the child care teachers. Pseudonyms are used to maintain confidentiality.

Stimulated Recall Interviews

Stimulated recall interviews were used to find out what child care teachers believed about toddlers' learning. Each child care teacher was videoed on one occasion within her program, during a morning session. The video focused on the interactions with toddlers during routine events (meal times, nappy change times, arrivals, departures) and non-routine play events (indoor or outdoor free play and activity times).

This video footage was then used as a focus for discussion in the stimulated recall interviews. The child care teachers were provided with a copy of the video tape prior to the interview, as well as a copy of the basic set of questions about children's learning. Semi-structured interviews were used to ask the following questions about the child care teachers' beliefs about toddlers' learning. Each of the interviews was tape recorded and transcribed verbatim.

1. Can you describe how you think toddlers learn?
2. Can you think of an experience you have had with a child in your care where you really noticed that he or she had learned something?
3. How do know when children have learned something?

Rather than using interviews alone to investigate child care teachers' beliefs as is often the case in personal epistemology research, we asked teachers to reflect on their beliefs as they were enacted in practice (as evident in the videos). This enabled us to make judgments about the extent to which their beliefs were reflected in their practices.

Analysis of the Interviews

The transcripts of each of the interviews were analyzed for common themes within and across the three questions relating to toddlers' learning. Comparison across categories, refinement of categories, exploration of relationships, and patterns across categories helped to provide us with an understanding of what the child care teachers thought about children's learning (Maykut & Morehouse, 1994). This process is described as deductive analysis because the categories were derived from the literature (Marshall & Rossman, 1999).

Table 7.1   Description of Child Care Teachers.

Child care teacher	Description
Bryony	Bryony has completed a Diploma of Child Care and Education (2 years). She has worked in child care for 4 years and has been at her current center for 3 years.
Catherine	Catherine is completing a Diploma of Child Care and Education (2 years). She has worked in child-related fields for more than 20 years. She has been at her current center for 1 year.
Kelly	Kelly has completed an Associate Diploma in Child Studies (2 years). She has worked in child care for 7 years and has been at her current center for 1 year.
Helen	Helen has completed a Diploma of Child Care and Education (2 years). She has worked in child care for 2 years during which time she has been at her current center.
Claire	Claire has completed an Associate Diploma of Education (Early Childhood—2 years). She has worked in child care for 12 years and has been at her current center for almost 4 years.
Rhonda	Rhonda has completed a Bachelor of Speech Therapy and an Associate Diploma of Child Care (2 years). She has worked in child care for 12 years and at her current center for less than 1 year
Dimity	Dimity has completed a Diploma in Children's Services (2 years). She has worked in child care for 3 years, and at this center for 1 years. She is studying for a Bachelor of Early Childhood.
Carol	Carol has completed the Diploma of Child Care and Education (2 years), and has worked in child care for 11 years. She has been at this center for 4 years.
Curstin	Curstin has completed the Diploma of Child Care and Education (2 years), has been in child care for 8 years, and has worked at this center for 3 years.
Patricia	Patricia has completed the Associate Diploma in Social Studies-Child Care (2 years) in New South Wales in 1993. She has worked in child care for 8 years and has been at this center for 1 year.
Diane	Diane has completed the Diploma of Early Childhood Education (2 years). She has worked in child care for 10 years and has been at this center for 3 years.
Nancy	Nancy has completed a Bachelor of Teaching (3 years) and has worked in child care for 13 years and in the current center for 10 years.

The full transcript of the interview which also involved discussion of the practices observed on the video was scanned for other comments by the child care teacher that might help to further clarify their beliefs about toddlers' learning. In this way, a social constructivist perspective of learning formed the basis of the analysis as we looked for beliefs enacted in practice. Further, the nature of the interview questions helped to reveal the influence of contexts on beliefs. The first more abstract and theoretical question was: "Can you describe how you think toddlers learn?"; followed by "Can you think of an experience you have had with a toddler in your care where you really noticed that he or she had learned something?"; and "How do know when toddlers have learned something?" These final questions had a more practical orientation, reflecting the contextual influences on beliefs.

FINDINGS

The child care teachers described beliefs about learning that ranged from instructivist to constructivist beliefs (Katz, 2002; McQuail et al., 2002). An instructivist position was one in which toddlers' learning was determined and dependent upon adults, with no acknowledgement of the child's cognitive processing. Child care teachers who were considered to hold a constructivist position responded with statements that indicated that toddlers created their own understanding and played an active role in the processing of information. A number of the child care teachers are described as holding mixed beliefs in which children created their own understandings but also required strong adult direction in their learning.

The findings revealed contextual influences on individual's construction of beliefs. Many of the child care teachers answered the first more abstract and theoretical question: "Can you describe how you think toddlers learn?" by indicating that children learn through their own actions and create their own understanding. However, this was not supported by their responses to the questions, "Can you think of an experience you have had with a toddler in your care where you really noticed that he or she had learned something?" and "How do know when toddlers have learned something?" These questions had a more practical orientation, reflecting the contextual influences on beliefs. The overall beliefs about toddlers' learning held by each child care teacher are summarized in Table 7.2. These beliefs are then explored in detail for each child care teacher.

Instructivist Beliefs about Toddlers' Learning

An instructivist position views toddlers' learning as managed and dependent upon the actions of adults. From this perspective, there is no discussion of children as being cognitively competent. Diane and Patricia described predominantly instructivist views about how toddlers learn. Diane said that adults need to provide children with challenges and positive role models:

> I think it's important to show a good example and be a positive role model, because they learn from everything that they see us doing and

Table 7.2   Beliefs About Toddlers' Learning

Instructivist	Mixed			Constructivist
Diane Patricia	Curstin Kelly Dimity	Helen Nancy Bryony	Claire Catherine	Rhonda Carol

their parents doing. And that age, between 15 months and two year olds, they just pick everything up so fast, especially language and you know. Yeah so I just think that's how they do it. And again if you make the experiences more challenging and more fun, then they want to do it, but if you just, plop the play dough on the table and there it is, then they'll go and play with it for a couple of minutes and then they'll go off to something else. But if you put other things out there with the play dough and put the play dough in like home corner for something different or just trying different things in a pretty normal activity just makes it more interesting and then they want to do things.

However, in addition to learning by adult role models, she also describes how toddlers can be encouraged to be active in their exploration of the environment, in this case, at the play dough table. This activity did not include a view that toddlers learn by constructing their own understanding.

Patricia also described predominantly instructivist views about toddlers' learning. She emphasized that children are visual learners, explaining that she needed to have visual aids to maintain their attention at group times. The specific contextual example she provided of a toddler having learned something was one of role modeling in which a child was imitating the adult's actions.

We've just being doing themes on animals and we have got quite a few different animals up all over the walls, and I've been pointing to different animals asking them what they are and one of the little girls who has just moved in from the nursery into my room . . . although she hasn't any language skills as yet, she was able to use the motion of a trunk to say that it was the elephant, which is just something that I'd always did, use my hand as a trunk and they all do that, because it's funny, every time there's an elephant, they'll all go "Bbbbrrrrrrrrr" (and makes arm movements like an elephant's trunk). So I know that they understand what an elephant is.

These teachers with predominantly instructivist beliefs viewed toddlers' learning as adult-managed and did not describe participatory views of children's learning. The examples provided by these teachers demonstrated support for these adult-centered beliefs, with a focus on children modeling adult behaviors.

Mixed Beliefs about Toddlers' Learning

Mixed beliefs refer to beliefs that children are both active in creating their own understandings and also require strong adult guidance in their learning. Teachers with mixed beliefs gave responses to the initial question about beliefs about how toddlers learn that were focused on the importance of play and exploration in children's learning, which appeared to be a constructivist perspective. However, this was not always evident in how they responded to the remaining questions in which they implied that learning was managed by the actions of the adults. In these cases, these child care teachers were described as holding mixed beliefs.

While acknowledging that toddlers can learn through their own actions in the context of play and exploration, teachers with mixed beliefs indicated that adults were responsible for the direction of children's learning. Curstin, Kelly, and Dimity were described as holding mixed beliefs but they were more instructivist in their expressed beliefs than constructivist. Curstin stated:

> Obviously they learn by repetition and being able to see things happen and learning by touch and feeling and tasting and basically through all their senses, just as adults do. But obviously even more so because children draw everything in, that's why you need to be so careful when you're around children because you're a good example. You're providing experiences which are very much child friendly that . . . Obviously you provide things that are appropriate to their age and their skills, so they can learn for themselves having put something together or how to stack something up. So basically just through doing, having hands on experience, it's the best, that's the best way I think.

Overall, her responses indicated that toddlers' skill development is dependent on the environment which is provided by the adult. Children are active in their learning but the focus seems to be on what the adult, rather than the child, does in this learning process.

Kelly acknowledges that toddlers are active in their learning, however, she displays a very adult-dependent understanding of learning by also emphasizing role modeling: . . . "Children learn from us. I believe in that strongly because like I said before, we are so influential in those children's lives and they also learn from their peers in terms of negative behaviors."

Dimity, while acknowledging that toddlers learn by experimentation and investigation and from each other, used contextual examples which also implied a belief that the child's learning was promoted and dependent on the adult and identified the importance of being a good role model.

So I guess you really need to role model the right things for children because they're always watching what you do, and what you say, and they learn through experimentation. It's important to let children try things providing it's not that dangerous so they can investigate things for themselves and I don't believe in just handing things to children on a platter, giving them answers to something, you're saying well prompt them with a question, you know, or 'why do think that's happening' and how, you know like getting them to think about it. I think that's the best way for them to learn, for them to have to think about it and you know, problem solve.

In addition to learning as role modeling, Dimity described a view of active learning in which children process information and solve problems. This processing of information was not so evident in the earlier responses of Curstin and Kelly.

Helen and Nancy also held mixed beliefs. They identified that toddlers have their own way of learning but that this learning may be managed by adults or from modeling adults' actions. Nancy implies an adult dependence for understanding: . . . "They learn by seeing other people by, you know, role modeling . . . my big word is scaffolding by, like being supported in their skill, they learn through kindness, through patience." She also saw a place for explicit management of learning by adults as indicated in the following quote.

One of the children in particular has a lot of problems sharing his personal space and the likes and, at one stage, we'd been working so hard, like I mean for two or three weeks now we've been working constantly with him, lots of one-on-one, lots of positives . . . because he used to be a biter, at least an eight times a day biter, and we'd got it down to just two times a day. We were just, "Wow, this is great."

Helen also expressed a belief in active learning through play and exploration but emphasized the adult role in managing the learning: . . . "They learn through play . . . but I let them explore on their own, before I interfere. Let them try and see what they can do." This response indicates an appreciation of the toddler being active in their learning. However the contextual examples provided by Helen below about knowing when a child has learned something were focused on the adult role in managing that learning process and less about toddlers' capacity to be autonomous learners.

Toilet training. I'll use James again because he's a perfect example. We were toilet training him, and, every time, the child did a wee on the toilet we'd get really excited and my assistant and I would give him a stamp. And we just continue it. Now he got to the point where he actually wears trainer pants throughout the day even at sleep time, without getting wet, and that's just the biggest achievement.

Bryony was described as having mixed beliefs. Like Helen, Bryony considered that toddlers learn through play, hands-on experience and the senses: . . . "Playing with each other, interactions, from the senses you know like watching, hearing, feeling, touching, a lot of that." The context specific examples she provided about when children had learned something were adult-directed activities, with a focus on group times, and examples were about specific cognitive knowledge (e.g., counting, knowing the letters of the alphabet).

Claire and Catherine held mixed beliefs but with a stronger focus on constructivist beliefs. Claire identified observing, listening and play with peers as how toddlers learn. The adult role was to provide support for learning through explanations and emotional support. The child's body language was identified by Claire as a means by which the child indicated that he/she were making meaning in learning and through which a sense of achievement could be evident.

> When a child comes into child care and doesn't want to be there and wants her mother, and she will cry for her mother. We will repeat that Mummy will be coming back after sleep time, and we're going to have a little play now and do we think we can come into the sandpit or would we like to have a swing. Often there's lots of crying and some-times they can be very silent but inside they're crying and, you can watch their body. It's really quite tense . . . But, one day they will come and say, "Mummy's coming after sleep time." And you sort of think, wow, they know and you say "Oh that's right" and, you try to sort of say "Well everybody's Mummy's coming," you know "Yes Peter's Mummy's coming after sleep time too, and Mary's Mummy's coming after sleep time." And you really know that they understand that and, you know, from there you'll see their body relax.

Catherine in her responses indicated that toddlers learn through play, by doing things and making mistakes: . . . "I believe play is very important, by discovery, searching for answers, communicating with each other . . . just asking questions, getting solutions." Catherine indicated she does a lot of listening and guiding to help children learn.

In summary, most of these child care teachers with mixed beliefs acknowledged the role of play, hands-on experiences or sensory exploration in toddlers' learning. However, most of the child care teachers who were considered to hold mixed beliefs placed greater emphasis on the importance of adults as role models. Often the examples provided from the child care context were at odds with teachers' initial descriptions of their beliefs about children's learning. These examples indicated that learning was managed by adults and that group times and adult-directed experiences were the most important times for learning. There was less evidence throughout the responses to suggest participatory learning in which toddlers could also be agents of their own learning.

Constructivist Beliefs about Toddlers' Learning

Constructivist beliefs are those beliefs about learning in which toddlers are viewed as active agents in the construction of their own knowledge. Carol and Rhonda were considered to hold strong constructivist beliefs. They acknowledged that toddlers learn through their senses and from hands-on exploration but emphasized children's active construction of their own knowledge.

Carol was the only child care teacher who provided a very strong constructivist response to all three questions. In response to the question, "Can you describe how toddlers learn?" she said:

> I think children learn all the time, that there's no particular way they learn. I think every child learns differently, just as every adult learns differently and that most children are active learners, but there are quite a lot of children that are passive learners. They'll sit and watch and be away from the rest of the group and then all of a sudden they'll just get up and do something. And you wouldn't even realize that—well you don't know—but they've obviously been processing all that information in their head and then when they're ready, they just get up and do it.

This focus on "processing all that information in their head" provides an indication that children are capable cognitive beings. Carol also suggested that toddlers learn from how people respond to them.

> I saw a child set the table and (she) put out four chairs around the table. (She) went and got three dolls and sat them at the table; put out four plates, four knives, four forks, four of everything, one on one correspondence and then sat in the other spot, and we just went "Wow!"

These quotes indicate that children have the ability, from an early age, to adjust to the different values of each context to which they are exposed. She provided an example of a child's learning through demonstrating an understanding of a situation where the learning was transferred from another context and demonstrated through play.

Rhonda, in response to the question, "Can you describe how toddlers learn?", indicated that she scaffolded children's learning but sought to help children make their own connections:

> To assume that because the child's under two will best learn only by touching tasting and smelling is an over-generalization. I think that it's lovely to offer an idea from as many facets as possible. When they have absorbed something they have indicated it to me, I've reached them. How important it is doesn't matter, but I've just stretched that little neural track just that little bit.

In an example of when she has noticed a toddler had learned something, Rhonda provided an example of learning a physical skill.

> And by being there, encouraging and sometimes not helping. Saying "Oh you can do it. You can do it, just hold on with two hands." Of course you're hovering, the whole time, with that hand to catch them just in case it goes wrong. But you don't let them see that, they have to build up their own confidence.

These teachers who were described as holding constructivist beliefs viewed children as cognitively competent and active in their own learning. The examples from the child care context provided by these teachers provided support for their understanding that children learn through participation in their social context.

DISCUSSION

The nature of child care teachers' beliefs about toddlers' learning ranged from instructivist to constructivist in nature (Katz, 2002; McQuail et al., 2002), although a mixed set of beliefs prevailed. In response to the first question "Can you describe how you think toddlers learn?" many indicated that children learn in a constructivist way. Individuals with such beliefs were considered to view knowledge as constructed and tentative rather than absolute and received by external authorities (Kuhn & Weinstock, 2002). Often this view of learning was not evident in their responses to the remaining questions, "Can you think of an experience you have had with a toddler in your care where you really noticed that he or she had learned something?" and "How do know when toddlers have learned something?" These questions often reflected the contextual influences on beliefs suggesting that toddlers' learning was the result of adult management and not participatory in nature. In most cases the examples provided were more about adult initiations and not toddler initiations. For example, some child care teachers provided examples about identifying colors or numbers on flash cards, counting, knowing the alphabet, learning a song, completing a puzzle, or recognizing their belongings. The formal learning evident in the examples and the "ownership" taken by the adults of children's learning suggested that learning involved the transfer of knowledge from the adult to the child, with little active participation in the learning process. These beliefs did not reflect constructivist or evaluativistic beliefs but rather an instructivist or objectivist perspective (Kuhn & Weinstock, 2002). Rogoff et al. (1998) suggest that "in societies that segregate children from adult context" (p. 236), as in child care which is an adult managed institution, there needs to be clarification on how participatory learning can be promoted by helping children to be responsible for their own learning.

It is possible that the foregrounding of instructivist views evident in the responses of these child care teachers is related to the pervasive cultural view that teaching is a transmissive process. Such views do not address the need for participatory learning nor provide balance between children's and adults' roles (Rogoff, Mosier, Mistry, & Goncu, 1998). Australia, along with other countries such as the Netherlands, New Zealand, Portugal, Spain, and the United Kingdom, has been described as promoting a mixed approach to early childhood education involving both constructivist and instructivist approaches (McQuail et al., 2003). Such mixed approaches are evident in a focus on both the holistic development of children and emergent literacy in early childhood settings. These broader cultural views and approaches are likely to influence the beliefs held by teachers in child care settings. For example, the more instructivist views evident in the broader cultural context may also be evident within the practices in centers, and subsequently teachers may find themselves enacting more transmissive approaches in order to "fit in" with the culture of that center. This suggests a social-constructivist perspective of learning, in which cultural and social contexts play a role in the construction of knowledge and beliefs. In this way epistemological beliefs are socially constructed rather than psychological in nature.

It is also possible that the nature of child care qualifications influences such beliefs. Most of the teachers in this study were two-year trained (Diplomas in Child Care). Only one held a four-year qualification. Locke and Ginsborg (2002; cited in McQuail et al., 2002) indicate that child care workers with lower qualifications are more likely to be focused on prescribed literacy and numeracy outcomes as evidence of learning for young children. Further, we know that the quality of adult-child interactions has been found to be associated with the educational qualifications of the child care teacher (McMullen & Alat, 2002). The level of qualification and the ability to be reflective about practice is also linked to the nature and level of epistemological beliefs (Hofer & Pintrich, 1997). Pre-service courses and professional development programs for child care teachers need to encourage participants to explicitly reflect on their beliefs about children's learning and their role to support that learning. Child care vocational training needs to promote adequate reflection in order that there is greater understanding about children as participatory learners and to support the development of a theoretically informed knowledge base about toddlers' learning. Rather than conceiving of learning as instructivist activity through the transmission of knowledge, it is important that support for learning is child-centered, constructivist, and based on interactional exchanges to promote participatory learning.

Early childhood pre-service education has a poor record when it comes to influencing change in pre-service teachers' beliefs in general, reporting difficulty in supporting students' acceptance of newer knowledge about children, and philosophies of practice (McMullen & Alat, 2002). It is suggested that early childhood teachers often maintain the beliefs about what it means to be a teacher and how children learn which they held when they entered their training courses and which were formed during their own educational experience in school. In the current study, the child care teachers' emphasis on their role in managing the learning means that they did not appear to have a clear understanding of constructivist practices or a depth of understanding of how children learn. These understandings need to be developed in professional training programs and in ongoing professional development activities. These findings support a need for future research to explore how beliefs about how children learn can be developed and reflected in practice in early childhood programs.

NOTES

1 The authors acknowledge the contribution of Margaret Brannock to the analysis of aspects of this data.

REFERENCES

Arredondo, D. E., & Rucinski, T. T. (1996, November). *Epistemological beliefs of Chilean educators and school reform efforts.* Paper presented at the Tercer Encuentro National de Enfoques Cognitivos Actuales en Education. Santiago, Chile.

Berthelsen, D., & Brownlee, J. (2005). Respecting children's agency for learning and rights to participation in child care programs. *International Journal of Early Childhood, 37*(3), 49–60.

Berthelsen, D., Brownlee, J., & Boulton-Lewis, G. (2002). Caregivers' epistemological beliefs in toddler programs. *Early Child Development and Care, 172,* 503–516.

Berthelsen, D., Irving, K., Brownlee, J., & Boulton—Lewis G. (2002). *Caregiving styles in infant child care programs.* Brisbane: Centre for Applied Studies in Early Childhood. Queensland University of Technology.

Brownlee, J., & Berthelsen, D. (2008). Developing relational epistemology through relational pedagogy: New ways of thinking about personal epistemology in teacher education. In M. S. Khine (Ed.), *Knowing, Knowledge and Beliefs. Epistemological Studies Across Diverse Cultures* (pp. 399–416). Amsterdam: Springer.

Brownlee, J., & Berthelsen, D. (2004). Working with toddlers in child care: Personal epistemologies and practice. *European Early Childhood Education Research Journal, 12*(1), 55–70.

Brownlee, J., Boulton-Lewis, G., Berthelsen, D., & Dunbar, S. (2008, in press). Investigating epistemological beliefs in vocational educational for child care workers: New ways of thinking about learning and training. *The Australian Educational Researcher.*

Chan, K., & Elliott, R. (2004). Relational analysis of personal epistemology and conceptions about teaching and learning. *Teaching and Teacher Education, 20*(8), 817–831.

Cost, Quality, and Child Outcomes in Child Care Centers Study Team. (1995). *Cost, quality, and child outcomes in child care centers: Public report.* Denver, CO: Economic Department, University of Colorado at Denver.

Daniels, D., & Shumow, L. (2003). Child development and classroom teaching: A review of the literature and implications for education teachers. *Journal of Applied Developmental Psychology, 23,* 495–526.

Edwards, S. (2003). New Directions: charting the paths for the role of sociocultural theory in early childhood education and curriculum. Contemporary Issues in Early Childhood, 4 (3), 251–266.

Hofer, B. and Pintrich, P. R. (1997). The development of epistemological theories: Beliefs about knowledge and knowing and their relation to learning. *Review of Educational Research*, 67, (1), 88–144.

Karp, N. (2006). Designing models for professional development at the local, state and national levels. In M. Zaslow & I. Martinez-Beck. (Eds.), *Critical issues in early childhood professional development* (pp. 225–230). Baltimore, PA: Brookes.

Katz, L. (2002). Program content and implementation. In *OECD thematic review of education and care policy—Background report: United States of America*. Washington, DC: OERI, US Department of Education.

Kowalski, K., Brown, R. D., & Pretti-Frontczak, K. (2005). The effects of using formal assessment on preschool teachers' beliefs about the importance of various development skills and abilities. *Contemporary Educational Psychology*, 30, 23–42.

Kuhn, D., & Weinstock, M. (2002). What is epistemological thinking and why does it matter? In B. Hofer & P. Pintrich (Eds.) Personal Epistemology: The psychological beliefs about knowledge and knowing. Mahwah, NJ: Lawrence Erlbaum.

McMullen, B. M., & Alat, K. (2002). Education matters in the nurturing of the beliefs of preschool caregivers and teachers. *Early Childhood Research in Practice*, 4 (2) 22 pages. Retrieved January 25, 2006, from http://ecrp.uiuc.edu/

McQuail, S., Mooney, A., Cameron, C., Candappa, M., Moss, P., & Petrie, P. (2002). *Early Years and Childcare International Evidence Project: Child Outcomes*. London: DfES.

Marshall, C., & Rossman, G. (1999). *Designing qualitative research*. Thousand Oaks, CA: Sage Publications.

Maykut, P., & Morehouse, R. (1994). *Beginning qualitative research*. A philosophic and practical guide. London: Falmer.

Nyland, B. (2003, February). *Infant programs in Australia child care centers: Are there gaps in pre-service training of child care staff?* Paper presented at 8th Australian Institute of Family Studies Conference.

Perry, W. G. (1970). *Forms of intellectual and ethical development in the college years*. New York: Holt, Rinehart and Winston.

Phillips, D., Mekos, D., Scarr, S., McCartney, K., & Abbott-Shim, M. (2001) Within and beyond the classroom door: Assessing quality in child care centers. *Early Childhood Research Quarterly*, 15 (4), 475–496.

Pianta, R. (2006). Standardized observation and professional development. In M. Zaslow & I. Martinez-Beck. (Eds.), *Critical issues in early childhood professional development* (pp. 231–254). Baltimore: Brookes.

Rogoff, B. (1990). *Apprenticeship in thinking: Cognitive development in social context*. New York: Oxford University Press.

———. (2003). *The cultural nature of human development*. New York: Oxford University.

Rogoff, B., Mosier, C., Mistry, J., & Goncu, A. (1998). Toddlers' guided participation with their caregivers in cultural activity. In M. Woodhead., D. Faulkner, & K. Littleton. (Eds.), *Cultural worlds of early childhood*. New York: Open University.

Rolfe, S., Nyland, B., & Morda, R. (2002). Quality in Infant Care: Observations on Joint Attention. *Journal of Australian research in Early Childhood Education*, 9 (1), 86–96.

Shonkoff, J. P., & Phillips, D. A. (Eds.) (2000). *From neurons to neighborhoods: The science of early childhood development*. Washington, DC: National Academy Press.

Vartuli, S. (1999). How early childhood teachers beliefs vary across grade level. *Early Childhood Research Journal*, 145 (4), 489–514.

Young, R. & Collin, A. (2004). Introduction: Constructivism and social constructionism in the career field. *Journal of Vocational Behavior*, 64, 373–388.

8 In Support of a Relationship-Based Approach to Practice with Infants and Toddlers in the United States

Mary McMullen and Susan Dixon

Until about the last two decades, American infants and toddlers were cared for and educated almost exclusively by their mothers or very close relatives or neighbors. This was typically done in the child's home and, of course, payment rarely if ever exchanged hands. It is becoming increasingly typical for children under the age of three years to receive some type of care and education services at the hands of paid professionals and, although this sometimes still occurs in family homes, it now also happens in a variety of other settings (Vandell, 2004). Nearly half of all infants and toddlers in the United States are in some form of regular non-parental care by the time they are nine months old (Kreader, Ferguson, & Lawrence, 2005), for an average of 32 hours per week (U.S. Census Bureau, 2005). As Dombro and Lerner (2006) informed us, "Most families today share the care of their babies and toddlers with someone else—often an early childhood professional, a teacher, or a family child care provider. Each family and professional must learn to work and make decisions together to support the child's healthy development and to ensure the family's well-being" (p. 29).

Thus, it is now common for multiple relationships to form between and among professionals and other adults who function in the various roles that touch the lives of infants, toddlers and their families. It is these individuals who need, as Dombro and Lerner (2006) stated: "to work and make decisions together," (p. 29) both with each other as colleagues, as well as with families in order to achieve common goals in providing optimal support. The potential challenges, obstacles, and even discomfort of engaging in such relationships that cross professional and philosophical boundaries are outweighed by the potential benefits. Shared interests, goals, and concerns, encourage new ways of thinking about issues, professional roles, and the important work we do with infants and toddlers and their families.

Relationships, positive and negative, have long-lasting impact on infants' and toddlers' ability to develop, learn, and regulate their own emotions (Bowman, Donovan, & Burns, 2001; Shore, 1997). Infants and toddlers learn in the context of important relationships. As Shore (1997) said, "the best way to help very young children grow into curious, confident and able learners is to give them warm, consistent care so that they can form secure attachments to those who care for them" (p. 29). Researchers from multiple disciplines including psychology, education, the social sciences, biology, and neuroscience have supported the preeminent role of relationships in the health and well-being, as well as in learning, growth, and developmental outcomes for young children. One of the core concepts of healthy outcomes stated in *From Neurons to Neighborhoods* (Shonkoff, & Phillips, 2000) is: "Human relationships, the effects of relationship on relationships, are the building blocks of healthy development" (p. 4).

In this chapter, we articulate our notions of a relationship-based approach with infants and toddlers and offer it to readers, not as something new, but as a consolidation of current understanding of best or recommended practice in the early childhood education and care (ECEC) of infants and toddlers, birth to age three, in the United States. We do so from the perspectives that we reflect in the practices we describe throughout the text, as well as from the context of being long-time professionals within the field of ECEC. Both authors actively work in pre- and in-service professional development programs and in the preparation of ECEC practitioners. We have each worked in our various roles for over 20 years, one as an early childhood education generalist, and the other in special education. The first author spent the early years of her career as an infant and then toddler caregiver and teacher, later as a preschool teacher, and then early childhood education program director, before becoming an early childhood professor and researcher. The second author is a speech pathologist and early intervention specialist who, along with being a therapist, has spent her career working as a trainer and instructor with pre- and in-service ECEC professionals.

In this chapter, we start by discussing the multiple contexts of ECEC for infants and toddlers in the United States, and the various spheres of interactions that exist within each child's universe of relationships as we elaborate upon our model of a relationship-based approach. We discuss relationship as the intersection of behaviors related to and in common with three types of practices. These are mindful, reflective, and respectful practices (as depicted in Figure 8.1.). We assert these are critical elements in the formation and growth of healthy relationships. Further, we define aspects of these three practices that we consider particularly relevant in the lives of infants, toddlers, and their families as they relate to ECEC in the United States and also provide information about the professional organizations that support such practices. Finally, before offering suggestions for engaging in a relationship-based approach in our daily life and work with infants and toddlers and their families, we present some of the challenges that the United States faces for the full implementation of such practices with infants and toddlers.

We are mindful that we are bounded by our own North American and Western perspectives but we believe that our ideas have general applicability across cultures and contexts of practice. From our perspective, a relationship-based approach with infants and toddlers, first and

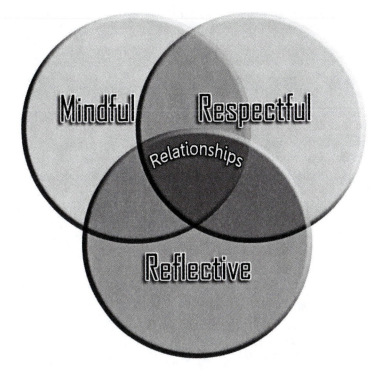

Figure 8.1   Relationship as an intersection of mindful, reflective, and respectful practices.

foremost, recognizes the inherent worth of every child as they are in the here and now. We add our voices to those of Moylett and Djemli (2005) who urged us to recognize infants and toddlers as "human beings rather than human becomings" (p. 65). Valuing children in such a way means that we acknowledge their individual rights as citizens to be happy and healthy, and to feel successful in their day-to-day lives. Thus, rather than focusing so much on the future, as we Americans often do, and worrying about how a child may someday "turn out," in our view, a relationship-based approach is concerned with the well-being of child who is with us, now, in the present. However, while focusing on the present, we must simultaneously, but not singularly, be mindful of the future and help the infants and toddlers with whom we work to develop and learn in ways that will ensure their ongoing and continued well-being within the contexts in which they will live and learn beyond our own classrooms and care environments.

Secondly, a relationship-based approach is one that values and respects each relationship partner within the multiple spheres of interaction in our own universes of relationships. Whether it is our relationships with infants and toddlers, parents, or other professionals, we believe that we build our most trusting and productive relationships between and among those individuals with whom we establish a reciprocal feeling that each relationship partner is valued as competent and worthwhile. Further, we believe that it is these trusting relationships that are most rewarding to all relationship partners, adults and children, but specifically, it is through such relationships that infants and toddlers are provided with the optimum opportunities to learn and develop.

The pre-eminent role of relationships in contributing to healthy and positive development and learning outcomes is a common theme arising in the research literature, among leading scholars, and from birth to three practitioners (Bowman et al., 2001; Shonkoff & Phillips, 2000; Shore, 1997). We deconstruct "relationships" into three elements, mindfulness, reflection, and respect, each of which is discussed separately later in this chapter. We again acknowledge that while relationship models for ECEC are not necessarily new, we believe that our ideas offer a somewhat different way of thinking about the relationships, what they mean in our lives, and ultimately, how they impact the infants, toddlers, and families with whom we work.

THE MULTIPLE AND VARIED CONTEXTS OF INFANT AND TODDLER CARE AND EDUCATION IN THE UNITED STATES

The contexts of care and education for infants and toddlers have broadened during recent decades. Many infants and toddlers now come into contact not only with their direct care providers but also with members of the wider community. Each member of the community also has the potential to contribute to young children's care and education. As infants and toddlers move into the community, the libraries, parks, church programs, museums, and the many other settings which they encounter in their daily lives become settings in which care and education is provided.

We support an expanded notion of what "care and education" means with children under three and where it may occur. It involves all adults, whether professionally trained or not, who touch the lives of infants, toddlers, and their families on a regular basis, in whatever context in which they encounter them. We see these contexts in which adults have the opportunity to impact the care and education of infants and toddlers as fitting primarily into four categories. Because we are writing about more formal systems of care and education, the examples provided for each category identify specific professional roles of individuals who are specially trained for work with families and young children:

(1) *The home*: Professionals who go into the homes of infants and toddlers include early interventionists, visiting health nurses, home visitors, doulas, and nannies;

(2) *The care and education setting:* Professionals who work in these contexts include caregivers, teachers, administrators, and early interventionists who work in schools, centers, and family child care homes;

(3) *The community:* There are at least two categories of professionals who touch the lives of infants and toddlers in our communities: (a) those who work directly with infants and toddlers and their families in settings such as libraries, museums, parks and recreation programs, and (b) those who provide resources or support services through, for example, medical programs, court systems, and family resources centers; and

(4) *The academic or professional development setting:* The professionals in this context are those who deliver mentoring or education services related to practice with infants and toddlers and their families, such as trainers, consultants, and college instructors.

With the recognition of the expansion of the contexts in which infants and toddlers are impacted by ECEC programs the realization that the potential number of relationships formed with and around infants and toddlers grows as well. Infants and toddlers are members of families who are, in turn, part of larger extended families and their daily experiences extend into neighborhoods and communities. Infants and toddlers have many spheres of interactions not previously available to them on a regular basis.

For example, the caregiver in the child care center, knowing that toddlers in her classroom are exploring the idea of how plants grow, takes the class on a walk to a nearby greenhouse. There, the horticulturist becomes a member of the toddlers' educational team. The horticulturist learns from the caregiver and one of the children's early intervention specialists, a speech therapist who came along on the visit, how to adapt her communication and presentation style for young children when they visit her greenhouse. In another scenario, an infant with disabilities has early interventional therapists who come to her home, as well as to her family childcare home setting. A relationship team forms, comprised of the young child, her family, the therapists, the family home care provider, as well as various medical care providers. The number of individuals involved on this team is extensive.

In Figures 8.2., 8.3., and 8.4,. we demonstrate the complexity of the interactions and potential relationships that may subsequently impact the lives of infants and toddlers using one infant or toddler and her family as an example. In Figure 8.2., the infant/toddler and her family are placed at the center, surrounded by the primary spheres of interaction, which in this example include extended family, friends and neighbors, community members, and members of her church, as well as her caregiver from her child care center, early intervention therapists who visit her both at home and in her child care program, as well as those involved in her medical care.

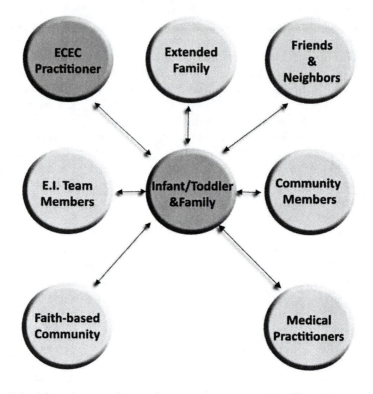

Figure 8.2   The primary spheres of interaction connected to the infant/toddler and family.

Taking just the sphere from Figure 8.2. showing the caregiver from our example, Figure 8.3. shows that the caregiver too has numerous spheres of interaction, each with the potential to impact the care and education of the infant/toddler and family. We consider this a secondary sphere of interaction, because it involves relationships between and among the adults. This is one step removed from the caregiver's primary relationships with the child and her family. In the example in Figure 8.3., these relationships include the caregiver's center director, her co-teacher and other colleagues from her program, the instructor for the course she is taking at the university toward her Master's degree in early childhood education, the licensing representative from the state who visits her room periodically, the children's librarian at the local library in her community, and an early intervention team that consists of a speech and language pathologist, a developmental therapist, an occupational therapist, and a physical therapist.

Finally in Figure 8.4., taking the example one step further, we depict the universe of potential relationships that may form around a child and her family. Clearly in our example, some of the relationships depicted are more

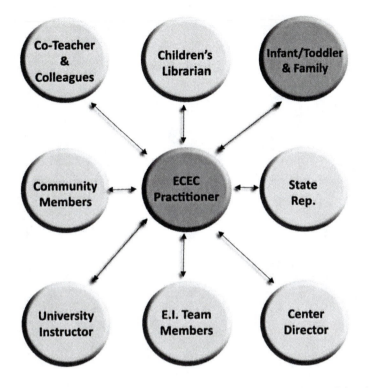

Figure 8.3 The secondary spheres of influence in the infant/toddler and family's life, those connected to one of the primary spheres of influence, the caregiver.

primary in that they involve direct, frequent, and regular interaction with the child and/or her family, and others that are one or more steps removed. The three levels of relationships (primary, secondary, and tertiary) are captured in the examples presented in Figures 8.2., 8.3., and 8.4., and are used to remind us of the complexity of the relationships involved in the care and education of infants and toddlers.

THE INTERCONNECTIVITY AND RECIPROCITY OF RELATIONSHIPS

The multiple and varied contexts and patterns of interactions and connections typify those that affect the lives of infants and toddlers today. Through these interactions, infants and toddlers are exposed to a wide variety of unique and different individuals who form networks of knowledge and experience that benefit the infants and toddlers in the present and into the future as they learn and grow. It is, as a part of these networks that young children also learn about human relationships and behaviors,

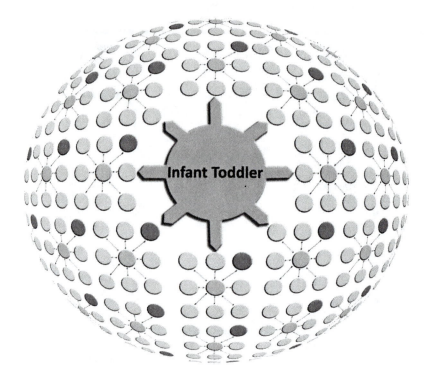

Figure 8.4   The universe of potential relationships surrounding the infant/toddler and family.

negative and positive. In their summative remarks in *Neurons to Neigh-borhoods* (Shonkoff, & Phillips, 2000), the authors stated that the well-being and "well-becoming" (p. 413) of young children are dependent on two essential conditions, the first of which is the need for stable and loving relationships, and the second being the need for a safe and predictable environment that provides a range of growth-promoting experiences.

Our belief in the interconnectedness across the various social contexts in which infants and toddlers experience life is highly reminiscent of the ecological perspective described and elaborated by Bronfenbrenner (1979). In this model, development and learning occur for infants and toddlers through relationships within overlapping and interactive systems. Bronfenbrenner described ecological systems in which children have the potential to establish very direct and immediate face-to-face relationships within the microsystem to the more distal relationships impacting on the child through the macrosystem or broader culture and society. Secondary (mesosystem) and tertiary (exosystem) levels link to one another and have the potential to influence development and learning in both positive and negative ways.

Similar ideas to Bronfenbrenner were presented from noted ethologist, Hinde (1987), who promoted a dynamic engagement model across three levels of increasing complexity. Hinde spoke of the influence on the individual and how in turn, the individual acted on all others in the system. The three levels of dynamic engagement involve basic interactions, then relationships, and finally social groups. As an ethologist, Hinde stressed that what the individual brought to the environmental system in terms of their own biology and how that biology was changed as the individual encountered various social engagements in different contexts.

An examination of organizational systems within the business world is also useful when thinking about the systemic nature of relationships. Consultants, for instance, believe that the free flow of information across networks of employees can change organizations (Senge, 1990; Wheatley, 1992). Networks are seen as powerful systems which can never fail. As each resource is added to the network, knowledge and options for all members increase in a geometric progression. Being members of such networks in working with infants and toddlers allows each person involved to be both a teacher and a learner. The influence, interconnection, and interaction of these spheres can support and enhance the lives of infants and toddlers as they become part of the universe of relationships that swirl around them in their daily lives. Ideally, this interconnectedness supports and enriches the lives of infants and toddlers and their families.

Bronfenbrenner's ecological framework, Hinde's theory, and the business networks model discussed above are all systems models. Any change in one part, or one relationship, or any interaction pattern within any of these complex systems is likely to have a wider impact, touching other relationship partners within the entire system. Such a ripple effect also exists within the relationship-based model that we are proposing and that is illustrated in Figures 8.2., 8.3., and 8.4. The model depicted the primary and secondary spheres of interaction and the universe of relationships surrounding the infant/toddler and family.

SPECIFYING THE ELEMENTS OF A RELATIONSHIP-BASED APPROACH

The relationship-based approach we described for infants and toddlers in ECEC (see Figure 8.1.) is built upon three key elements of practice including mindfulness (being in the moment), respect (taking into account beliefs and cultures), and reflection (a thoughtfulness before, during and after our actions) (McMullen, & Dixon, 2006). The manner in which mindfulness, respect, and reflection intersect and overlap defines the relationship-based approach that is the basis on which professionals work with one another. Through this approach it is possible "to establish close communication with families and work together with them toward positive outcomes for children's identity, sense of belonging, and cultural competence" (Gonzalez-Mena, 2001, p.368). The trio of elements is critical to creating an atmosphere and environment in which infants and toddlers may experience the world as a trustworthy place. This trust contributes to a sense of well-being, vital to helping infants and toddlers experience life to the fullest, in the here and now, and that optimizes the likelihood of healthy development and learning outcomes. A safe and healthy physical, social, and instructional environment; appropriate assessment, evaluation, and curricular decisions; family involvement practices are all dependent on healthy relationships between infants and the adults that care for them.

THREE CRITICAL ELEMENTS OF RELATIONSHIP-BASED PRACTICE

Each of the three elements of a relationship-based approach is described more fully in the following sections.

Mindful Practice

Mindfulness, being fully present with an infant or toddler, is a cornerstone of successful, meaningful interactions with children birth to three years. However, all of our interactions with those within our spheres of interactions deserve attention. Conversations with parents, colleagues, students, instructors, or community members all require that professionals are fully attentive and engaged as relationship partners.

The skills we find essential in relationships with infants and toddlers are easily and almost necessarily translated to all other relationships. Being responsive to the needs of infants and toddlers depends on an awareness of a level of non-verbal communication which allows infants and toddlers to participate in interactions as opposed to being recipients of them. The wiggles, smiles, and grimaces that let us know an infant's or toddler's state of being and allow us to create the type of interactions and environments which comfort and instruct at the same time, are the beginnings of complex communication systems. "Two people become companions on a mutually created journey through time. Interpersonal communication can be seen in spontaneous, resonant communication that flows freely and is balanced between continuity, familiarity, and predictability on one side and flexibility, novelty and uncertainty on the other. Neither partner of a dyad is fully predictable, yet each is quite familiar" (Siegel, 1999, p. 335). It is within that balanced flow that the mindful practitioner relies on continuity, familiarity, and predictability to support their relationship partner in flexible, novel, and uncertain situations. In the absence of mindful practice, novelty and uncertainty can overtake the interactions. For children, secure attachments form in responsive, trusting relationships and lay the foundation for the curious, motivated explorer who is open and able to establish reciprocal relationships with those around her (Bowman et al., 2001). Those relationships further provide the context for participation in the learning opportunities available.

Not only must the practitioner be mindful of the infants and toddlers in his or her setting, but also of the adult members of the care and education team. We are all communicating all the time. Words are only the most explicit surface of the messages. When we are mindful of what is being communicated by our own interactions both at and below the most superficial levels, we notice the impact that we are having on our conversational partners. What we do affects those around us, and reciprocally, these interactions provide us with the information that we need to engage in the next key component of relationship-based practice, reflection.

Reflective Practice

Reflective practice, or thinking before, during, and after our actions and interactions, clearly overlaps with mindfulness. The ability to understand that our personal characteristics and interactional styles influences the way those around us interact with us, our abilities to be an observer of those exchanges, and our capacities to respond and modify them in the future are also more overarching pursuits (Heffron, Ivins, & Weston, 2005; Norman-Murch, & Ward, 1999).

In entering into a cycle of self-inquiry, we explore those elements of our practice, including the struggles, dilemmas and difficulties, as well as the successes and celebrations in more depth than is possible in the moment of living them. It allows us to learn from our own experiences and practice, and apply that to our relationships with those in our spheres of interaction. Why did that activity fail today when it was such a resounding success yesterday? How can I make sense of the meeting we just attended? Did I listen openly so that I really heard what she had to say, or was I just listening for what I wanted to hear? Is there a way that I can make this work better for everyone next time? Have I learned anything from prior experiences that might inform me now? Reflective practice means not just having the fleeting thoughts as we run through our day but spending the time necessary to put them in the context of our practice and create new knowledge from thinking through the ideas.

Reflection may be, but is not necessarily, an isolated pursuit. Involving families, colleagues and other members of our spheres of interaction with whom we have established mindful, respectful relationships in the reflective process increases the impact of our discoveries. We can share the processes of inquiry with our essential relationship partners. Reflecting together with families or team members allows the group to examine issues or ideas which impact them directly. The reflective piece of this equation nurtures relationships and allows relationships to grow by ensuring that practices are purposeful and well-considered.

Respectful Practice

The United States is one of the most ethnically, racially, linguistically, and culturally diverse nations in the world. The ECEC professional encounters family and community cultures that differ from her own everyday and must be willing to face these differences among the children, families, and professional colleagues with whom she works as assets, not deficits. She demonstrates this perspective by showing that she values the characteristics, beliefs, and behaviors of the children and families and other relationship partners within her sphere of interactions. In all of actions and communications, the caregiver demonstrates that she sees each and every one, including the infant or toddler, as competent, with worthwhile contributions to make.

It is necessary to support infants' and toddlers' full participation in his or her home culture if the expectation is optimal development (Gonzalez-Mena, 2000). It is unreasonable to expect an infant or toddler to acquire new skills or knowledge while learning new cultural norms at the same time. For the optimal development and learning to occur, educators must accept the legitimacy of children's home language, respect (hold in high regard) and value (esteem, appreciate) the home culture, and promote and encourage the active involvement and support of all families, including extended and non-traditional family units. When early childhood educators acknowledge and respect children's home language and culture, ties between the family and programs are strengthened. This atmosphere provides increased opportunity for learning because young children feel supported, nurtured, and connected not only to their home communities and families, but also to teachers and the educational setting (National Association for the Education of Young Children, 1995, par.6 & 7).

A philosophy of respect in infant and toddler care and education requires that all children under the age of three, whether on a typical developmental path or with a disability, have access to child care, education and community membership, and the right to a full and meaningful life. In the United States, there is a firmly established service system for children with documented disabilities. Services for infants and toddlers are federally mandated and are available through a "statewide, comprehensive, coordinated, multidisciplinary, interagency system that provides early intervention services for infants and toddlers with disabilities and their families" (U.S. Department of Education, 2007, p. 26503). Core principles of early intervention in this country rest on principles of inclusion and family partnerships in the process. Both principles embody the philosophical basis of respect for individual differences, and the child and family's right to full participation within their community. For infants and toddlers, services are provided either at home or in community-based programs where children who do not have disabilities are enrolled, and the full involvement of families in setting priorities, planning, and participating in intervention is encouraged.

Respect in relationships allows us to approach the issues we hold in common as professionals within our spheres of interaction in new and different ways. Rather than compromise, which implies that both sides have to give up something to gain something, Gonzalez-Mena (2001) characterized this new or different way as "the third space," or the place in which we can resolve "conflicts by embracing contraries" (p. 370). In the third space, multiple perspectives in relationships are valued, as is holistic ("both/and") rather than dualistic ("either/or") thinking and problem solving (Barrera, Corso, & Macpherson, 2003; Bredekamp & Copple, 1997; Gonzalez-Mena, 2001; Rogoff, 2003). Holistic thinking moves us away from positioning ourselves as "right" and others with whom we are working as "wrong." In this third space all members of a respectful working relationship have the potential to come away winners; but more importantly, the infants and toddlers and families with whom we work benefit when we engage in an holistic relationship-based approach in dealing with the issues in the day-to-day professional lives.

SUPPORT FOR ELEMENTS OF A RELATIONSHIP-BASED APPROACH IN THE UNITED STATES

Mindfulness, respect, and reflection as the three elements of relationship-based care are currently at the heart of many of the major theories and models supported by ECEC professionals in the United States. Such approaches are advocated by the most influential professional organizations that support infant and toddler care and early education in the United States (e.g., National Association for the Education of Young Children [NAEYC], the Program for Infant/Toddler Care [PITC], and Zero to Three).

NAEYC articulates the philosophy of developmentally appropriate practice for children birth to age eight in the United States, with a separate statement for birth to three-year-olds (Bredekamp & Copple, 1997). This philosophy is influenced by key ideas from Jean Piaget's Cognitive Development Theory, Lev Vygotsky's Sociocultural Theory, John Dewey's Progressivist Movement and Theory of Pragmatism, Erik Erikson's Psychosocial Development Theory, and Maria Montessori's work (see Mooney, 2000). Developmentally appropriate practice takes a holistic perspective on development, reminding us not to just focus on the isolated achievement of academic or cognitive milestones but on the "whole" child, including social, emotional, communication, and physical domains as well. In addition, culture and community play a central role in determining what is "appropriate" about the practices in which we engage with both individual children and groups of children.

A fundamental aspect of developmentally appropriate practice for infants and toddlers, as described by NAEYC, is the formation of trusting relationships, as described by Erik Erikson (Bredekamp & Copple, 1997). NAEYC espouses the centrality of relationships in the achievement of healthy growth, development, and learning outcomes; this includes the relationships between infants and their caregivers, among child peers, between caregivers and families, and between colleagues engaged in caregiving. These relationships are explicated in most of the practices suggested by the philosophy of developmentally appropriate practice (Dodge, Rudick, & Berke, 2006; Greenman, Stonehouse, & Schweikert, 2008; Honig, 2001; Koralek, Dombro, & Dodge, 2005). For example, developmentally appropriate practice urges us to be focused and deliberate (mindful and reflective) in how we set up the environment and in the planning of day-to-day interactions. A focus on relationships is also seen in the organization's rationale for low caregiver to child ratios and small recommended group sizes.

PITC also has a clear focus on the planful, reflective behaviors associated with our definition of a relationship-based approach prominently displayed on their website—"care should be based on relationship planning—not lesson planning" (PITC, 2008). Close ties to the philosophies and work of Magda Gerber and Emmi Pikler (Gerber & Johnson, 1997) are also evidence of PITC's focus on mindfulness. This philosophy of mindfulness with infants and toddlers noted by Gerber (cited in Weaver, 2002) indicates that when we engage in routine caregiving practices with infants and toddlers that it is important to: "'unbusy' your head and 'unbusy' your body. Be fully there, interested only in your baby for that time" (p. 5).

Of the three elements identified in the relationship-based approach, PITC places most emphasis on the formation of respectful relationships with infants and toddlers and their families as the critical element in defining best practices for children under three years (Lally, Griffin, Fenichel, Segal, Szanton, & Weissbourd, 2003; Lally, Mangione, & Greenwald 2006). PITC has promoted important ideas about how relationships can be facilitated through daily caregiving routines, through ensuring continuity of care by allowing infants and toddlers to remain with the same caregiver(s) over longer periods of time and through primary caregiving models in which infants and toddlers are assigned to one caregiver who is primarily responsible for their care and education. Sensitively responsive care is a cornerstone of best practices promoted by PITC. Such care also reflects highly respectful practice (Gonzalez-Mena & Eyer, 2007). To be sensitively responsive (i.e., to be able to read and respond appropriately to the verbal and non-verbal communications of infants and toddlers, caregivers must take the time to form caring and close relationships with them). We must also be mindful or "in the moment" in order to be responsive to our relationship partners.

Zero to Three is an organization dedicated to the professional development of practitioners working with infants and toddlers. Like NAEYC and PITC, it emphasizes trusting, respectful relationships. Zero to Three also promotes the reflective cycle as a key to forming and maintaining relationships. According to Zero to Three, relationship-based practice is characterized by self-awareness, careful and continuous observation, and respectful, flexible responses that result in reflective and relationship-based programs (Zero to Three, 2008). Zero to Three expands our notions of reflection as indicated by Parlakian (2001) who identified reflection as: " . . . stepping back from the immediate, intense experience of hands-on work and taking the time to wonder what the experience really means . . ." and to ask ourselves . . ."What does it tell us about the family? . . . About ourselves?" (par 2).

It is important to point out that these organizations, and the philosophies they promote which influence contemporary beliefs and practices about infant and toddler care and education in the United States are influenced by theoretical ideas beyond the United Stated. Most notable among these outside influences comes from recent examination of the work of Emmi Pikler from Hungary, primarily interpreted by the RIE organization (Resources for Infant Educarers) and Magda Gerber (Gerber & Johnson, 1997). Other influences on practice in the United States come from Reggio Emilia and other Italian models for infant and toddler care and education (Gandini & Edwards, 2000). More recently the work done in Great Britain in the development of the *Birth to Three Matters Framework for Effective Practice* (Abbott & Langston, 2005) has also had an influence.

CHALLENGES TO IMPLEMENTING A RELATIONSHIP-BASED APPROACH IN THE UNITED STATES

The behaviors and practices described within a relationship-based approach align with other perspectives on quality in ECEC which are typically discussed in terms of either process or structural variables (Cryer, & Clifford, 2003; Lally et al., 2003; McMullen, 1999). Structural variables are easiest to regulate but also have less direct impact on the child. Structural variables include group size, ratio of adults to infants and toddlers, and the stability and the qualifications of the staff. Process (or dynamic) variables are more difficult to regulate because they relate directly to interactions but they are important because they have more direct impact on practices with infants and toddlers. Process factors involve the nature of the relationships and communications between and among caregivers and infants and toddlers, as well as the relationships and communications with colleagues, administrators, parents, community members, and others. These very directly align with a relationship-based model.

High quality care related to a relationship-based approach is achieved when group sizes are small, ratios between caregivers and children are low, infants and toddlers are able to remain with the same highly qualified caregivers for longer periods of time, communications are positive and effective, and caregivers are sensitively responsive in their practices. However, too few infants and toddlers in the United States experience the high level of quality that is indicative of relationship-based practices. The Cost, Quality and Outcomes Study Team (1995) found only 8% of infants and toddlers in the United States were experiencing high quality ECEC settings. A full 40% of infants and toddlers in the United States were found to be in "poor" quality settings. Poor quality was defined by criteria that indicated that the children were at risk in terms of health and safety. Unfortunately, there is no evidence that progress has been made in the past decade to improve this situation.

Assuring quality in ECEC for infants and toddlers is problematic in the United States for a number of reasons, the largest of which is that there is no coherent centralized national system for monitoring the quality of care. In fact, there is no centralized educational system in the United States for children from birth through school-age. Thus, neither the U.S. Department of Education nor the U.S. Department of Health and Human Services (the federal agency responsible for the health and welfare of its citizenry) is responsible for ECEC for children under the age of three. There are two notable exceptions to this lack of government oversight. These are Head Start which provides care, education, and social services to children in poverty and the U.S. military child care system. These national ECEC programs are managed at least in part by federal regulations (Center for the Child Care Workforce, 2004).

Although there is no nationwide centralized system to cover infants and toddlers in ECEC, the 50 individual states of the United States each have their own regulatory bodies, rules and systems of oversight of children in out-of-home care. State governments hold firm to their rights to develop, implement, and oversee the laws and regulations about care within local communities. However, state regulations are widely characterized as assuring only minimal standards of quality, typically addressing only the most basic health and safety concerns (Apple, 2006; Azur, LeMoine, Morgan, Clifford, & Crawford, 2002).

One possible contributor to the lack of a coherent system overseeing ECEC for all U.S. infants and toddlers is a persistent attitude that national attempts to regulate interfere with parental authority, control, and choice. However, this attitude is at odds with a position that assures the full rights of children as citizens in a modern democracy. Another negative and pervasive social attitude is that the care of infants and toddlers is something "anyone can do." Therefore, the professionalization of the field has been an uphill battle (Apple & McMullen, 2007; McMullen & Alat, 2002).

As discussed earlier in this chapter, the United States does have a federally mandated system for infants and toddlers with disabilities, but this too is not a centralized, nationally regulated system. The implementation of early intervention (birth to three) services is determined by individual state interpretation of the federal law across each of the 50 states. Thus, the greatest future challenge in the delivery of quality in these services for children with disabilities lies in the considerable variability which exists across states. The intent of the federal law was to deliberately build flexibility into the system to allow states to tailor their systems to meet local needs. However, decisions made at local levels are not always found to reflect the best interests of infants, toddlers and their families (Spiker, Hebbeler, Wagner, Cameto, & McKenna, 2000).

Despite a lack of a coherent regulated system in the United States for infant and toddler care and education, there are national voluntary systems of accreditation. The largest of these accreditation systems is organized through NAEYC. According to Apple (2006), "In contrast to state child care regulations, NAEYC's voluntary accreditation for ECEC programs provides quality criteria, rather than minimum standards. The research on the NAEYC accreditation consistently indicates that accredited programs are of higher quality than nonaccredited programs" (p. 536).

CONCLUSION

In this chapter, we asserted that relationships should be at the heart of best practice in infant and toddler care and education in the United States. We described the behaviors that are associated with mindful, reflective, and respectful practices that are central to the formation, growth, and nurturing of positive relationships. Such relationships create interpersonal systems which promote a healthy sense of well-being, as well as the optimal growth, development and learning outcomes for infants and toddlers in care settings.

Establishing and maintaining positive relationships is not always easy. It certainly takes more effort with some of our relationship partners than with others. There are also numerous other challenges within the systems of care within the United States in order for full implementation of a relationship-based approach to be successful. However, summarizing from what we presented earlier, we can make suggestions about this process, whether between ourselves and infants and toddlers and their families, or among one or more of the many other relationship partners in our spheres of interaction.

Be mindful by:

- Being fully present in the moment with your relationship partner.
- Being a responsive communicator, attentive to and aware of the impact of our own and our partners' verbal and non-verbal messages.

Be reflective by:

- Being aware of how our own background, beliefs, and experiences shape and filter our perceptions of other's behaviors and influence our own responses and behaviors.
- Being deliberate in our actions and communications, considering beforehand what we will do and say, paying careful attention to how

it is interpreted, and engaging in critical self-assessment following each encounter or behavioral episode.

Be respectful by:

- Valuing and honoring the differences in our relationship partners, and treating them all as competent and worthwhile.
- Being more holistic in our thinking and engaging in "both/and" ways of approaching issues and problems rather than more dualistic "either/ or" or "right/wrong" thinking.

Infants and toddlers in the United States experience a range of care and education experiences. From the nature of the settings to the number and quality of the relationships, the diversity seen across the country is both a tribute to the best possible circumstances and a condemnation of a system of care and education that lacks the ability to monitor itself and assure even the basics in healthy and safe environments. Because we believe that "children learn in the context of important relationships" (Shore, 1997, p. 29), we have proposed that children exposed to positive, caring relationships that nurture their current well-being are more likely to have healthy growth and more positive developmental and learning outcomes. By remembering that each facet of every child's life is integrally connected with all others and that, within each sphere of interaction is the potential for relationships that will play a formative role for them now and in the future, we begin to create the types of experiences we want for all children.

REFERENCES

Abbott, L., & Langston, A. (2005). *Birth to three matters: Supporting the framework of effective practice*. Maidenhead, Berkshire, England: Open University Press.

Apple, P. (2006). A developmental approach to early childhood program quality improvement: The relationship between state regulation and NAEYC accreditation. *Early Education and Development, 17*(4), 535–552.

Apple, P., & McMullen, M. B. (2007) Envisioning the impact of caring and just decisions that determine early childhood professional development pathways. *Contemporary Issues in Early Childhood Education, 8*(3), 255–264.

Azur, S., LeMoine, S., Morgan, G., Clifford, R., & Crawford, G. (2002, Winter). *Regulation of child care*. Chapel Hill, NC: National Center for Early Development and Learning. Early Childhood Research and Policy Briefs. Retrieved January 28, 2008, from http://www.fpg.unc.edu/~ncedl/PDFs/RegBrief.pdf

Barrera, I., Corso, R., & Macpherson, D. (2003). *Skilled dialogue: Strategies for responding to cultural diversity in early childhood*. Baltimore, MD: Brookes Pubishing.

Bowman, B., Donovan, M. S., & Burns, M. S. (Eds.) (2001). *Eager to learn: Educating our preschoolers*. Washington, DC: National Academy Press.

Bredekamp, S., & Copple, C. (Eds.) (1997). *Developmentally appropriate practice in early childhood programs (revised edition).* Washington, DC: National Association for the Education of Young Children.

Bronfenbrenner, U. (1979). *The ecology of human development: Experiments by nature and design.* Cambridge, MA: Harvard University Press.

Center for Child Care Workforce (2004, October). *Current data on the salaries and benefits of the U.S. early childhood education workforce.* Retrieved January 30, 2008, from http://www.ccw.org/

Cost, Quality, and Child Outcomes Study Team (1995). *Cost, quality and child outcomes in child care centers.* Denver, CO: Department of Economics, University of Colorado at Denver.

Cryer, D, & Clifford, R. (Eds.) (2003). *Early childhood education and care in the USA.* Baltimore, MD: Brookes Publishing.

Dodge, D. T., Rudick, S., & Berke, K. (2006). *The creative curriculum for infants, toddlers & twos.* Washington, DC: Teaching Strategies.

Dombro, A. L., & Learner, C. (2006). Sharing the care of infants and toddlers. *Young Children, 61*(1), 29–33.

Gandini, L., & Edwards, C. P. (2000). *Bambini: The Italian approach to infant/toddler care.* New York: Teachers College Press.

Gerber, M., & Johnson, A. (1997). *Your self-confident baby: How to encourage your child's natural abilities from the very start.* New York: Wiley Publishing.

Gonzalez-Mena, J. (2000). *Multicultural issues in childcare.* New York: McGraw-Hill.

———. (2001). Cross-cultural infant care and issues of equity and social justice. *Contemporary Issues in Early Childhood, 2*(3), 368–371.

Gonzalez-Mena, J., & Eyer, D. W. (2007). *Infants, toddlers, and caregivers* (7th ed.). New York: McGraw Hill.

Greenman, J., Stonehouse, A., & Schweikert, G. (2008). *Prime times* (2nd ed.). St. Paul, MN: Redleaf Press.

Heffron, M. C., Ivins, B., & Weston, D. R. (2005). Finding an authentic voice. Use of self: Essential learning processes for relationship-based work. *Infants & Young Children: An Interdisciplinary Journal of Special Care Practices, 18*(4), 323–336.

Hinde, R. A., (1987). Individuals, relationships, and culture: Links between ethology and the social sciences. New York: Cambridge University Press.

Honig, A. S. (2001). *Secure relationships: Nurturing infant-toddler attachment in early care settings.* Washington, DC: NAEYC.

Koralek, D. G., Dombro, L, & Dodge, D. T. (2005). *Caring for infants and toddlers.* Washington, DC: Teaching Strategies.

Kreader, J. L., Ferguson, D., & Lawrence, S. (2005, August). *Infant and toddler child care arrangements. National Center for Children in Poverty.* Retrieved January 26, 2008, from http://www.nccp.org/publications/pub_628.html.

Lally, J. R., Griffin, A., Fenichel, E., Segal, M., Szanton, E., & Weissbourd, B. (2003). *Caring for infants & toddlers in groups: Developmentally appropriate practice.* Washington, DC: Zero to Three.

Lally, J. R., & Mangione, P. L., & Greenwald, D. (Eds.). (2006). *Concepts for care: 20 essays on infant/toddler development and learning.* San Francisco: WestEd.

McMullen, M. B. (1999). Characteristics of teachers who talk the DAP talk AND walk the DAP walk. *Journal of Research in Childhood Education, 13*(2), 216–230.

McMullen, M. B., & Alat, K. (2002). Education matters in the nurturing of the beliefs of early childhood professionals. *Early Childhood Research & Practice, 4*(2), Retrieved March 23, 2008, from http://ecrp.uiuc.edu/v4n2/index.html.

McMullen, M., & Dixon, S. (2006). Building on common ground: Unifying the practices of infant toddler specialists through a mindful, relationship-based approach. Research in review. *Young Children, 61*(4), 46–52.

Mooney, C. G. (2000). *Theories of childhood: An introduction to Dewey, Montessori, Erikson, Piaget, and Vygotsky.* St. Paul, MN: Redleaf Press.

Moylett, H., & Djemli, P. (2005). Practitioners matter. In L. Abbott & A. Langston (Eds.), *Birth to three matters: Supporting the framework of effective practice* (pp. 56–67). London: Open University Press.

National Association for the Education of Young Children (NAEYC). (1995, November). *Responding to linguistic and cultural diversity: Recommendations for effective early childhood education.* Retrieved January 30, 2008, from http://www.naeyc.org/about/positions/PSDIV98.asp.

Norman-Murch, T., & Ward, G. (1999). First steps in establishing reflective practice and supervision: Organizational issues and strategies. *ZERO TO THREE/ National Center for Clinical Infant Programs, 20*(1), 10–14.

Parlakian, R. (2001). *Look, listen, and learn: Reflective supervision and relationship-based work.* Washington, DC: Zero to Three. Retrieved April 12, 2008, from   http://www.zerotothree.org/site/PageServer?pagename=ter_key_reflec_ blocks.

Program for Infant/Toddler Care (PITC). (2008, April). *The PITC philosophy.* Retrieved April 13, 2008 from http://www.pitc.org/pub/pitc_docs/about.html.

Rogoff, B. (2003). *The cultural nature of human development.* New York: Oxford University.

Senge, P. (1990). *The fifth discipline: The art and practice of learning organizations.* New York: Doubleday.

Siegel, D. J. (1999). *The developing mind: How relationships and the brain·interact to shape who we are.* New York: Guilford Press.

Shonkoff, J. P., & Phillips, D. A. (Eds.). (2000). *From neurons to neighborhoods: The science of early childhood development.* Washington, D.C.: National Academy Press.

Shore, R. (1997). *Rethinking the brain: New insights into early development.* New York: Families and Work Institute.

Spiker, D., Hebbeler, K., Wagner, M., Cameto, R., & McKenna, P. (2000). A framework for describing variations in state early intervention systems. *Topics in Early Childhood Special Education, 20,* 195–207.

U.S. Census Bureau (2005, October). *Who's minding the kids? Child care arrangements: Winter 2002.* Retrieved January 26, 2008, http://www.census.gov/ prod/2005pubs/p70–101.pdf.

U.S. Department of Education (2007, May). *Early intervention program for infants and toddlers with disabilities; Proposed Rule. Federal Register, 72*(89), 26456–26503. Retrieved May 28, 2008, from http://www.ed.gov/legislation/ FedRegister/proprule/2007–2/050907a.pdf.

Vandell, D. L. (2004). Early child care: The known and the unknown. *Merrill-Palmer Quarterly, 50*(3), 387–414.

Weaver, J. (Ed.). *Dear parent: Caring for infants with respect (2nd edition).* Los Angeles, CA: Resources for Infant Educarers.

Wheatley, M. (1992). Leadership and the new science: Learning about organization from an orderly universe. San Francisco: Berrett-Koehler Publishers.

Zero to Three (2008, April). *Zero to Three.* Retrieved April 13, 2008, from www. zerotothree.org/

9 Looking and Listening for Participatory Practice in an English Day Nursery

Paulette Luff

This chapter considers the importance of observant, attentive, respectful, and responsive work with babies and toddlers, especially those who spend time in group day care. It highlights the significance of various positive relationships, between children and adults, arguing that these relationships encourage young children's participation in their day nursery community and enhance their care and education. The observations of practice discussed in this chapter stem from a larger research study of case studies of practice carried out in three different early childhood settings. Illustrative examples of practice used in this chapter stem from observations of daily life in one small day nursery that was a participant centre in the research. The main aim of the chapter is to identify key ways in which early childhood practitioners enable very young children's active, participatory learning. The title of the chapter reflects two meanings: first, the observational role of the researcher to be alert to instances of participation by looking and listening carefully; and, second, the role of the practitioners to be effective in facilitating children's participation through careful looking and listening.

THEORETICAL PERSPECTIVES

While this chapter is primarily practical in its focus, it is based on understandings drawn from sociocultural theory (e.g., Rogoff, 1990, 2003). Insights from such a theoretical perspective inform this chapter. Babies and very young children can be viewed as active members of social groups. There are many implications of viewing young children in this way—for nurturing and for learning; together with understanding the significance of the contexts in which care and education occurs (Selby & Bradley, 2003). Each of these issues are discussed briefly and revisited in the subsequent discussions on practice.

From their earliest days, human infants show evidence of their predisposition to be social by showing distinct preferences for human faces (Fantz, 1961; Johnson & Morton, 1991); voices (Aslin, Jusczyk, & Pisoni, 1998;

DeCasper & Fifer, 1980); a capacity to imitate facial expressions (Meltzoff & Moore, 1977, 1997); and feeding in burst-pause patterns (Kaye, 1977; Wolff, 1968). They rapidly begin to relate to their carers. From an early age, babies actively elicit responses from their carers through social smiling and turn-taking in shared interactions (Bruner, 1983; Murray & Andrews, 2000; Trevarthen, 1979, 2001). In these ways, babies show that they possess agency, efficacy, and growing competence in dynamic, social interactions, and transactions.

This view of young children, as active in making connections with people, implies a right that they be listened to and attended to: "Babies and infants are entirely dependent on others, but they are not passive recipients of care, direction and guidance. They are active social agents who seek protection, nurturance and understanding from parents or other caregivers, which they require for their survival, growth and well-being" (Convention on the Rights of the Child [CRC], 2005, p. 8). This view of children has implications for pedagogies for participation for the youngest children in the nursery. If learning is viewed as a social process, through which meanings are constructed in shared contexts, then adults and children should have the opportunity to engage in interactions and be open to what they understand from one another (Bruner, 1995; Smith, 1999). Particularly when working with the youngest children, this also implies a need for awareness on the part of adults of young children's often powerful emotions and a capacity to share, contain and respond to young children's feelings (Elfer, 2007; Reddy & Trevarthen, 2004; Trevarthen, 2001).

In supportive homes, it is the parents, and other relatives who respond to babies and young children's emerging personalities and who engage them in the culture of the family. Thus, a child gains social understandings and a range of other skills through the opportunities afforded in the family environment (Dunn, 1988; Parker-Rees, 2007). Can group care provide similarly enabling surroundings where babies and young children can learn in this participatory manner? There has been extensive debate about the suitability of group day care for babies. Consensus in this debate·is that all care environments should be made of high quality in order to provide satisfying experiences for the youngest children (Dowling, 2005). Thus, on a day to day basis, the emphasis in activities should be on how interactions between adults and children can provide a context for active growth while also instilling positive dispositions for future social participation and learning.

THE CONTEXT FOR EARLY CARE IN THE UNITED KINGDOM

In the United Kingdom since 1997, there has been considerable government interest and investment in early childhood services and considerable challenges associated with policy changes. Policies have been driven by ambitious targets to eliminate child poverty by the year 2020, together with an aim to raise overall educational attainment through a focus on the early years of education. These initiatives have been described and discussed elsewhere (e.g., Penn, 2007; Pugh, 2006). In this section, several key points on policy are highlighted that have had a direct impact upon group care with very young children.

An emphasis upon parental participation in the labor market has led to a very large increase in the number of full-day care places available to parents (National Audit Office, 2004). All nurseries, whether in the public, voluntary or private sector, are subject to registration and inspection by the Office for Standards in Education (Ofsted). According to judgments by Ofsted, based upon the National Standards that set the minimum requirements for provision of services, the majority of full day care settings are found to be of good quality with some services identified as being of outstanding quality (Ofsted, 2007). However, there is concern as to whether settings that are merely satisfactory in meeting the standards can provide sufficient nurture for very young children (Dowling, 2005). The Early Years Foundation Stage (Department for Children, Schools and Families, 2008) sets out a regulatory and legal framework for early childhood education and care for children from birth to age five years, in England, together with guidelines for about its implementation. Of particular relevance to this chapter is a requirement in this framework for all children to have a designated key person as a carer; together with commitments to fostering holistic development and promoting positive interactions within a supportive environment. While this framework was broadly welcomed, concerns were expressed about its statutory nature and its inconsistencies between advocating a child-centered approach while mandating prescribed learning outcomes, including goals for reading and writing, to be reached by the age of five.

THE RESEARCH STUDY

The observations discussed in this chapter form part of the data from a larger set of case studies of practice carried out in three different early childhood settings involving 11 newly qualified practitioners for the early years and their understandings and use of child observations in their practice (see Luff, 2008). One finding from the larger study was that, even when no formal observations of children were documented, practitioners were often highly observant and responsive to the children in their care. Moreover, this informal observant practice was shown to be very important for enhancing relationships with children, families, and colleagues (Luff, 2008). The findings suggested the importance of relationships for enabling shared learning.

The examples discussed in this chapter stem from two, day-long observations sessions recorded in the "under-twos" room of a small (36 place) London day nursery, towards the end of the one-year research study. The first observation is focused on a nursery worker called Kel, aged 20 years, and the second observation on Mij, aged 19 years. At the time of these observations, Kel and Mij had been employed at the nursery for nine months. Kel has supervisory responsibility for this nursery room, which catered for up to nine babies and children less than two years, at any one time. There was also a third member of staff that allowed for a ratio of one adult to three children. On both observational occasions, there were only six children attending who ranged in age from eight to 20 months. This allowed the researcher who was usually a more active participant observer, to withdraw and watch the day proceed. These two observations were seen and analyzed within the context of a longer association with this day nursery over the course of the research study that enhanced the authenticity of the research. While acknowledging an inevitable mutual influence between the researcher and the research context (Edwards, 2004), Kel and Mij were well used to the presence of an observer and the researcher can confirm that the observed practice reported in this chapter was consistent with behaviors witnessed on other occasions.

The analysis from these two observations sessions informs the remaining sections of this chapter. The sections are organized using three key themes: adult and child relationships; relationships between children; and relationships between adults involved with the children. These themes were chosen in recognition of the centrality of social experiences for babies' and toddlers' learning and serve to illustrate how significantly relationships contribute to participatory learning and form a basis for participatory pedagogy for "people under three" (Goldschmied & Jackson, 2004).

Instances of sensitive and participatory practices with babies and young children, highlighted in the analyses are not unique. Similar examples have been documented in other publications that have focused on the development of effective ways of working with babies in English early years settings (Abbott & Langston, 2005; Forbes, 2004; Gillespie Edwards, 2002; Manning Morton & Thorp, 2003, 2006). These particular examples are offered in response to a call for "studies which document very young children's participation in their natural habitat" (Parker-Rees, 2007, p. 12) and in support of the view that the voices of the youngest children may be heard and understood through attending to their interactions with others (Elfer, 2005, 2007).

ADULT-CHILD RELATIONSHIPS

Relationships between adults and very young children attending early childhood settings are frequently discussed in terms of attachment theory and the importance of the emotional security provided to each child and family by a key person (Elfer, 2007; Elfer, Goldschmied, & Selleck, 2003; Goldschmied & Jackson, 2004). While agreeing that consistent care and special attention are essential to well-being, when focusing upon participatory learning the emphasis changes slightly and includes consideration of the significance of care-giving relationships for the shared development of knowledge and understandings. Bruner (1972) highlighted very young children's "tutor proneness," an eagerness to learn through active engagement with familiar adults (p. 697). Trevarthen (2001) also argues that babies seek companionship and cooperative intersubjectivity and are highly motivated to engage in reciprocal communications for learning. Within families, dance-like interactions (Murray & Andrews, 2000; Stern, 1985), in which babies lead and parents follow, are highly effective in fostering development and learning. In child care environments outside of the home it may not be so easy to provide opportunities for these attuned interactions (Elfer, 2007). Parker-Rees (2007) fears that in day care settings it can "be difficult to achieve the depth of shared experience and easy companionship which allows young children to engage in bold and confident social participation" (p. 12).

Research into the effectiveness of early childhood care and education (e.g., Pascal & Bertram, 1997; Siraj-Blatchford, Sylva, Muttock, Gilden, & Bell, 2002; Smith, 1999; Woodhead, 1996) continually highlights the importance of interactions between adults and children, especially those characterized by periods of joint attention and shared meaning-making. Where adults are engaged in offering consistent, receptive, and responsive attention, children are shown to thrive and to learn. Payler (2007) identifies how children's involvement in learning processes is shaped by the pedagogies of their early childhood settings and the ways in which these open or restrict space for participation. Bae (2007) speaks, similarly, of how spacious dialogical patterns provide children with opportunities for self-expression while narrow, adult dominated patterns are more restrictive. What might such open, spacious, participatory interactions look like between adults and very young children? The following examples are offered as possible answers.

ADULT-CHILD INTERACTIONS

Sophie and Kel

Kel sees Sophie, aged 18 months, reaching up to place a toy car in a garage which is on top of a storage unit. In response to Sophie's one word, "car," Kel lifts the garage down onto the floor and says in response, "Sophie is playing with the car!" Just a little later, Sophie hands Kel a toy car, again saying, "car." This time Kel repeats the word, takes the car and hides it behind her back. Kel then stretches out her arms towards Sophie with closed fists saying, "Where's it gone?" Sophie laughs and points at Kel's right hand and says, "That!" When Kel opens her hand to reveal the car Sophie takes it and they both smile.

Throughout the whole nursery day, Sophie uses her emergent vocabulary to elicit this type of playful response. When they are singing songs, Kel reacts to Sophie rolling her hands by leading a "roly-poly" rhyme followed by "Wind the bobbin up." During a pause between songs Sophie says, "Baa, baa," to which Kel responds, "Do you want to do Baa, baa black sheep?" When Sophie nods emphatically they sing it. At lunch time Sophie teases Kel by saying that her ice cream dessert is "hot," and also by calling Kel "Mummy!" and then "Daddy!" When Kel shakes her head and everybody laughs, Sophie repeats loudly, "Daddy! Daddy!" and smiles at Kel. Both these small jokes continue for the rest of the afternoon, for example, when Kel is washing Sophie's face she asks her whether the flannel is hot or cold.

The playful relationship is seen during a physical play time, too, when Kel is sitting on the ground and Sophie runs up and rolls over Kel's legs and then runs round and round. Kel catches Sophie and gives her a hug and they both laugh. There is a different, but equally trusting and affectionate, encounter a little later when Sophie slips on the slide. She cries a little and rubs her head and arm then goes over to Kel and points to her head. Kel gently rubs Sophie's head and she is immediately reassured and runs back to the slide, laughing. Similarly, when Sophie is barefoot, playing with soft foam shapes on the carpet, she comes near to Kel and points to her toes. Kel makes a sympathetic response, rubbing Sophie's toes and saying, "Remember you've got no shoes!" to which Sophie nods and says, "Shoes."

It is clear that Sophie and Kel have developed a positive relationship in which both feel confident. Sophie is a skilled contributor to these interactions and knows how to participate effectively and to elicit responses from Kel. Kel is gentle, receptive, and prepared to take Sophie's lead. The communication between them seems to exemplify the mutual recognition that is characteristic of open, spacious pedagogical interactions. The shared humor is a particularly appealing feature of these encounters. Loizou's (2005) research suggests that very young children gain satisfaction and enjoyment from violating the expectations of their caregivers, as Sophie does when she calls Kel "Daddy!" This suggests that humor is an important tool for the development of empowered young learners.

While Kel allows Sophie to initiate interactions and matches her responses accordingly, Kel's colleague, Mij, also acts as "playmate and companion in meaning" (Trevarthen, 2004, p. 2) for the children but behaves differently. As the babies and toddlers in Mij's care choose to play with different activities, including the sand pit and a toy kitchen, she follows each child's lead but also adds elements to their play. This is illustrated in the following examples, taken from episodes playing with stickle bricks (a simple, brightly colored plastic construction toy with pieces that fix together easily).

Mij and the Stickle Bricks

When Jesse moves towards the door, carrying the stickle bricks box by the handle, Mij says, "Where are you going?" and "Bye, bye!" Jesse comes back and kneels on the mat. He picks up a brick. Mij sits by him and helps him to press two bricks together. He laughs and Mij smiles. When he manages to fit two bricks together by himself, Jesse laughs again and Mij smiles and claps. He presses more bricks together, still smiling, and then stands up and picks up the box by the handle. Mij asks him if that's how his mummy carries her shopping bag. Jesse kneels down again and Mij sits alongside him pressing bricks together. Jesse makes speech-like sounds and looks at Mij and she replies to him. Mij pushes the stickle brick car that she has made towards Jesse and he takes it. He pushes it backwards and forwards and then breaks it up, pulling it apart brick by brick and dropping the bricks onto the mat.

Later, they play a different game with the same bricks. This time Jesse posts a stickle brick down the front of his vest. Mij joins in and, taking turns, they fill the front of his vest (which is quite loose fitting and tucked into his trousers) with stickle bricks. Mij smiles and Jesse laughs and pulls the bricks out one by one. Jesse then begins to post more bricks into his vest.

With Jean-Paul, who is a few months younger than Jesse, the interaction is different. It is initiated again by the child and Mij picks up on Jean-Paul's cue and creates a simple game. Jean-Paul comes up and stands close to Mij who is sitting down. They smile at each other. Jean-Paul stands in front of Mij and raises his face to look up at her. Mij lowers her head so that their foreheads touch, gently, and they both smile. Jean-Paul then sits beside Mij and leans back against her legs. Mij presses some stickle bricks together and he takes them. Jean-Paul turns around and raises his face to Mij who bends towards him. Jean-Paul takes a brick from Mij's right hand and picks up another brick from the floor in front of him. He presses the two together. Jean-Paul then puts the bricks onto his head. Mij holds them, helping the bricks to balance there. Jean-Paul tips his head and Mij says, "Ooo!" when the bricks fall off. They take turns in placing bricks on his head and he smiles as he shakes each of them off.

In these sociable games, the children are active in constructing the opportunities for learning and the adult is, likewise, active in her responses. This corresponds well to the view of Trevarthen (2003) of the child seeking communicative contact "matched by the motives to share creativity and teach in the adult" (p. 239).

Both Kel and Mij recognize babies and young children's participation, offering many opportunities for the children to take the initiative and attending and responding to their cues. Thus, they foster reciprocal relationships, provide the children with emotional support, encourage communication, and promote developing competence. In addition to interacting with each child as an individual they also promote wider relationships within the day nursery community.

CHILD–CHILD RELATIONSHIPS

When considering the care of babies and toddlers the emphasis is often upon adults as having key person roles and the relationships between individual children and the adults. The examples of Kel's interactions with Sophie and Mij's games with Jesse and Jean-Paul, in the previous section, indicate that it is possible for close personal relationships to be built and maintained in a nursery group. The significance of relationships between very young children are more rarely discussed, despite more than twenty years having elapsed since Schaffer's (1984) call for a polyadic approach to the study of human development.

Children under three years of age are often characterized as egocentric, playing alone or in parallel with others, and not yet capable of sustained friendships. This view is challenged by the observations of sibling relationships and early peer relationships, in which children were seen to possess social and emotional understandings and to be responsive to the feelings of others. Selby and Bradley (2003) argued that babies possess a general relational capacity and, even at six months of age, are capable of simple communication within a group. The research by Rayna (2001) also showed that even very young children are interested in and understand other children's ideas and emotions and may demonstrate quite sophisticated imitative and interactive behaviors. In day care settings, the importance of peer relationships has often been underestimated but they provide an important source of support and stimulation for children of all ages (Penn, 1997).

The focus for this section is on children's developing awareness of each another and of mutual participation. Although the first example provided is of an interaction between children, the observational data on which this chapter is based focused upon the adults. The subsequent examples, therefore, exemplify ways in which the practitioners work to foster positive relationships between babies and toddlers.

Just as the young children in the research of Dunn (1988, 1993) knew how to manipulate and tease others in this day nursery, they also understood each other well. Jesse is very fond of his soft face flannel which he uses as a comfort object. Owyn, who is the same age, upsets Jesse by trying to snatch the brick box away from him. He then manages to placate Jesse by handing him the flannel. On another occasion, Owyn cheekily takes the flannel causing Jesse to scream loudly. Jesse himself instigates a similar incident when he picks up one of Sophie's shoes and runs away with it, laughing, as she follows protesting, "Shoes!" In both cases the adults quickly notice what is going on and the children respond to requests to return the items.

Observant attention and interventions by the adults before arguments escalate often serve to facilitate positive behavior and mediate peer interactions. When Jesse and Sophie want the same car they both hold onto it and tug, with Jesse pulling and screaming assertively and Sophie also refusing to let go. Kel resolves the situation by offering another car, which Jesse takes. She tells them that there are plenty of cars and they can both play. Likewise, when Sophie jumps off the slide and bumps into Jesse, Kel notices him raise his arm to retaliate and quickly stretches out to hold his arm gently and reassure him that it was an accident.

While effective behavior management like this is important, there are many other ways in which the practitioners assist cooperation and awareness of others. Kel, arriving for her late shift, greets every one of the six children present in the room in some way. Children's names used in these greetings are important in fostering their sense of belonging. At group singing time, the adults sing "Polly put the kettle on" inserting each child's name in the song in turn. When singing this song, Mij looks at each child as his or her name is being sung, making eye contact and smiling. With ratios of three children to each adult, staff become skilled at working with the small groups of children. The following three examples illustrate Kel's abilities as a facilitator.

Kel with Groups of Children

From a secure position on Kel's knee, nine-month-old Jem sits up very straight and watches the older children in the playhouse intently, following them with his eyes. Kel joins in the game and includes Jem in the conversation saying, "I want some pizza and Jem wants some pizza." When the piece of pretend pizza is offered, Jem reaches out to take it.

Owyn and Jesse begin to build a tower with the soft blocks, Kel holds the bricks steadily as they build the first few blocks then, as the tower becomes too tall for them to reach the top, she continues to pile the blocks as they watch. On cue, Jesse and Owyn then knock the tower down and they all laugh and applaud. Sophie runs over and the building process starts again. The mood is very lively and playful but never out of control.

Jesse picks up a large piece of A1 sized sugar paper from the drawing area and waves it, then begins to walk around waving the piece of paper which is very large and difficult for him to manage. Kel tells him to be careful and not to step on Jem, who is lying on the floor nearby. Owyn watches and smiles and when Jesse puts the paper down. Owyn takes it and waves it, just as Jesse was doing. Kel watches them carefully, now making sure that Owyn doesn't step on Jem. Moments later Kel helps Jesse pick up the large felt pens which have fallen on the floor. Owyn joins in and Kel encourages him to match the pens and the lids. As Owyn does this, Kel hands the torn paper to Jesse and asks him to take it and put it in the bin. Kel then turns and says, "Hi!" to Jem who has managed to crawl across the room and she smiles at him, aware of this achievement.

Jesse and Owyn's play with the paper is not stopped, even though the way that they use it is very different from what the adult intended. Imitation, both in terms of the adult imitating the children and also the children copying one another, is a feature of all three of these examples of this group play. Parker-Rees (2007) highlights the salience of this type of mutual imitation for building relationships between adults and babies and its value for the active construction and enjoyment of shared cultures.

A sense of shared culture and community is also fostered between the babies and the other children in the nursery. While the babies get ready to go out, Mij speaks to the older children and tells them where the babies are going. Similarly, when some of the older children leave to go out shopping, Kel calls good bye to them and the youngest children join her in waving them off.

The older children in the nursery engage with the babies and toddlers and show interest and delight in their progress. The mealtimes are communal and provide opportunities for informal interaction. The under-twos have their own table, a round table so that the children face one another during the meal. It is visited by older children especially at the end of lunch time when they are getting up to wash their hands. They stop by the table and discuss with Kel the fact that Jean-Paul can now feed himself. Chanel, one of the oldest children in the nursery, tells Kel that when she is older she is going to "be a teacher and have a baby in my buggy" and work at the nursery with Kel. Later, she asks Kel "Can Jem crawl now?"

These examples of sociable interactions within the nursery community are very interesting, particularly for those working within a care and education system which emphasizes the profiling of the progress of each individual child (DCFS, 2008). Evidence from a recent large scale study (Kutnick & Brighi, 2007) indicates that early years practitioners tend to focus on each child's individual development and are rarely proactive in promoting children's social competence during peer play or in enhancing children's group learning. While the study by Kutnick and Brighi focused on practices with slightly older children than in this study, the practices described here show that adults can do a lot to promote both children's self-awareness and their capacity to participate with others within a nursery group.

ADULT–ADULT RELATIONSHIPS

The argument presented, in this third section, is that relationships between the adults in an early childhood setting are also vital in supporting very young children's participatory learning. Communication between adults and children, as discussed above, must be paralleled in the ways that the adults themselves interact. Carers who listen to and value one another and show respect provide important role models for children (Manning Morton & Thorp, 2003). Relationships between members of staff are also an essential source of mutual support and nurture for those involved in the emotional labor of caring for babies and young children (Hochschild, 1983). This can be a challenging and psychologically demanding task (Elfer, 2007). Gibbs (2006) stressed that the educator's role is based upon relationships and should be about establishing a strong personal and professional identity which may then provide a secure basis for developing connections with others and interacting effectively with children, parents, and colleagues. Day nursery staff in England tend to have a low professional status with their work being recognized and valued by children, parents, and families but not necessarily respected by the wider society (Albon & Holland, 2006; Burgess-Macey & Rose, 1997). The examples presented here show how both Kel and Mij operate in a highly professional manner: in their interactions with one another; in the support and recognition they offer to child care students working in the nursery; and in the ways in which they relate to the children's parents.

Supportive Colleagues

Mij and Kel are friends but they avoid the temptation to chat socially while they are working with the children. They do share jokes, for example, laughing when Kel changes Jesse and realizes what he has been playing with because he has sand in his nappy. There is evidence of their care for one another when Kel returns from lunch complaining that her eyes are itching and Mij sends her to wash them. When Kel is saying good bye to Mij, as she leaves at the end of her shift, another affectionate incident occurs. As the children join in and wave, Sophie says "Mij!" Kel excitedly calls after Mij saying, "Sophie said your name!" and she encourages Sophie to repeat this new word.

These positive interactions also extend to other colleagues. There is evidence of respect and shared working, including checking with one another before leaving the room for any reason, or when making a change to the activities, such as getting the slide out for a while before lunch. When there are tasks to be done, for example moving between the two rooms during the quiet time after lunch in order to maintain supervision of the children and cover staff breaks, they ask politely and negotiate solutions. There are also brief conversations about the activities, about the children and what they have been playing with, and about the content of children's daily record sheets. The back door to the nursery opens from the under-twos' room. This is not a public entrance but is used by staff. For safety reasons, it is kept locked from the inside and so every time somebody needs to come in or leave a member of staff has to open or close this door. This can be quite disruptive to the work of the under two's room but Mij and Kel smile at those they let in and always exchange a few pleasant words.

Legitimate Peripheral Participation

This friendly and encouraging attitude is maintained towards students working in the nursery on work placement for their Diploma in Child Care and Education (the same qualification that Kel and Mij recently attained). They are made welcome in the team and are well supported. As a part of their course, they have to complete written observations of the children and both Mij and Kel discuss these with them. Kel talks to one of the students who is uncertain about how she can record Jem's language development, and later in the day invites the student to observe and record as she interacts with him, encouraging him to vocalize. The other student gives Mij a copy of her observation of Jem's motor skills and Mij thanks her, looks at it and recognizes its contribution, promising to include the observation in Jem's record folder. There is also discussion of the children's growth, when the student comments that Jem couldn't crawl last week but now he can, Mij carefully describes the progress that Jem has made during the week. Similarly, at lunchtime, Kel answers the students' questions about what the babies eat.

In keeping with a model of situated learning within the workplace (Lave & Wenger, 1991; Wenger, 1998), the students learn by engagement in the social practices of the nursery. They are attentive to what is going on and tend to imitate Kel and Mij in their actions, for example, when Kel applauds Jem, who has managed to pull himself forwards to reach a ball, the students join in. When, at tea time, Mij uses a spoon to break the fruit salad into smaller pieces the students do the same. One student asks whether the babies can eat this fruit with their hands but accepts Mij's decision that spoons are needed because the dessert is quite juicy and sticky.

The students are involved throughout the day. They are even asked for their suggestions for animals and animal sounds for "Old MacDonald had a farm" during singing time. Mij and one of the students creates a game for Jesse, using a long cardboard tube, in which Mij and the student take turns to put to their ear or speak down. They joke is that Jesse might utter one of his ear piercing screams during the game. Sometimes responsibility is handed over to a student but Mij and Kel are watchful and step in when needed. Students also take the initiative offering to undertake tasks and noticing when children need their noses wiped. While a tendency for child care students to copy and reproduce the practice seen in their work placement setting has been noted (Alexander, 2002; Colley, James, Tedder, & Diment, 2003), in this center there seems to be potential for richer learning by the students through meaningful professional collaboration within a learning community.

Partnerships with Parents

Just as Kel and Mij take their cues from the babies and children and respond accordingly, the same sensitivity is seen in their interactions with parents. In the morning Mij deals differently with each of the children's carers. For the child whose relative brings him, she checks who will be picking him up at the end of the day. She spends time with Jem's father gaining important information for a smooth handover of care from home to nursery, discovering when Jem woke up and when he last had his milk. When his father leaves, Mij encourages Jem to wave goodbye. With a third child, whose busy mother puts him down on the floor in the baby room and rushes off quickly, Mij exchanges a warm smile.

Similarly, at the end of the day, Kel acts in response to the parents' cues. Simple daily record sheets, listing what the child did, what they ate, when they slept and times of nappy changes are given, as a written record of the child's day, and verbal anecdotes about each child are also shared. When Jean-Paul's mother and siblings arrive, they are made very welcome. Kel speaks with his mother and then goes to get a bottle of milk. Jean-Paul's mother then sits on the sofa to feed him while his older brother and sister run around the room and build tall towers with the soft blocks. Kel reassures her that the children's lively behavior is fine and the family stays for about half an hour and leave when they are ready. Later in the evening when Jesse's parents arrive, Kel talks with them about his day. They discover that his precious flannel has been mislaid and Kel searches for it all around the under-twos room, and goes through the laundry pile before finding it tucked in between the piled up soft shapes and a sofa.

These relationships with parents seem relaxed and supportive. The parents are in control during the times of transition, when they leave their children at nursery and when they collect them, while the staff use these times to engage in a friendly way and to share information. Working with parents in this way fosters confidence and enriches the child's experience of nursery (Gillespie Edwards, 2002) and thus facilitating participation.

Babies and young children are likely to be highly sensitive to the quality of relationships between the adults who care for them. Kel and Mij's positive interactions with one another, with students, and with parents are important in providing role models for the children and, perhaps more significantly, a warm and calm atmosphere in which everybody feels comfortable to participate and learning can occur.

CONCLUSION

In summary, all these observations of practice begin to provide clues about ways in which participatory learning can be fostered with the youngest children in group care settings. Selby and Bradley (2003) proposed that if we recognize infants' abilities as active members of groups, we are better able to think of ways to enhance the quality of their time at nursery. The manner in which adults relate to children, the ways in which relationships between children are encouraged, and the importance of positive and productive relationships between adults are of high importance. All of these require further consideration and research in order to identify clear strategies for participation. There are, undoubtedly, implications for the education and continuing professional development for early years practitioners. This presents an important challenge for those of us who agree with Nutbrown (1996) that "young children are entitled to respectful attention in all they do and their educators must collaborate to examine their work and beliefs in order to ensure that the rights of the youngest children are secured" (p. x).

REFERENCES

Abbott, L., & Angston, A. (2005). Birth to three matters. Maidenhead: Open University Press.

Albon, D., & Holland, P. (2006, August). *"I'm now seen as a professional": Multiple perceptions of the professional within the early years workforce.* Paper presented at the 16th European Early Childhood Education Research Association. Reykjavik, Iceland.

Alexander, E. (2002). Childcare students: Learning or imitating? *FORUM: for promoting 3–19 Comprehensive Education, 44* (1), 25–27.

Aslin, R. N., Jusczyk, P. W., & Pisoni, D. B. (1998). Speech and auditory processing during infancy: constraints on and precursors to language. In D. Kuhn & R. Siegler (Eds.), *Handbook of child psychology: Cognition, perception, and language* New York: Wiley.

Bae, B. (2007, August). *Children's participation: Focus on dialogical patterns in early childhood institutions.* Paper presented at the 17th European Early Childhood Education Research Association Annual Conference, Prague.

Bruner, J. (1972). The nature and uses of immaturity. *American Psychologist, 27* (8), 1–22.

Bruner, J. S. (1983). *Child's talk.* Oxford: Oxford University Press.

———. (1995). From joint attention to meeting of minds: an introduction. In: C. Moore & P. J. Dunham (Eds.), *Joint attention: Its origins and role in development.* Hillsdale, NJ: Lawrence Erlbaum.

Burgess-Macey, C., & Rose, J. (1997). Breaking through the barriers: Professional development action research and the early years. *Educational Action Research, 5* (1), 55–70.

Colley, H., James, D., Tedder, M., & Diment, K. (2003). Learning as becoming in vocational education and training: Class, gender and the role of vocational habitus. *Journal of Vocational Education and Training, 55* (4), 471–496.

Convention on the Rights of the Child (CRC) (2005). *Implementing child rights in early childhood.* General Comment No. 7. New York: United Nations.

DeCasper, A. J., & Fifer, W. P. (1980). Of human bonding: newborns prefer their mothers' voices. *Science, 208,* 1174–1176.

Department for Children, Schools and Families (DCSF) (2008). *The early years foundation stage.* London: DCFS. Retrieved January 17, 2008, from http://www.standards.dcsf.gov.uk/eyfs/

Dowling, M. (2005). *Young children's personal, social and emotional development (2nd ed.)* London: Paul Chapman Publishing.

Dunn, J. (1988). *The beginnings of social understanding.* Oxford: Blackwell.

———. (1993). *Young children's close relationships.* London: Sage.

Edwards, A. (2004). Understanding context, Understanding practice in early education, *European Early Childhood Education Research Journal, 12* (1), 85–101.

Elfer, P. (2005). Observation matters. In L. Abbott & A. Langston, A. (Eds.), *Birth to three matters.* Maidenhead: Open University Press.

———. (2007). Babies and young children in nurseries: Using psychoanalytic ideas to explore tasks and interactions. *Children and Society, 21,* 111–222.

Elfer, P., Goldschmied, E., & Selleck, D. (2003). *Key persons in the nursery.* London: David Fulton Publishers.

Fantz, R. (1961). The origin of form perception. *Scientific American, 204,* 66–72.

Forbes, R. (2004). *Beginning to play.* Maidenhead, United Kingdom: Open University Press.

Gibbs, C. (2006). *To be a teacher: journeys toward authenticity.* Auckland, New Zealand: Pearson Education.

Gillespie Edwards, A. (2002). *Relationships and learning.* London: National Children's Bureau.

Goldschmied, E., & Jackson, S. (2004). *People under three: Young children in day care* (2nd ed.). London: Routledge.

Hochschild, A. R. (1983). *The managed heart: Commercialisation of human feeling.* Berkley, CA: University of California Press.

Johnson, M. H., & Morton, J. (1991). *Biology and cognitive development. The case of face recognition.* Cambridge, MA: Blackwell.

Kaye, K. (1977). Towards the origins of dialogue. In H. R. Schaffer (Ed.), *Studies in mother- infant interaction.* London: Academic Press.

Kutnick, P., & Brighi, A. (2007). The role and practice of interpersonal relationships in European early education settings: Sites for enhancing social inclusion, personal growth and learning. *European Early Childhood Research Journal, 15* (3), 379–406.

Lave, J., & Wenger, E. (1991). *Situated learning: Legitimate peripheral participation,* Cambridge, UK: Cambridge University Press

Loizou, E. (2005). Infant humor: The theory of the absurd and the empowerment theory. *International Journal of Early Years Education, 13* (1), 43–53.

Luff, P. (2008). Looking, listening, learning and linking: Uses of observation for relational pedagogy. In T. Papatheodorou, & J. Moyles (Eds.), *Learning together in the early years: Relational pedagogy.* London: Routledge.

Manning Morton, J., & Thorp, M. (2003). *Key times for play: The first three years.* Maidenhead, UK: Open University Press.

———. (2006). *Key times: A framework for developing high quality provision for children under three years.* Maidenhead, UK: Open University Press.

Meltzoff, A. N., & Moore, M. K. (1977). Imitation of facial and manual gestures by human neonates. *Science, 198,* 75–78.

———. (1997). Explaining facial imitation: A theoretical model. *Early Development & Parenting, 6,* 179–192.

Murray, L., & Andrews, L. (2000). *The social baby: Understanding babies' communication from birth.* Richmond, United Kingdom: CP Publishing.

National Audit Office (NAO) (2004). *Early years: Progress in developing high quality childcare and education open to all.* London: HMSO.

Nutbrown, C. (1996). *Respectful educators-capable learners: Children's rights and early education.* London: Paul Chapman.

Office for Standards in Education (Ofsted) (2007). *Quality of childcare provision as at 30 September 2007.* Retrieved November 19, 2007, from http://www.ofsted.gov.uk/

Parker-Rees, R. (2007). Liking to be liked: Imitation, familiarity and pedagogy in the first years of life. *Early Years, 27* (1), 3–17.

Pascal, C., & Bertram, A. D. (1997). *Effective early learning: Case studies of improvement.* London: Hodder and Stoughton.

Payler, J. (2007). Opening and closing interactive spaces: shaping four-year-old children's participation in two English settings. *Early Years, 27* (3), 237–254.

Penn, H. (1997). *Comparing nurseries. Staff and children in Italy, Spain and the UK.* London: Paul Chapman.

———. (2007). Childcare market management: How the United Kingdom government has reshaped its role in developing early childhood education and care. *Contemporary Issues in Early Childhood, 8 (3),* 192–207.

Pugh, G. (2006). The policy agenda for early childhood services. In G. Pugh & B. Duffy (Eds.), *Contemporary Issues in the Early Years (4th edn.).* London: Sage.

Rayna, S. (2001). The very beginnings of togetherness in shared play among young children. *International Journal of Early Years Education, 9* (2), 109–115.

Reddy, V., & Trevarthen, C. (2004). What we learn about babies from engaging with their emotions. *Zero to Three, 24* (3), 9–15.

Rogoff, B. (1990) *Apprenticeship in thinking: Cognitive development in social context*. New York: Oxford University Press.

———. (2003). *The cultural nature of human development*. New York: Oxford University Press.

Schaffer, H. R. (1984). *The child's entry into a social world*. London: Academic Press.

Selby, J. M., & Bradley, B. S. (2003). Infants in groups: A paradigm for the study of early social experience. *Human Development, 46*, 197–221.

Siraj-Blatchford, I., Sylva, K., Muttock, S., Gilden, R., & Bell, D. (2002). *Researching effective pedagogy in the early years. Research Report RR356*. London: Department for Education and Skills.

Smith, A. (1999). Quality childcare and joint attention. *International Journal of Early Years Education, 7* (1), 85–98.

Stern, D. (1985). *The interpersonal world of the infant*. New York: Basic Books.

Trevarthen, C. (1979). Communication and cooperation in early infancy: A description of primary intersubjectivity. In M. Bullowa (Ed.), *Before Speech: The Beginning of Human Communication* (pp. 321–347). Cambridge, UK: Cambridge University Press.

———. (2001). Intrinsic motives for companionship in understanding: Their origin, development and significance for infant mental health. *Infant Mental Health Journal, 22*, 95–131.

———. (2003). Infant psychology is an evolving culture. *Human Development, 46*, 233–246.

———. (2004). *Learning about ourselves, from children: Why a growing human brain needs interesting companions*. Perception-in-action Publications, University of Edinburgh. Retrieved January, 16, 2008, from http://www.perception-in-action.ed.ac.uk/publications.htm.

Wenger, E. (1998). *Communities of practice: Learning, meaning and identity*. Cambridge, MA: Cambridge University Press.

Wolff, P. H. (1968). The serial organization of sucking in the young infant. *Pediatrics, 42*, 943–56.

Woodhead, M. (1996). *In search of the rainbow: Pathways to quality in large scale programmes for young disadvantaged children*. The Hague, The Netherlands: Bernard van Leer Foundation.

10 Dialogue, Listening and Discernment in Professional Practice with Parents and their Children in an Infant Program

A Canadian Perspective

Enid Elliot

(in consultation with Heather Kay and Wendy Ready at Options Child and Family Centre)

This paper is based on the work in a young parent program in Victoria, British Columbia. In 1972, *Girls' Alternative Program* (GAP) was created to provide a venue for young women who did not "fit in" to the regular high school setting. At first, the program was run out of a series of houses operating with meager resources. Eventually, it gained credibility and moved into a small vacant school building with a staff of counselors and teachers. In the early 1980s, another element was added to the program for young women who became pregnant during their high school years, called Options for Pregnant Teens. The girls (the term 'girls' has always been used despite a strong feminist awareness within the program) continued to come to their regular school bringing their infants with them until it became too difficult for them to focus on their studies, at which time they dropped out. With the addition of Options Child and Family Centre in 1989, girls could continue their educational program with their babies and toddlers close by.

Counselors, community agencies, friends or family who are familiar with GAP refer girls to the program. Many of the girls come with difficult life challenges—mental health issues, involvement with drugs, at-risk for sexual exploitation, poverty, and family instability. A majority of the girls are of European heritage with one third being of First Nations heritage. The school provides life skills training and counseling, as well as an educational program.

Options Child and Family Centre was the first program for infants and toddlers on Vancouver Island. Lacking any local models we consulted with people who had knowledge and experience in group care for infants. Since then, experience, reflection and ongoing questioning have helped the program grow and mature for the past twenty years.

LOOKING BACK AT UNDERSTANDINGS GAINED

Over the years, the program has developed a philosophy that has evolved from a primary focus on the babies to one embracing whole families creating a vibrant community of parents, educators, and children. Experience, theory, staff reflection, and discussion have informed the growth of the program, an ongoing evolution influenced by individual babies, mothers, and staff. Through the process of writing this chapter we have begun an articulation of the different strands of thought and influences at work in the program. In turn, this reflection this has led us to re-examine some of our practices.

Staff has remained remarkably constant as the program has been built. While rapid turnover of staff due to low wages and devaluation of the work in Canadian child care programs is of concern across the country (Beach, Bosica, Bertrand, Forer, Michal, & Tougas, 2004), the *Options* staff have remained with the program a long time with four of the seven being there over fifteen years. This consistency helps the philosophy and practice become richer as staff deepen their own thinking and knowledge.

While working on this chapter I went to the staff at *Options* to ask particularly about democratic practices within the program. Staff had not particularly framed their creation of relationships or community in this manner, but saw that it might fit. In our first discussion we defined democratic practice simply, as providing the space for children's and parents' voices to be heard and acknowledged. Over time, the staff had learned ways to encourage building a sense of community by respecting each child's voice, each parent's voice, as well as honoring their own. Our subsequent conversations began to give further shape to the ideas of democratic practice. When providing space for voice while creating cohesion within a group, tensions inevitably rise and finding a balance is a constant struggle. While a democratic ideal might exist, the tensions and struggle for balance between individual and community challenge staff in the program to continually reflect and re-evaluate their practice.

DEVELOPING COMMUNITY

Entering a child care program babies are beginning their participation as members of the larger community beyond their family. The child care setting can provide a community in which babies and toddlers begin to experience participating in a group, an early childhood community. Actively creating community became a value of *Options Child and Family Centre* as we began to embrace the young mothers as part of the program and increasingly worked closely with the school programs to support the young women in their lives.

Democratic values are part of being a Canadian citizen ("A look at Canada: What does Canadian citizenship mean?" 2008); the belief that everyone has a right to be heard is a part of the Canadian social contract. Practicing with these values in mind can provide a framework for creating community in a child care setting. Ideal beliefs and values about community may be difficult to translate into practice and to articulate these values that the child care setting espouses, as well as what values a child experiences in that setting may or may not be congruent. Values of community, including that everyone respects others' perspectives can be important guides to practice.

Traditionally in Canada children's voices are not included in the landscape of community decisions. On the whole, young children are not seen as competent to contribute ideas or thoughts on issues that might affect them. Yet while a baby's speech may be rudimentary, it is clear that she has many ways to communicate and, in order for us to include her in the community, we must be able to "hear" her. By observation of body language, facial expression, and through ongoing relationships, we are sure that babies can communicate their voice as the following vignettes from observations at *Options* illustrate.

> Ann, eighteen months old, arrives in the morning and empties the shelves, then turns to the nearest newly-walking baby and gives her a shove; next, she sees a doll on the floor which she picks up and flings across the room. With this difficult entry into the group she announces her frustration and fear, and even her sadness. Physically articulating her feelings, thoughts, and anxieties is the language she uses in this situation.

> Sam is inconsolable when his mother leaves. He stays by the door, crying, refusing any solace for the first few minutes.

> Asha has a blanket that is calming and soothing for her. It is never far from her reach and she happily drags it everywhere. Sara comes into the center in her mother's arms. With her eyes, bright and round, she's kicking her legs and squealing. There is a big smile on her face as her arms wave towards her caregiver.

Within our early childhood communities we need spaces for everyone, spaces where we can strive for democratic ideals, places where children's voices can be heard and where people are free to speak. As Gunilla Dahlberg and Peter Moss (2006) say, "all children are embarked on a course of making meaning of the world" and they have "the democratic right to be listened to and to be a recognized citizen in the community" (p. 13). They also speak of the possibility of places for children that "can be understood, first and foremost, as forums, spaces, or sites for ethical and political practice" (Dahlberg & Moss, 2005, p. 157). Moss (2006) expands the concept to "democratic political practice" and suggests that early childhood programs could be places of democratic practice; it is "a choice we make." We can provide spaces for children where their presence is noted, their voices heard and their differences respected, and we can practice "democracy as a form of living together" where there is a democratic ethos of listening and dialogue (p.36). The possibility is there.

Too often, our early childhood programs are defined in technical terms of practice, such as places where practice is developed in order to create a desired outcome, like school readiness or overcoming social risk. Curricula focused on limited outcomes prescribe and describe ways to act and speak, and seems to be concerned with controlling adult behavior in order to control children's behavior; when one is slavishly following prescribed curricula, there is little time for curiosity about the meaning behind the children's behavior or questions with which children are struggling. To avoid becoming places of control and prescribed practices, we can create community in our early childhood programs that consciously make space for questioning, reflecting and finding one's place in the group. Within the framework of a community that honors all participants, we can introduce children and their families to concepts of democracy. Here, a goal for caregivers becomes seeing children as active participants in their environments. These concepts of questioning, reflecting and community membership provide us with goals of honoring diversity, learning to listen to each other, listening to ourselves and respecting all of our community members. These broad goals can give meaning and direction to our practice.

In community we can come together; *com* means *with*, and *unis* means *unity* or *one*. While community unifies a group of people, it continues to be made up of individuals, each coming with their own voices. Thus the tension vibrates between the individual members and the members as a group. Another analysis of the word community is rather than *unis*, we can see the second syllable as *munis*, meaning *gift*. Community, by coming together with common purpose, can provide space and support for individuals to find and raise their voices and bring their gifts. An early childhood setting can provide space encouraging community that honors all its participants and benefiting everyone.

Within community we may find relationships of intimacy and emotion, those kinds of relationships that might be within a family, between friends or between educator and child. From these are built relationships of community. Within North American society, our focus on the individual often masks the presence of the interdependent relationships of community. Huebner (1999) reminds us that "the relationships of community, wherein we join hands and voices to do something in and of the world . . . they weave us into the external worlds of others—the worlds of work, of recreation, and celebration" (pp. 391–392).

SOCIOCULTURAL ORIENTATION

Within relationships and community we grow both by influencing and being influenced. The interplay between and among individuals makes both relationship and community complex; these negotiations are not simple and often need to be approached carefully. Within community-based environments, children learn and grow from their interactions with other children and with adults. By listening to children and to each other, building a web of relationships, adults are provided opportunities to learn more of children's lives and are challenged to understand others more deeply.

Learning to listen to others and learning to participate in a community provides children with the knowledge that their contribution is valued and they have a voice to be shared. By viewing children as competent people with valid and clear perspectives on their own lives, educators become committed to providing space for children's thoughts and ideas, recognizing that children can make choices, form relationships, and have theories and ideas that can enrich the communal, but not prescribed, curriculum.

Rogoff (2003) emphasizes in her sociocultural theory that people participate in valued cultural activities and practices, adopting, transforming, and extending them over time. Through participation, the practices and the participants are mutually constituted, each influencing and transforming the other. Children, parents, and educators can participate together in a community with the early childhood educators, establishing the milieu into which families arrive. Democratic values are familiar to Canadian families, but encountering them in an early childhood setting that values children's voices may create some dissonance for parents who might not have listened carefully to babies.

Since the early childhood educators create the child care environment, they also have the power to define how democracy is enacted. Along with their commitment to creating space to listen to the children and their parents, educators must also stay open to challenges to their concepts of democracy. For example, discussing this chapter with *Options* staff opened up ideas for further discussion as tensions were discussed and further possibilities envisioned.

IN THE BEGINNING

As described by Penn (1999), we found that Magda Gerber and her mentor, Emmi Pikler, had a philosophy and approach that appealed to us. Hungarian pediatrician Pikler began to develop her ideas of respecting infants and their innate abilities in the 1930s. In her work with parents and babies, she emphasized the capability of the infant, believing young children to be competent, and that infancy was a stage of life with experiences as vital and meaningful as those of adults. After World War II, Pikler became the director of the Loczy Institute, an orphanage in Budapest. Concerned about the results of observational studies that pointed to poor development among children living in orphanages, Pikler (1979) believed she could devise a system that respected the needs and the strengths of the babies. She wrote that infants need an intimate, stable, adult relationship that support an infant's abilities; this became the leading principle of the infant care at

Loczy. Relationships were to be formed "during the physical contacts, i.e., dressing bathing, feeding, etc. when the adult and child are in intimate personal contact" (Pikler, 1979, p. 91). Focusing on the routines of caring, she developed a primary caregiving system where infants were diapered, fed, and comforted primarily by a familiar adult.

Magda Gerber trained with Pikler and brought her ideas to the United States when she fled Hungary after the revolution in 1956. Through her work with parents and infants, she set up a program called *Resources for Infant Educarers* (RIE) (Gerber, 1979). Like Pikler, Gerber had a philosophy of respecting babies and recognizing their many abilities, believing that having a consistent, or primary, caregiver promotes security in the child.

We learned from Magda about caring for babies and toddlers with respect for their many capabilities; her teaching stretched our thinking and encouraged us to look at infants with "new eyes." Using these ideas, *Options* developed a system of primary caregiving for the babies. In a description of primary caregiving, Bernhardt (2000) wrote:

> In the primary caregiving model, each caregiver or teacher within a larger group is assigned primary responsibility for a specific group of children. For example, in an infant care room with a ratio of three to one that serves 12 babies, each caregiver is responsible for the care of the same three children every day. This does not mean the caregiver cares exclusively for the same three children; rather, that she has principal responsibility for the few children in her direct care. (p. 74)

Without thoughtfulness and reflection, this model, like any other model, can become a straitjacket limiting thinking rather than expanding it. This primary caregiving system requires that staff work as a team and communicate closely and thoughtfully about the working day. By focusing on each baby's messages, encouraging them to listen to each other, and responding as befits the individual and the group, we tried to establish individual and communal dialogues with children. This was the beginning of our democratic practice in the infant/toddler room.

CREATING DIALOGUE

Being in dialogue with babies and with each family meant continually challenging ourselves to reflect and respond in unique ways to each parent, family, and child. Asking, wondering, and speaking with children and families led us to understand their situations more fully and with a deeper understanding of the issues we can respond to. As MacNaughton (2005) says, "relationships are notoriously difficult to control and predict. Techniques that work with one person fail with the next, irrespective of their age and their contexts" (p. 193). We do not always know what we should do and we must acknowledge our own uncertainty and doubt. "Listening to a baby involves transformation and risk-taking" suggests Wright (2007, p. 18). We have to set aside judgments and think more deeply about what we are doing, aware of the multiple truths and complexities of families and children. Our dialogue with babies and the families must also fit within the group context. Relationships radiate in multiple directions and are constantly constituting and re-constituting our community and practice. Balancing individual dialogues with communal discussions can create tensions and finding balance can be tenuous, as the following vignette from *Options* shows:

> Early in the history of *Options Child and Family Centre*, we had a baby who had not rolled over by nine months. We wondered if we should intervene and considered what the intervention might look like. His mother was young, not interested in our ideas and we found developing a dialogue with her was difficult and slow. At this particular time, the mother was coping with a great many issues in her life. We wondered if we should add to her stress and possibly disrupt our emerging dialogue with her by suggesting our worry that her baby was not rolling over, especially as she had not indicated to us that she had any concern; she had other issues on which she was focused. We informally asked an occupational therapist what they thought we should do and received a suggestion or two, but she acknowledged that there was not much more she would or could do. We implemented her suggestions and waited only two weeks, at which point the baby rolled over, began to pull to stand and began to crawl. Around that time the mother started to develop a warmer relationship and deeper dialogue with her child's caregiver.

Since the time of that vignette, we have moved even further from making assessments and judgments of babies and their mothers. Infants may come with specific diagnosis and concerns, but diagnosis can be mistaken and we still need to find out what a particular diagnosis might mean for this particular family, this particular baby, and her care in our program. For example, the child who came to us with brittle bone disease did not break all her bones when she started to crawl; the toddler whose speech was "delayed" understood everything and when she did speak, used full sentences. Each child is different and each child and family will have and find their strategies for coping with the world.

Through dialogue we can begin the journey of developing relationships with babies and families. Over time, with opportunities for discussion, sharing of stories and perspectives, trust can be built. While these are individual dialogues and relationships they impact our community. Mothers watch to see how others are treated, and each relationship impacts the other. At *Options*, we avoid policies and procedures manuals preferring to negotiate with families, finding out what they might want and why and together finding ways to make things happen. Some limits exist, as children must be protected from harm and so must all the other participants in our community as much as possible. When families, babies, and staff feel safe they are more likely to add their voice to the ongoing community discussion. It takes careful listening and observation to invite those voices to be heard. As Freire (2000) describes it—"a dialogic relationship—communication and intercommunication among active subjects who are immune to the bureaucratization of their minds and open to discovery and to knowing more . . .". (p. 99)

LISTENING INTO RELATIONSHIP

Through the first couple of years, we focused simply on caring for the babies; the mothers seemed more peripheral to the job. None of us had cared for infants in a group setting before so the babies were challenged enough for the first year. The practical issues of bottles, formulas, support for breastfeeding, diapers, and three babies crying at once faced us at the outset. While we never considered baby swings or jolly jumpers, we began to understand why other programs might adopt them. How to have time for each baby and how to balance those needs within the group was our primary question at that time.

Holding onto principles of respect and our belief in babies' considerable abilities, we negotiated the challenges of feeding, comforting, and diapering a group of babies. By staying away from baby devices we were forced to focus on the babies, who they were and what our relationships with them could be. We soon began to adapt Magda Gerber's ideas to our situation. While we agreed that babies were best served by putting them in situations where they experience their own abilities as fully as possible, such as refraining from placing a baby in a sitting position until they can get to that position themselves, we began to realize in order to mesh with the care found at the babies' home, we needed to be philosophically pragmatic and flexible. We found babies preferred care that was familiar, or as familiar as possible. If they were in a sitting position often at home, they often liked to be in that position in our program, at least in the beginning of their time with us.

To understand the babies and what they need, we needed to listen carefully to both babies and parents. Carlina Rinaldi (2005) defines listening "as sensitivity to the patterns that connect, to that which connects us to others; abandoning ourselves to the conviction that our understanding and our own being are but small parts of a broader, integrated knowledge that holds the universe together" (pp. 19–20). While she acknowledges that listening is difficult and requires paying attention to all our senses and emotions, when we share and find the time to really hear another person, we are changed and our understanding is enlarged.

Listening to babies we must bring ourselves into the exchange. Babies are *listening* all the time to everything—the conversations we have with them, the conversations we have with their parents and among ourselves. They also listen to what we do not say, what we avoid or do not notice. Babies and toddlers pay close attention because that is how they learn about and begin to understand the world. When we listen to babies we begin to provide them with a space to have a voice, to have a presence. When babies begin to communicate with us, we can begin to understand the world they are seeing and experiencing; it enlarges our view of the world.

As we became practiced in listening to the babies, we understood how to care for them in unique and individual ways. For example, one primary caregiver wrapped a particular baby up snugly in a blanket for his nap. Once settled with him in a rocking chair, she also draped a flannel cloth around his face. Throughout the process he was quiet and peaceful and after a few minutes went to sleep. When asked why she did this, she explained that she had noticed he liked to feel different textures and when he went to sleep he often had a cloth in his hand and rubbed it on his face. One day, she had found he had fallen asleep with a terrycloth bib pulled up over his face. So afterwards she draped a cloth around his face, which he enjoyed, and she could still see his face, which she enjoyed. Gerber (1979) talked of paying attention to the babies we look after: "It is full, unhurried attention. Under the right circumstances it is a peaceful, rewarding time for both parties because, ideally, it is a time of no ambivalence, one for open listening, taking in the other person, trying to fully understand the other's point of view" (p. 21).

This attentive presence helps caregivers find a path to relationship. Paying attention to the other person is not always comfortable. The words attend and tension share a common root, *tendere*, meaning to stretch. To really attend to or pay attention to another person, we must stretch ourselves, and really strain to listen, to see, to feel—it is not a casual process.

Routines of changing, feeding, and sleeping can be places to create space for listening, for honoring children's participation in the routine. Explaining that you are changing a wet diaper to the baby and allowing space for the baby to help with the process demonstrates to the baby that you are concerned with their input, that you are listening to them. Even small babies can help shift their weight as you remove a diaper. Waiting a minute after you have informed a baby that you will pick him up allows time for a baby to indicate whether he is ready to be picked up. This small space of time acknowledges that his participation is valued.

Parents need the respect, time, and space to develop their voice and to believe that their voice will be heard and honored and their relationship with their baby will be validated. As the principles of respect challenged us to re-think our approach with parents, we began to listen more deeply to the parents, trying to understand their situations. We tried to suspend judgment and to listen for the fuller story.

Wendy, an educator who has worked with *Options* off and on for twenty years, says that we had to:

... put aside or compromise some of our ideas of what quality care was and change tactics on how to teach parents. We moved the notion of respect for the babies into respect for the moms as well. We worked on building trusting relationships with families so doors to communication could be opened and flow more easily when an issue arose that needed addressing. We now saw the moms as capable and competent too and as our mindset changed so did our connections.

Moss (2006) says that practitioners: "bring an important perspective and a relevant local knowledge to the democratic forum [of the early childhood program], they also recognize they do not have *the* truth nor privileged access to knowledge" (p. 9).

Listening carefully to mothers or other family members demonstrates there is space for their voices while it enriches our understandings of our community. Both assumptions and judgments can hinder dialogue and relationship building. Judgments can obscure the voice of the other person in a dialogue; in judgment, we may make statements that reflect our bias and silence the other person who may not hear her reality reflected. Assumptions can give us lenses to make judgments. The assumption that a young mother is incompetent or that children are at risk will weight our discussions with parents. In order to stay present to the other person with whom we are in dialogue, we must stay open to them and continually wonder what we do not understand. Ultimately, we may need to make a judgment of incompetence or risk, but hopefully with as much dialogue and knowledge as possible.

In order to be willing to speak, parents must feel safe; they must feel that who they are and what they say is respected. Through dialogue that strains to hear the other, information and perspectives are shared. By holding an attitude of uncertainty we can deepen our practice and create communities where power is shared and voices can be heard. Listening to the babies, toddlers, families, and each other became a key issue in developing a network of relationships. Listening offers a welcome into a relationship that is built by all the participants; doing this over time builds connections and a continuing narrative.

REDEFINING THE EXPERT ROLE

The mothers in our program were young. All were under nineteen and attending the alternative educational program that was down the hall from the baby/toddler program. As mentioned, working with young mothers was new to all of us. At first we were intimidated with the idea of forming relationships with these young women—as early childhood educators, we were not used to working with youth, but they were also mothers and the mothers of the babies in our program. As a staff dealing with young parents, we found that we had assumptions and misconceptions to put aside. Uncovering and acknowledging our assumptions has become an ongoing process. Over time and with reflection, we realized that we needed to move from the position of experts with a mission to change the parents as described by Penn (2005).

The expert practitioner may hold a vision of the "good parent" or the "normal parent," claiming the "truth" about the child, and the knowledge of how to interact with the child, and what is "good" for the child. Holding this vision she waits for or makes the opportunity to "educate" the parent. This is probably one of the more insidious early childhood "identities" and it is difficult to relinquish. The expert narrative is based on the "truths" of child development. Over the years, child development has defined children according to ages and stages. Categories of children and families have been created in relation to a norm that defines an age or stage. Assessments are done in order to pinpoint a child's progress toward some future goal. Early childhood educators have used child development as both their yardstick for practice as well as the backbone of their professional knowledge (Bredekamp & Copple, 1997; Singer, 1992; Weedon, 1987). Working from a sociocultural stance, we began to see ourselves as co-creators of an environment with the children and families, bringing our own particular knowledge and experience with us. Our knowledge became less judgmental and more facilitative and became grounded in our experience of creating spaces for infants and toddlers. Using a perspective that includes democratic ideals, we tried create a community that had a place for everyone.

By moving away from child development theories and focusing on relationships, the *Options* staff had an opportunity to understand the issues and situations with which mothers were coping and to hear the values that guided these young mothers in their parenting. By listening closely, we began to uncover some of the multiple 'truths' and some of the complexities that the role of expert can obscure. Relationships usually have a reciprocal aspect to them where each member shares strengths and weaknesses. The role of expert suggests that there are "no chinks in one's armour." Freire (1970) reminds us to recognize our own ignorance and value the contribution of others. By believing in others' strengths, we create space for their voices.

Relationships work in multiple ways and community can affect us all. Wendy tells this story:

> I was helping a child (two years old) who was very, very upset when his grandpa dropped him off. It was his last day with us, his caregiver was sick and his mom had been missing for several weeks. He said few things with words but volumes with his body and heart. "Mum, mum, mum" he kept repeating as his back sank against my chest. Holding him very gently he relaxed his body as his heart poured open. His head rested between my shoulder and chin and I leant the side of my head towards him. I just let him cry and release. I could feel his anguish and

my heart felt for him. Acknowledging his grief opened up some of my own and we met together in sadness. It was very profound, powerful and, in a way, beautiful. We both touched upon and realized what needed to be dealt with. He gave me such a gift that day. I am grateful to him for sharing his heart with me.

The practice of primary caregiving for babies revealed its importance for the moms as well, as they began to develop deeper relationships with the one person who was focused on their child. These were girls for whom traditional learning structures had not worked and we had to be creative. We wrote and performed rap songs about little things like being quiet when walking past the nap room. We offered snacks to the mothers. We went out for coffee and breakfast just to chat and get to know each other. We had family potlucks where staff family came as well. We became more like a big extended family, sharing life together. We allowed ourselves to be fallible.

At *Options*, we encouraged mothers to feed their babies formula or to breastfeed. Knowing that the nutritional needs of an infant are specific and critical to good growth we had a policy of not allowing juice for the infants. Understanding that juice is cheaper and that the mothers had very limited incomes, we tried to have extra formula donated in order to offer it to families, giving it to mothers as they might need it. But things did not always work as we might like. After three years of operating *Options*, we had a mother, father, and three-month-old baby begin the program. They insisted that the baby did not like formula and so they only gave it to him at night, feeding him juice throughout the day. When we explained our policy and said that the baby needed to have formula for proper nutrients, they left the program. We never had a chance to develop a relationship and to create a dialogue that might have been more useful. We had not allowed a place for their voice.

RESPONSIBILITIES OF LISTENING

In relationship we are called to respond to what we hear or understand from the other person. At the root of *responsibility* is *response* or to *answer* (Fowler & Fowler, 1964), the ability and obligation to respond in words or action. In response to our dialogue, in response to what we hear, we act and demonstrate our commitment to that person. When babies experience being heard and sense that someone is listening they can become active members of a community. The attention necessary to listen to a baby is considerable; this is not a moment to relax.

At *Options* the room was divided more or less down the middle with the youngest babies on one side and the older toddlers on the other. One afternoon while many of the babies were napping, staff decided to move the room divider, allowing the baby side more space as the babies were all beginning to move and some were walking. One of the children who had just begun to walk woke up and upon coming into the room he burst into tears, not stopping until the staff figured out that he was upset with the room change and returned the room to its original set up. They rearranged the room the next day while he was awake and participating in the move. The child had become a key contributor to the decision making process—local democracy in action.

Presently, a new outside space is being planned at *Options* and the children are contributing their ideas and preferences. Alison Clark and Peter Moss (2001) used a multi-method approach, the Mosaic approach, including observation, photos, mapping, conferencing, in order to listen to many "voices" of young children about issues that concern them (Clark, 2007; Clark, Kjorholt, & Moss, 2005; Clark & Moss, 2001). Building on the Mosaic Approach, the educators have been finding ways to listen to the toddlers' preferences in the outside space. Noting their movement in the outside space and their interest in various materials, the educators are exploring possibilities for design through their observations and conversations with the children.

Listening is not passive; it requires attempting to understand the babies and toddlers as well as responding to their communications. Paying attention to the mothers while listening to the babies can stretch and challenge educators. A young mother's focus may not seem to connect with her baby and an educator may have to strain to hear the threads of connection. By finding the threads and understanding which ones connect mother and child, educators can find ways to help weave stronger webs of connection. A listening presence truly appreciating another, appreciating their situation and their struggles, can provide encouragement. The Catholic theologian Henri Nouwen (1975) writes that healing is possible with "the full and real presence of people to each other" (p.95).

When we enter into relationships we enter into a space of uncertainty. Relationships have their own map and journey and each one is different. Once the journey is embarked upon the destinations are unknown. When we respond to what we have heard, or what we think we have heard, we are demonstrating the depth of our listening, and our appreciation for another's viewpoint. In responding, we are vulnerable to misinterpretation; we may have not heard a child or parent correctly or we may have imposed our own agenda on top of their words. But responding, making a mistake and stopping to listen again we indicate our desire to be in an authentic dialogue and to journey with someone with care.

PHILOSOPHY AND MISSION STATEMENTS—VISIONING IDEALS

Since the program began, *Options* has had a philosophy and mission statement. A year before this chapter was written, the staff rewrote the original philosophy. While there are consistent themes of respect and caring that

run through both documents the wording suggests a different attitude has evolved. The original philosophy statement was:
As early childhood educators we believe in:

- Fostering respect and respecting the developmental process of each child and their family;
- Supporting others and supporting ourselves in order to recognize and to discover their and our potential;
- Providing an environment that is nurturing, caring, flexible and responsive to individual needs.

In this original philosophy statement and the subsequent mission statement and program objectives, there was no mention of community and power appears to rest solely with the educators who appear to be solely in charge of the process.

The most recent philosophy statement says: "As Early Childhood Educators/Caregivers we believe in celebrating, honoring and respecting each child and family while nurturing their growth and connectedness." In this statement, there is a shift to connection that suggests community. The mission statement goes on to say that staff is committed to providing a compassionate and nurturing community. There is a more inclusive feel to the latter statement.

A philosophy statement is written for a program stating explicit values while other values are implicit within the statement. The process of writing a philosophy and thinking carefully about values can be illuminating for the staff. Within the second philosophy statement, more attention to inclusion is found, for example, "providing an inclusive environment which respects and honors diversity." Particulars can also be found that speak to listening and paying attention to individual children and "allowing the children to be the guide and taking our cues from them." The statement in the philosophy of: "valuing the contribution of each mom and using this to build a relationship built on trust and respect" expresses a belief that influence goes both ways within a relationship.

While the philosophy has seemingly broadened and deepened, what would a philosophy look like that included all the voices within a community? How would the families articulate the philosophy and what are the children's understanding of it? Young mothers may not be interested in exploring philosophical beliefs and babies are at the beginning of their participation in community but to speculate on their views could add another dimension. Working within the program and discussing staff practices and values has heightened awareness of this particular ideal. Striving to provide space for each individual's presence and voice can create difficulties. It is not easy to decide what the appropriate voice is or the appropriate message. When one person overshadows another there must be some discernment as to how to pay attention to each individual.

CONCEPT OF DISCERNMENT

Using discernment, we discriminate between our relationship with this child and that child, and justify a particular response as more appropriate. A definition of discernment is the perception of that which is obscure (Fowler & Fowler, 1964) and it is our discernment that uncovers the hidden strengths and wisdoms of the parents and children with whom we are in relationship. Discernment may nudge us to look deeper into situations exploring issues of power and hidden assumptions.

In our relationships, we create dialogues and then must listen in order to understand each other through what Habermas (1984) would call communicative empathy—'I have to want to understand what you say in order to communicate.' Discernment is an element of that desire to want to understand our dialogues, what we are hearing from families, as well as examining the context within which the dialogues take place. As Huebner (1999) says, "discernment is inherently a community activity" (p. 394); it helps us to contextualize our understandings or our attempts to understand families and children.

Michelle, an educator at *Options*, spoke of welcoming Nia, a new twelve-month-old child who had never been away from her mother. Disconsolate at being left in the center, Michelle tried to comfort Nia, going to her to pick her up or consoling her in some physical way but Nia was clear she did not want to be touched or consoled. Michelle felt helpless and yet wanted to respect Nia's communication. She sat nearby, a calm presence ready to comfort when it was wanted. This went on for several days before Nia came and sat with Michelle. Michelle did not impose a standard response to Nia, but discerned the response that fitted for Nia in this situation. Michelle listened to Nia and discerned she needed a different response than the natural impulse to pick up the child.

The discernment does not measure Nia's response to separation from her mother against how Michelle felt she should react. Rather, it gauged the response for which this particular child called. Discernment goes past judgment and turns listening into an act of appreciation. As we appreciate the uniqueness that child or parent bring to our relationship with them we can appreciate their contribution, the gift they bring to us.

TENSIONS

Working with a vision or ideal we are at times faced with tensions that are part of being in community. We cannot always actualize our ideal, it eludes us. The situation can be constantly in flux. For example, an educator with a group of three children understands that two of them are ready to go outside. The third child is busy with her own project and is not ready. How to decide what to do? The educator speaks to the group, explaining that one of them is not ready to head outside, can the other two wait. But she could also explain to the one who is busy that it is time to go outside, as the other two are ready. It may depend on the children—to need to hear that they must wait at times or the one may need to learn that she has to put her interests secondary to the group. Other things may influence the decision, the educator's particular needs, the situation with other children and educators, what was decided last time.

Balancing multiple relationships can create tensions, and managing the relationships with parents, children, and co-workers takes reflection and careful thought (Elliot, 2007). Working within the tensions, recognizing them, using them as a basis for ongoing dialogues is part of being in community. The educators are older than the mothers, more experienced, and have been with the program for many years: these qualities give them considerable power within an early childhood context. Ideally, they may envision sharing power, but they are in the program all day with the babies and they have the ongoing history with the program. While sharing power may be a value, there is the pragmatic piece that this is the early childhood space and ultimately the educators will decide and ultimately the babies and families will leave, so the power is never even. Realizing the inequity may be a step to using that power carefully.

Tensions provide opportunities for re-evaluation and discussion. As the program evolves with the experience of different families and children and different educators, tensions will be inevitable. Keeping the broad view, re-examining the philosophy and practice will keep the work dynamic. Democratic practice may be one framework but there is also a need for further reflection on the role of ethics in the discussions.

THE ROLE OF ETHICS

In a community made up of multiple relationships, we can be faced with moral dilemmas as well as tensions, and there are often no clearly correct answers. Relationships can be guided by a sense of caring, that responds within the context of a particular relationship. Wendy says:

We are almost non-hierarchical among the day care staff. We know there are bigger systems in place that we have to work within but amongst ourselves we are constantly checking in and running things past each other. Our decisions are group made. We are respectful of each other and the impact a decision can have on everyone involved. It's a balance between consensus and maintaining your sense of self too. We try really hard to be non-judgmental knowing there is always more to people and situations than just our program can see or deal with. We believe in the big picture and have faith in the positive. We go with the flow being available and ready when needed, treating others as we would like to be treated. The children also have a great deal of say in how their day unfolds. They make decisions about their care and activities.

Whenever we interact with others we must strive to act ethically. Philip Hallie (1997) says " . . . ethics is nothing more or less than the sporadic human effort to see and to treat all human lives as equally precious" (p. 6). Levinas (1987) tells us to approach the Other with respect, understanding that we cannot know the other person but we are obligated to attempt to understand. He goes on to speak of the ethics of an encounter and being responsible to the Other. To be responsible means we are answerable; to be answerable we must be appropriately responsive. The difficulty is that each situation and each person requires a different response. We must be attentive and present to the situation and the person. It requires that

> . . . learning to be part of the world rather than trying to dominate it—on learning to see rather than merely look, to feel rather than touch, to hear rather than listen: to learn, in short, about the world by being still and opening myself to experiencing it. If I realize that I am an organic part of all that is and learn to adopt a receptive, connected stance, then I need not take an active, dominant role to understand; the universe will, in essence, include me in understanding. (Delpit, 1995, p. 92)

The rules are slippery, changing with the situations and the people. Conversations, listening to another's point of view and responding with respect keeps our own perspective from becoming too narrow and self-absorbed. To do so we must continually challenge others and ourselves. The conversations, far from offering answers, acknowledge the complexities of life and explore possibilities of a delicate balance. We are a step nearer to creating local democratic early childhood programs when we create communities that are based on relationships of dialogue, listening, and discernment.

CONCLUSION

Options Child and Family Centre is a local response to a mandate for a program for young mothers and their babies. Within the program they have attempted to connect values of caring, relationship, and community into a framework of listening, dialogue, and discernment. Using this framework, educators work towards creating a community valuing the presence of every member, reflecting democratic values that are part of the Canadian society. Traditionally children's voices have been left out of concepts of democracy in the belief that they were unable to contribute. At Options we have found that babies have ways to inform and educate us as to their perspectives and views on their lives and experiences. As we practice including children's voices, their parents' voices we will gain experience in handling the inevitable tensions and contradictions that in turn will inform further thinking. Sharing our experiences has possibilities of deepening our thinking on this work.

The process of writing this chapter has given us an opportunity to think about infant care, democratic practice and what it means to us. As the author of this chapter I was concerned with including the voices of practitioners who think deeply about their work with infants and toddlers. Reflecting on their work in terms of democracy was new to the educators. While this perspective is just one lens with which to look at practice, it provided a useful view for evaluating the space given to children's voices and the voices of their families. Ideals can be guides and can illuminate ignored spots of practice.

The process of listening to children and families, entering into dialogues and using discernment in response provide possibilities for creating a community where democratic principles are valued. Providing space and weight for all the voices produces tensions that can keep the community process dynamic. As children participate in community, expressing themselves and learning to listen to others they begin their own journeys towards participation in the greater community.

REFERENCES

A look at Canada: What does Canadian citizenship mean? (2008). Retrieved 19 May, 2008, from http://www.cic.gc.ca/english/resources/publications/look/look-03.asp.

Beach, J., Bosica, C., Bertrand, J., Forer, B., Michal, D., & Tougas, J. (2004). *Working for change: Canada's child care workforce.* Ottawa, Canada: Child Care Human Resources Sector Council.

Bernhardt, J. L. (2000). A primary caregiving system for infants and toddlers: Best for everyone involved. *Young Children, 55*(2), 74–80.

Bredekamp, S., & Copple, C. (Eds.). (1997). *Developmentally appropriate practice in early childhood programs* (Revised edition ed.). Washington, DC: National Association for the Education of Young Children.

Clark, A. (2007). *Early childhood spaces: Involving young children and practitioners in the design process.* The Hague, The Netherlands: Bernard van Leer Foundation.

Clark, A., Kjorholt, A. T., & Moss, P. (Eds.). (2005). *Beyond listening: Children's perspectives on early childhood services.* Bristol, UK: Policy Press.

Clark, A., & Moss, P. (2001). *Listening to children: The mosaic approach.* London: National Children's Bureau.

Dahlberg, G., & Moss, P. (2005). *Ethics and politics in early childhood education.* London: Routledge Falmer.

———. (2006). Introduction: Our Reggio Emilia. In C. Rinaldi (Ed.), *In dialogue with Reggio Emilia: Listening, researching and learning* (pp. 1–22). London: Routledge.

Delpit, L. (1995). *Other people's children: Cultural conflict in the classroom.* New York: The New Press.

Elliot, E. (2007). *"We're not robots": The voices of infant/toddler caregivers.* Albany, NY: SUNY Press.

Fowler, H. W., & Fowler, F. G. (Eds.). (1964). *The concise Oxford dictionary* (5th ed.). Oxford, UK: Clarendon Press.

Freire, P. (1970). *Pedagogy of the oppressed.* Harmondsworth, UK: Penguin.

———. (2000). *Pedagogy of the heart.* New York: Continuum Publishing.

Gerber, M. (Ed.). (1979). *Manual for Parents and Professionals.* Los Angeles: Resources for Infant Educarers.

Habermas, J. (1984). *Theory of communicative action* (T. McCarthy, Trans. Vol. Volume I: Reason and the rationalization of society). Boston, MA: Beacon.

Hallie, P. (1997). *Tales of good and evil, help and harm*. New York: Harper Collins Publishers.

Huebner, D. E. (1999). Religious education: Practicing the presence of God. In V. Hillis (Ed.), *The lure of the transcendent: Collected essays by Dwayne E. Huebner* (pp. 388–395). Mahwah, NJ: Lawrence Erlbaum.

Levinas, E. (1987). Collected philosophical paper (A. Lingis, Trans.). Dordrecht, Netherlands: Martinus Nijhoff.

MacNaughton, G. (2005). *Doing Foucault in early childhood studies: Applying poststructural ideas*. New York: Routledge.

Moss, P. (2006, August). *Bringing Politics into the Nursery: Early Childhood Education as a democratic practice*. Keynote address presented at the 16th Annual European Early Childhood Research Association conference, Reykjavik, Iceland.

Nouwen, H. J. M. (1975). *Reaching out: The three movements of the spiritual life*. New York: Doubleday.

Penn, H. (1999). *How should we care for babies and toddlers? An analysis of practice in out-of-home care for children under three* (Occasional Paper No. 10). Toronto, Canada: Childcare Resource and Research Unit, Centre for Urban & Community Studies, University of Toronto, Canada.

———. (2005). *Unequal childhoods: Young children's lives in poor countries*. London and New York: Routledge.

Pikler, E. (1979). A quarter of a century of observing infants in a residential center. In M. Gerber (Ed.), *A manual for parents and professionals: Resources for infant educarers* (pp. 90–92). Los Angeles: Resources for Infant Educarers.

Rinaldi, C. (2005). Documentation and assessment: What is the relationship? In A. Clark, A. T. Kjorholt & P. Moss (Eds.), *Beyond listening: Children's perspectives on early childhood services* (pp. 17–28). Bristol, UK: Policy Press.

Rogoff, B. (2003). *The cultural nature of human development*. Oxford, UK: Oxford University Press.

Singer, E. (1992). *Child care and the psychology of development* (A. Porcelijn, Trans.). London and New York: Routledge.

Weedon, C. (1987). *Feminist practice and poststructuralist theory*. Oxford, UK: Basil Blackwell.

Wright, S. (2007). Modes of being: Control, dissent, and listening in early childhood. *The first years: New Zealand Journal of Infant and Toddler Education, 9*(2), 17–20.

11 "If You Think They Can Do It— Then They Can"

Two-Year-Olds in Aotearoa[1] New Zealand Kindergartens and Changing Professional Perspectives

Judith Duncan

Through a combination of practitioner research and collective teacher discussions, a small group of kindergarten teachers in Aotearoa New Zealand engaged in rethinking their teaching practices with two-year-old children from a sociocultural perspective. We drew on a sociocultural theoretical approach to rethink and reframe teaching and learning because Fleer (2002, p. 2) identified that it offered "scope for building new foundations" not only for research but also in constructing and conceptualizing all aspects of pedagogy. In this way, sociocultural theory enables the construction of new understandings of participatory learning for children and an ability to shift the 'gaze' to the wider contexts which impact on teaching and learning experiences (Carr, 2001; Fleer, 2002, 2003; Fleer & Richardson, 2004).

In our research, reported here, we aimed to "build new foundations" and understanding for the teachers in order to support meaningful participatory learning for the two-year-olds who are now attending kindergartens in large numbers. The tool to accomplish this was developed as a partnership between two academic researchers (Judith Duncan and Carmen Dalli) and the teachers themselves, as researching practitioners.

Practitioner research is a key method in developing new understandings within professional practice (Goodfellow & Hedges, 2007). Practitioner research has changed the context of teachers' investigation of their teaching, and is being used more regularly to support teacher reflection on practice, transformative practices, and subsequent refinement of professional practices (Goodfellow, 2005; McLeod, 2000; Ponte, Beijaard, & Wubbles, 2004; Potter, 2001). These insights can be seen as "priceless wisdom" (Mitchell, 2003, cited in Goodfellow & Hedges, 2007, p. 206) where not only are new understandings gained but where the knowledge can become 'owned' by the teachers themselves, enabling a meaningful application of new principles and practices in the teachers' daily experiences (Loughran, & Northfield, 1998; Mitchell, 2001, 2003).

In this project we used a multi-layered investigation to inform this 'transformation.' Following an adaptation from Rogoff (1998 cited in Fleer, 2002, p. 5) we focused our analysis through three different lenses:

personal perspectives, interpersonal perspectives, and community/institutional perspectives—so as to be able to observe and conceptualize teaching and learning in a way that encompassed as many aspects of the process as possible. In this way, and in keeping with a sociocultural framework, our approach moved away from traditional child development positions, which has often observed the "isolated child" (Fleer, 2002, p. 6), to a more contextually and community based position enabling a wider understanding to be gained of both the child and the teacher's beliefs and pedagogy in the kindergartens.

CONTEXT FOR THE RESEARCH—KINDERGARTENS IN AOTEAROA NEW ZEALAND

As part of a two-year action research project, funded by the New Zealand Teaching and Learning Research Initiative[2], we explored the changing professional practice of a group of Aotearoa New Zealand kindergarten teachers with two-year-olds in their kindergartens. Over the two years of the study, a small group of teachers re-examined the experiences and abilities of the two-year-olds in their kindergartens and reflected on how to increase the participation and the possibilities for the youngest members in their early childhood education community. The study reported here was a partnership between the Dunedin and Wellington Kindergarten Associations[3], Dr. Judith Duncan (author) of the University of Otago and Associate Professor Carmen Dalli of Victoria University of Wellington.[4] Within both associations individual kindergarten teachers were involved in the research. Four kindergartens, with high numbers of under-three-year-old children were included as case studies, and all interested teachers from the associations were included in discussion groups aimed at examining and exploring the contexts and wider understandings of the two-year-olds. The focus was centered on supporting teachers in their thinking and their practice with two-year-olds in the kindergarten setting from "mission impossible" (Greenman, 2005, p. 138) to an understanding of these same children as capable and competent (Ministry of Education, 1996) and able to participate in the program alongside their older peers.[5]

Historically, Aotearoa New Zealand kindergartens have provided early childhood education for three and four-year-olds in local communities. Children in Aotearoa New Zealand begin school on, or near, their fifth birthday and, traditionally, kindergarten was the provider of early childhood education for the two years before school entry. As a general model kindergartens are administered by kindergarten associations, partly funded by government grants, and have early childhood trained teachers. While kindergartens can vary from area to area, most kindergartens have either a group size of 30 children and two teachers, or 45 children and three teachers. Traditionally, kindergartens hold sessions for older children (four- to five-year-olds) in the morning and younger children (three- to four-year-olds) in the afternoon. However, school-hour sessions are becoming common in many areas, as are family grouping, where the children attend together with their siblings and in mixed age groups for a six-hour day, modeled on the compulsory school-hour day (Duncan, 2007a). All kindergartens implement Te Whāriki—The New Zealand early childhood curriculum—(Ministry of Education, 1996) and teachers have access to regular professional development opportunities provided by localized early childhood providers and the associations themselves.

However, the scene for kindergartens has changed considerably over the last twenty years (Duncan, 2001, 2007b; Duncan, Dalli & Lawrence, 2007). With an increase in number of other high quality government subsidized early childhood education centers, parents have a wider range of services to choose from to meet their child and their families' requirements (Ministry of Education, 2007). No longer is kindergarten the dominant provider of early childhood education for three- and four-year-olds. This wider range of choices of early childhood centers to parents, combined with a falling population, has led to a decrease in enrollments at kindergartens. In a response to this, several regions in Aotearoa New Zealand have introduced under-three-year-olds in large numbers into their kindergartens to maintain sufficient numbers of children to keep the kindergarten open in any specific community. This change in age of attendees in kindergarten sessions has proven to be a challenge for teachers, more familiar with three and four-year-olds, in terms of their teaching practices, programming practices, and curriculum goals. Factors in the teaching environment, such as physical environments structured primarily for the older-age child, and large group settings of 30 to 45 children per session impact on the experiences of all the children but particularly on the very young child. These same factors have the potential to limit the experiences of the two-year-olds.

While this discussion focuses on the Aotearoa New Zealand kindergarten, the issues explored with the kindergarten teachers are transferable to other mixed age settings in early childhood, who also have large group sizes and low child to adult ratios (which occur in many sessional programs internationally). The challenges for teachers surround existing teaching beliefs and understandings of children, often in relation to the purposes of the educational setting that the teacher and child is positioned within. It is at this point of challenge that reframing and rethinking of teaching and learning becomes essential (Loughran & Northfield, 1998).

RESEARCH APPROACH: INVESTIGATING
TEACHING AND LEARNING EXPERIENCES

Using investigative qualitative research methods, we conducted case studies of 18 two-year-old children in four kindergartens, two in Dunedin and two in Wellington, over a two-year period. The kindergarten teachers reflected on the narrative observations of the case study children and their own teaching practices with the two-year-olds in their kindergartens. Parents of the case study children were involved in reflective discussions of their child's narrative observations.

These same case study teachers met with other teachers in their association for five cluster group meetings over the two years, to explore the research questions and to support best practice with two-year-olds across their association's kindergartens. These meetings were developed to engage the teachers in a "co-constructive learning culture" (Dahlberg, Moss & Pence, 2007, p. 135), to hold up pedagogy "for public consideration" (Mitchell, 2003, p. 12), and to build a "community of practice" (Anning, 2004; Boardman, 2003; Wenger, 1998) of teachers in kindergartens with two-year-olds. The sessions, held over the two years, were structured to reframe teachers' perspectives and beliefs about two-year-olds that worked to disadvantage the children or negatively impact on the teacher's pedagogical practices. At the same time the teachers in the cluster groups also identified the structures and beliefs that would need to be addressed at the wider society levels to ensure a safe and high quality educational experience for the two-year-olds who attend kindergartens.

PRAXIS IN ACTION: REFRAMING TWO-YEAR-OLD CHILDREN'S PARTICIPATION AND POSSIBILITIES

The discussion that follows is from the two case study kindergartens and the cluster group of teachers who participated from the Dunedin Kindergarten Association.[6] The teachers' journeys in personal reflective practice, joint reflection on center pedagogy, and self-study in co-construction with other teachers in the cluster groups over the two years indicated two themes which demonstrate praxis in action. These themes are: identifying the complexities and the possibilities of a participatory pedagogy with two-year-olds.

THEME 1: IDENTIFYING THE COMPLEXITIES

The complexities of working with two-year-olds in a large group size with a wide age range, with limited numbers of teaching staff, and often in an environment which had been built and resourced for three- and four-year-olds, were identified as the key complexities for two-year-olds in the kindergarten.

Numbers Do Matter

All the teachers spoke about the benefits of having more adults in the kindergarten because "under-threes need a lot more support." Teachers spoke about how much better it was for children when there were fewer in these sessions. We also observed the difference that smaller group numbers made to the individual case study children's experiences in the kindergartens. This was most noticeable in one of the case study kindergartens that repeatedly had fewer than 20 children (and two teachers) in most sessions. On the days that this increased to over 20 children (and two teachers), there was a recorded drop in the amount and the length of the interactions between the teachers and the children, and an increase in supervision, routine, and management tasks. Interactions were often more focused on instruction, guidance, and safety, where previously they had been on mastery, skill acquisition, and extending dispositions.

> *Teacher 1:* I think the amount of children that come in like—we had a group last year that we had about ten or fifteen new two-year-olds and it was—that was hard. If you're getting three or four at a time it's a lot easier I think. It definitely depends on how many you get at a time.

> *Teacher 2:* Especially after the Christmas term break. We had 23 under-threes [in a group size of 30 children and two teachers] last year and that was quite a different group. It was very busy—everyone seemed to be running from one thing to another.

The ratio of the two-year-olds to the over two-year-olds (children aged three to five years) was a significant factor in how the teachers perceived the experiences of the children and what they saw as possible at any one time. This ratio component went both ways: if the under-twos were in larger numbers than the over-twos then the teachers worried about the consequences of the increased attention to the two-year-olds' interactions, the environment adjustments, and the time taken with increased "care" duties that took them away from the older children. Over the two years of this research the case study teachers became increasingly concerned about the older children in their two-year-old afternoon sessions:

> *Teacher:* I was thinking of some of our older children that are almost four and you're still with some that aren't two and half . . . you know, they're [the four-year-old]s trying to play and they're actually looking for interactions with children . . . they're looking to talk with these children and play games with them and these little ones aren't at the same—they're not wanting to play with them and they don't talk back to them and they're, yeah, and they're saying: "Oh, they don't talk." And they're looking for those interactions and they're not necessarily getting it.

When the over-twos were a larger group than the under-twos then the teachers were concerned as to the levels of safety and suitability of the environment, the resourcing, and the ability of the younger children to access the program.

Structural Constraints

The suitability of the environment and the available resources were constantly discussed by the teachers. Structural factors are not always easy to modify or change—despite the wish by the teachers (and parents). However, that having been said, the complexities within the pedagogy itself were often associated with the teachers' own beliefs and perceptions of 'two-year-olds,' drawn from child development theory predating many of the teachers' own training and current professional development. This focus on 'ages and stages,' which the teachers themselves no longer applied to three and four-year-olds in their teaching practices, heavily influenced their thinking about these very young children in a way that, once made aware of, both surprised and saddened them. Such a frame of reference about two-year-olds led to teachers' high levels of anxiety of what the children 'could not do,' or the limits that the child's physicality brought to the provision in any particular session; for example, more complex equipment and resourcing for the older children in the program was seen as a problem and the teachers regularly discussed removing these in preparation for the arrival of younger children.

In one of the cluster group meetings (Cluster Group Discussion 1: Dunedin 2004) in early 2004 the teachers listed the programming difficulties in this way: *What we need to change for the two-year-olds?*

- Remove Lego—bring out the Duplo[7]
- Lower wooden planks (moveable outside equipment)
- Replace heavy metal spades with lighter plastic spades (for the sandpit)
- Sometimes cover the water trough
- Take away the more difficult puzzles
- Less equipment in total ('less is more')

The focus at this stage of the teachers' discussions was predominantly on safety issues and concerns at the level of competence that the younger children had not yet acquired. The two-year-olds exploration of the environment and their language abilities were repeatedly experienced as a constraint and difficulty within the program. One teacher expressed her frustration at trying to understand the beginning language of the two-year-olds and described how difficult it was to get it right for the child to feel listened to and understood—key aspects for feeling a part of a place and for building relationships with others. She finished her reflection with "two shots at it and then you're out," which was her experience of how often a child would or would not attempt to reconnect with the teacher after the teacher had been unsuccessful in understanding.

In the same cluster group discussion (Cluster Group Discussion 1: Dunedin 2004), referred to earlier, the teachers were asked to identify the behaviors that two-year-olds engaged in that the teachers would prefer they were not doing, and the list demonstrated that these two factors as the most difficult: *What do they do that we don't want them to do?*

- Put dough in the fish tank
- Harass the rabbit/Paint the rabbit
- Move things around
- Glue the puzzles
- Flood the hand basins/bathroom
- Hiding and going to sleep in a corner
- Eating on the run

This list, and the experiences behind them, demonstrates the complexities of managing large groups of children with few adults—the teachers wanted to be able to have meaningful engagements rather than the physical chaos that could often occur in the sessions. These daily struggles are mirrored in Greenman's (2005) challenge for early childhood education environments to support the growth and learning of two-year-olds in their settings:

> How do you develop an environment that allows for collecting, hauling, dumping, and painting (with the requisite tasting of the paint and experimenting with the logical primary canvas, namely themselves)? How do you allow the necessary robust, explosive, and occasionally clumsy motor learning with a group of amoral beings who are largely oblivious to the safety of others—a group, however, that often hums with a current of collective energy? In a group setting, how do you accommodate and support the wonderful, albeit erratic, *do-it-myself* desire and the equally developmentally important but often less wonderful assertion of "No!"—and still accomplish anything in a reasonable time frame? Finally, how do you muster up the time, let alone the patience and sensitivity, to help each child through the agony and ecstasy of toilet training? "Mission impossible" may in fact understate the situation. (Greenman, 2005, p. 138)

In several reported cases the actual physical positioning of the grounds in the kindergartens also introduced a range of complexities: either the large open size where children could not be easily seen, or grounds with steep landscape or multiple stairways. For example, many of the playgrounds in Dunedin are on hill suburbs and just negotiating the slopes, ramps, and steps was a major challenge for many children. The following discussion between teachers demonstrates these concerns:

> *Teacher 1*: Oh, I was just thinking how lovely it would be to have a playground that's just for little ones, with equipment that you wouldn't worry about being unsafe. Just height-wise, I'm thinking about the kind

of boxes and things that we've got that will be lower, or maybe have good steps up, inset into them and things, that they could still have lots of fun with, but were much more suitable for them.

Teacher 2: Not just only the equipment, but the actual layout of the land. You know, Dunedin being Dunedin, there's a lot of sites that are quite steep and difficult for little ones and while it might be challeng-ing—it's a bit more than just challenging really—it's too much.

In sharing our observations with the teachers, many of the observations had examples of the two-year-old struggling with aspects of the equipment and the environment. The teachers' sense of frustration was increased at not having been able to "be there at that moment," "not able to stand there for that length of time to help them across one more time," or "having moved away just before that happened." Despite the adjustments that most of the teachers had made to their environments for safety, the lack of adults in the environment left the teachers constantly 'on the run' to ensure that the chil-dren were safe at all times—particularly in the outdoor environment.

However, the focus on the 'ages and stages' of the very young child did not always lead to negative outcomes, for example, teachers were observed physically reassuring the two-year-old more regularly with hugs and cud-dles more than the older children. The teachers were full of the 'joys' of working with the younger children that directly contrasted with their expe-riences of the older children: the physicality of the hugs and reassurance, the feeling of being 'needed,' the length of time the child would remain in the kindergarten (until going to school) and the ability to get to know the child and the child's family over this period of time, plus the overall sense of being involved in so much of the child's growth and learning over these early years (see Duncan, et al., 2006 for full discussion).

THEME 2: POSSIBILITIES OF A PARTICIPATORY PEDAGOGY WITH TWO-YEAR-OLDS

The pleasure that working with the two-year-olds had introduced to the teachers, despite the complexities and concerns, led into discussion and reflections, with the teachers, on the possibilities for increased participatory pedagogy for the two-year-olds.

The Physical Environment

One of the resounding messages from the literature surrounding best environments for quality early childhood education is that the equipment and materials within the setting should allow children to be in control, to develop independence and a sense of autonomy (Douville-Watson, Watson & Wilson, 2003; Lally, Griffin, Fenichel, Segal, Szanton, & Weissbourd,

1995). The environment relays powerful messages to the child about whether adults consider that he or she is capable of successful independence and the type and variety of equipment and materials either promote the children's ability to independently impact the environment around him or her or communicate the idea of the child's dependence on others (Albrecht & Miller, 2000). One feature of this is that the equipment and furniture is recommended to be scaled to the size of the children using it. Albrecht and Miller (2000) note that children should be able to touch their feet to the ground when seated on chairs. While kindergartens are 'child-size,' traditionally the child has been a three or four-year-old, which has meant that some of the furniture and resources in the kindergarten are just too big—and feet don't touch the floor!

Photo 11.1 Two years old and feet don't touch the floor. (Photo taken by Judith Duncan)

Age-Appropriate Equipment "Down at Their Level"

The teachers regularly spoke about the modifications they had made, or needed to make, to the standard kindergarten physical environment, to ensure that age-appropriate equipment was easily accessible to the youngest under-three year-olds. These included moving the younger-age books and other equipment to the lower shelves where younger children could reach them easily and placing posters and pictures "down at their level."

The teachers from one of the Dunedin case study kindergartens looked at their own environment from a two-year-old's worldview and, using observation and a camera, saw their environment from a new perspective. Jan Taita (Head kindergarten teacher) describes it in her own words (all photos taken by Jan):

> I was spending some time with one of our two-year-olds and we were doing patterns on a peg-board and I realized that she couldn't actually see the shapes that we were talking about. I lifted it up for her so that she could see what she was working on. And then it dawned on me also that really this little girl couldn't see a lot of the things in the environment. I got down to her level on the floor and looked around the room and realized that we had a wee bit of a problem. So getting my camera out and following her around this day I realized that changes needed to be made.

At the play dough table she also wasn't able to reach the shapes and the rolling pins and things that are in the middle of the table—they were just out of her reach. We had also observed that the little ones would get up on the chair and get on the table to reach whatever was in the middle.

Photo 11.2 Peg board viewed from a two-year-old's height. (Photo taken by Jan Taita)

Photo 11.3   Play dough table from a two-year-old's height. (Photo taken by Jan Taita)

At the time I was lucky to have a student [in teacher training] with us who worked in another [center in an] under-threes room and I was talking to her about the height of the equipment and she talked about the height of the equipment in their [under-threes] room. And she invited me to go and have a look there, which I did, and took lots of photos and when we looked through them we realized that everything was a lot easier for them to access. So after discussing with the team we decided we were going to change things.

This photo reflects the first initiative that was implemented.

Photo 11.4   Puzzle tables. (Photo taken by Jan Taita)

We separated the tables. We usually had the two red ones together and the two purple ones together. The children can walk right round them now. They can reach all the things that are on the tables. We made changes to the play dough table as well and took the legs off and put the cushions around and the children have found this a lot easier.

Initially they [the children] jumped right up onto it, but that didn't last long. I know that some kindergartens do have low tables for their children but we don't, they're all the same height. So we lowered it and put the cushions around it, it is really good.

This example of observation, reflection, and change; and then further reflection demonstrated the willingness of the teachers in the project to begin to think not only about their own personal pedagogy, but their environments and their collective teaching pedagogy. In the style of self-study Jan and her teaching team presented this example to the other teachers in the Dunedin cluster group. While several kindergartens were already addressing some of these issues, it supported other teachers to become increasingly aware that the size of the equipment and the resources in

Photo 11.5 Play dough table. (Photo taken by Jan Taita)

their environments had been designed for older and bigger children, and some of their 'management' issues could be removed by changing their environment—by quite simple steps. For example, the following discussion between several teachers in the cluster group highlighted the shift that the teachers began to introduce:

Teacher: Even your furniture and things like that, sometimes the teeny little two-year-olds, their feet don't touch the floor or they can't reach right up to the painting. Some of the furniture for your little ones, it's still really big for them.

Teacher: They have to stand on things in the toilets.

Teacher: Or the water trough, they can't reach the water trough, so you need to put them up higher so they can get into it.

Teacher: And with the paints, when we first had two-year-olds they couldn't see what color they were using. That's really unsatisfying for them. It's just a whole lot of bottles—what does that mean? So we got some clear bottles so they could actually see and make choices. You know, if you get down to that height and you look at what's available, it's really interesting.

These are examples of the increased awareness of the different but complementary needs of children within the kindergarten. The decision to alter the furniture to enable the children to access the existing program, rather than withdrawing the materials from the program, or seeing the children as too 'small' or 'unable' to participate in the program, demonstrates an inclusive approach to these children. The perceptions and expectations of the teachers with regards to what the two-year-olds could and could not do were a key factor in these experiences of the children.

Equipping for the Youngest and Remembering the Oldest

Limiting the equipment available when the younger children were present, came to be acknowledged as reducing the opportunities for the older children in the session as well as limiting the learning appropriate use of equipment experiences for the younger child. This debate was significantly influenced by the age of the child. For example, for the kindergartens with the 'just-turned two-year-olds' limiting equipment for increased safety was of more concern than for the kindergartens that had the older two-year-olds, that is, those who were nearly three years-old. For those with the very young two-year-olds also, the teachers identified the need for bigger and more open areas for the children, to minimize the conflict between children from the uncoordinated movement and collisions that occur with groups of toddlers, and to allow for the 'transporting' of toys. This openness of space is also recommended in guidelines for environments for toddlers and the two-year-olds (Douville-Watson, Watson & Wilson, 2003; Greenman, 2005; Moore, 2001).

However, "having more than one thing out" was also seen as helpful because "some of them don't know how to share." The particular case of "transporting" equipment was highlighted because "they love transporting things from one place to another: it's the whole program" and if there were not enough of it, the danger would be that the older children would "lose" (or hijack!) the younger children's equipment. As a teacher sums up:

> I think having a lot of equipment also means there's less conflict. We've got a big area and they've got their own space and normally there's enough room for everybody that wants to play at that particular time. So that helps them in their relationships, so they're not actually fighting over a piece of equipment and that, you know, the environment is set up for a lot of children and so there is plenty there for them to choose.

However, thinking 'smarter' about what equipment and materials are in the program and where they are situated was a factor that made a key difference for both the teachers and the children in the kindergartens. By being selective and strategic in the resources they made available in the afternoon session the teachers found that they could avoid the environment taking over and the teachers having to spend the afternoon dealing with problems:

> Are the bikes a nuisance, you know, are the bikes too big? Should we just put them out? So it's those types of things. Otherwise, I think you can set yourself up to actually deal with problems all the time as opposed to really looking at what's actually suitable for the children who are here. . . . We thought, "We can't cope like this, we really have to sit back and say: What are we trying to achieve?" So it gets back to your planning and you're looking and thinking: "We've got too much. They can't make choices." So if you can get that nice balance there it means for your teaching, it's easy. *It's like less is more.* [emphasis added]

IF YOU THINK THEY CAN DO IT—THEN THEY CAN

Teachers spoke about their daily work with two-year-olds as something that in many cases their original teacher training had not prepared them adequately for. The teachers recalled the impact of their first experiences with two-year-olds in their program:

> *Teacher*: Your own expectations. It came up; we had quite a good discussion the last couple of days, about those who have trained years ago and those who have trained more recently, as to how you actually see the role. You know, see two-year-olds in the program. Whereas we were probably brought up with three to five year-olds and others are bringing up from the two to five. And it's a totally different perspective

and you have to grow into that and you can't just stick with your way and say: 'Well that's how I was trained.' That doesn't happen, that's not the reality of today. So you've actually got say: "Hey, well, where do my values and my place fit in with what's actually happening?"

Having professional support for this questioning and for building new teaching skills for the current context was a recurring discussion with the teachers who clearly understood that their expectations made a difference to children's experiences as well as their own. This is how one teacher expressed her understanding:

> *Teacher*: It's the teachers' expectations. If you expect them to be little babies and all those bla bla things, then that's what you will get. However, you do need to be realistic of what they can do and if you just set your expectation, like 'I expect you to sit down and eat your food'— eventually it will happen.

During one afternoon's observation, the impact of teachers' expectations was emphasized when a relieving teacher used language that continually reinforced the smallness of a child, and his 'inability' to undertake tasks. The data in the excerpt below demonstrate how the reliever's assumption about what the child was not capable of doing, based largely on his size and, possibly, lack of verbal interactions, reinforced 'help seeking' behavior in the child and removed any independent attempt at achieving a task that he had previously shown an ability to do: putting a ball through a hoop successfully. The case study child had also been previously observed engaging in problem-solving strategies for raising his own personal height by placing steps under the hoop to make it easier to reach. The following excerpt starts at a point when a group of three boys (all two-year-olds) had been playing with 'ride-ons' on the path and then had headed to a wood chip area:

> Relieving Teacher: "Boys, come over and bring them [ride-ons] back onto the path" (calling to them). The Relieving Teacher walks over and takes hold of one of the boys on a bike and wheels him onto the path. The other two boys follow. Once on the path, the case study child turns around and heads over to the grass area where another boy [three years old] is throwing a ball through a basketball hoop attached to the wall. The case study child grabs a ball and then calls out loudly (cry sound). He runs over to another Kindergarten Teacher who is standing alongside the sand pit. She bends down and looks him in the eye and asks him: Do you want to put the ball in the hoop? Meanwhile, the Relieving Teacher has moved over to the basketball hoop area and the case study child turns and runs over to stand beside her. He stands close and watches the three-year-old throwing a ball at the hoop several times. [Case study child] watches and laughs holding on tight to his ball the

whole time. Relieving Teacher (talking to the Case study child): "Is that too hard for you? Would you like a turn? I'll lift you up." She then lifts him up so that he can drop the ball into the hoop. They repeat this three times. Other children begin to gather and watch. The Relieving Teacher turns to talk with the other children who have gathered and she decides to get more balls from the shed. As she moves to the shed, the case study child calls out in a loud voice: "Lift me, help me." He continues to call out to the relieving teacher as she moves off to the shed and he runs after her holding the ball.

The excerpt above stands in contrast to the following one in which a teacher, from a case study kindergarten, who regularly observed the 'wisdom' and 'skill' of the two-year-olds that she worked with, recounted a moment in which she realized that her expectations of two-year-olds could be turned around from seeing them as lacking in skills or capabilities to seeing them as learners and teachers. The teacher recounted this example, at one of the cluster group meetings, which she had found beneficial for helping her reflect on her practice and changing her expectations of the capabilities of young two-year-olds. Michelle Butcher (in her own words):

I was still new to having two-year-olds in the program. I had asked [two-year-old child] to put his socks and shoes on because he was beginning to play on the wood chips and I was concerned that he might get splinters in his feet, after having been in the sand and having his shoes off. I really thought I was going to have to help him to put his socks and shoes on. But in the time that I was still fumbling around getting his shoelace untied he had very quickly got toes in the toe, heels in the heel. Next minute, he had a shoe on and just kept the shoelace done up, and I was still fumbling around, I think, with the shoelace. He had that on as well and before I knew it he had both shoes on. So it was just no barrier to him to be able to get back into the play. Whereas, sometimes you think with older children, even, shoes can be a barrier. So I learned a lot, very quickly, about two-year-olds and their competencies.

Later that same day with the same two-year-old, she says:

This child was having a look up in the tree. He spent time looking up into the branches of the tree. He listened and watched the leaves blowing in the wind. And he said: "shush." While holding his finger to his pursed lips, he talked in a whisper and told me that there were birds up in the tree, in a gentle way, so as not to frighten the birds. Another child was with him and was really intrigued and looking really carefully for the birds. And it was just one of those really superb, warm, fuzzy moments where all those things that we want for children to be imaginative and playful with their surroundings were happening and suddenly I wasn't the teacher, I was the learner with the teacher. It was fabulous.

Michelle's shift in perception enabled her to see the two-year-olds in her kindergarten as active participants engaged in the learning community of her kindergarten. Jan enabled the two-year-olds to engage more in the program by making substantial physical changes to the environment, thus assisting in more meaningful opportunities for participation for her two-year-olds also. Both of these examples are in contrast to the excerpt where the relieving teacher perceived the young child as incapable of managing by himself and, by physically intervening, created a reinforcement of depending on the adult 'to do it for you' rather than an environment and attitude of 'yes, I can do this myself.' While I have only presented these three examples, both the cluster discussions and the reflections with other teachers in the case study kindergartens provided numerous examples where the shift from "mission impossible" (Greenman, 2005, p. 138) to 'mission both possible and desirable' was occurring.

CONCLUSION

Working within a sociocultural approach to teaching and learning enabled the teachers to 'reframe' and 'rethink' both their teaching practices in individual kindergartens, and to begin to establish a community of learners within each association. The multiple lenses that sociocultural theory provided to examine children within their contexts in this project, (Rogoff, 1998 cited in Fleer, 2002) were used to support teachers' reflections on their teaching and their everyday constructions of children, and to change views and attitudes. These changes demonstrated the unique ways in which sociocultural 'ways of being' and 'ways of knowing' can reposition teachers and children within meaningful interactions that are supportive of positive learning and teaching relationships and environments.

Exploring the notions of 'being two'—what this means for children, teachers, and parents, has been central to this project. How the two-year-old in Aotearoa New Zealand is perceived, and what we feel or believe is the best practice and the best environments for a two-year-old, is an outcome of understanding about child development. Bloch and Popkowitz (2000, pp. 20–25) describe the theories and outcomes of child development and educational psychology as working to govern teachers' and parents' mentalities in both how they perceive children and for the consequences of the development of today's pedagogical practices. One of the reasons that may account for the anxiety and concern at two-year-olds attending kindergarten is the common understanding of the abilities, or lack of abilities, of two-year-olds which informs much of the thinking about children in this age group. This raises an interesting point for reflecting on how the discourses of 'ages and stages' are still dominating what constitutes 'good' or 'bad' practice—working as regimes of truth in early childhood education (Cannella, 1997; Duncan, 2005).

This project has enabled a community of teachers to gather together to self-reflect, collectively reflect and discuss, and to gain acknowledgement and recognition for the pedagogical work that they are engaging in their community kindergartens. Not only has this study provided insights for others with regards to the very young child in a mixed age, large group setting with low ratios, but it has validated and legitimated the experiences of those who are doing the work—right now! This legitimization and validation can be by itself a key in shaping and supporting improved or enhanced pedagogical practices and teacher role satisfaction (Loughran & Northfield, 1998, p. 7).

An additional consideration is that this study was funded and carried out over a two-year period (2004–2005) and this is an important factor in the reconsideration of participatory pedagogy for two-year-olds. The Dunedin teachers who participated in the complete two-year cycle of the study reported the impact on their teaching practices—both in gaining new insights into working with, planning, and providing for two-year-olds, and in their own ways of working as a team with the two-year-olds. Thus, time is a key factor for teachers—time to reflect, reflect again, discuss with others, try out, try out again, discuss and build communities of learning, and have the confidence to try one more time again. Often teacher professional development can be a short experience (evenings, a whole day or several days) with limited 'take-up' or long-term change or development. This project enabled a group of teachers to explore and examine their pedagogical practices intensely over a two-year period within a community of learners, some with more expertise at the beginning of the project but which was shared and then built up between many other teachers over the two years. We can see that the length of time involved in this project was a key support factor for bringing about the shift in pedagogy, which will be sustained over time for those involved in the project—both the teachers and their two-year-olds.

While the study itself was localized to a particular setting (kindergarten) within a particular country (Aotearoa New Zealand) the understandings gained from this study are applicable across early childhood settings internationally. Teacher perspectives and their 'communities of practice' can work to enhance all children's learning development and outcomes, but even more so for the youngest members of our centers, whether they be babies in nursery settings or two-year-olds in kindergarten settings. As Mad-Eye Moody (as mentor) reminds Harry Potter (as student) to maintain "constant vigilance" (Rowling, 2000) as early childhood practitioners our own 'constant vigilance' in reflecting on, and challenging our daily practices, as well as supporting our colleagues to do the same, will be a key for the best possible early childhood education provisions for the very young child.

NOTES

1. Aotearoa is the indigenous Mäori name for New Zealand.
2. This project was made possible by the *New Zealand Teaching and Learning Research Initiative*. This is a government supported research fund which seeks to bring together teaching practices and research for improved learning outcomes for children of all ages in educational settings in Aotearoa New Zealand. The focus is on supporting research that is carried out in partnership with teachers and researchers, with robust findings can inform teaching practices for other teachers—not just those involved in the research themselves. For more information on this grant and other projects see www.tlri.org.nz.
3. Kindergarten Associations are the umbrella management organizations that oversee the kindergartens in their geographical area.
4. The full research team of this project are: Judith Duncan, Carmen Dalli, Raylene Becker, Michelle Butcher, Kristie Foster, Karmen Hayes, Sue Lake-Ryan, Bev Mackie, Helen Montgomery, Penny McCormack, Raylene Muller, Rosalie Sherburd, Jan Taita, and Wendy Walker; with Chris Bowden, Kerry Cain, Helen Duncan, Julie Lawrence, Karen McCutcheon, Renate Simenaur, and Jessica Tuhega.
5. The full report, Duncan et al. (2006). *Under three-year olds in kindergartens: Children's experiences and teachers' practices,* is available electronically at: www.tlri.org.nz
6. The Wellington kindergartens and cluster sessions are not included here in this discussion. Information from the Wellington teachers can be found in the full report: Duncan et al. (2006), *Under three-year olds in kindergartens: Children's experiences and teachers' practices.* Available URL: www.tlri.org.nz
7. Both Lego and Duplo are trade names for plastic building blocks. Lego are the smaller size, and Duplo is designed for the very young child.

REFERENCES

Albrecht, K., & Miller, L. G. (2000). *The comprehensive toddler curriculum. A complete interactive curriculum for toddlers for 18 to 36 months.* Redmond, WA: Exchange Press Inc.

Anning, A. (2004, November). *Knowing who I am and what I know: Developing new versions of knowledge in early childhood group settings.* Paper presented at the Strengthening Early Childhood Communities Conference, Palmerston North, New Zealand.

Bloch, M. N., & Popkowitz, T. S. (2000). Constructing the parent, teacher and child: Discourses in developme–nt. In L. Diaz Soto (Ed.), *The politics of early childhood education* (Vol. 10, pp. 732). New York: Peter Lang.

Boardman, M. (2003, December). *Learning communities contribution to educational improvement: Joint participation for mutual gain in early childhood education.* Paper presented at the Annual Conference of the New Zealand Association for Research in Education and the Australian Association for Research in Education, Auckland, New Zealand.

Cannella, G. S. (1997). *Deconstructing early childhood education. Social justice and revolution.* New York: Peter Lang.

Carr, M. (2001). A sociocultural approach to learning orientation in an early childhood setting. *Qualitative Studies in Education, 14*(4), 525–542.

Dahlberg, G., Moss, P., & Pence, A. (2007). *Beyond quality in early childhood education and care: Languages of evaluation.* London: Routledge.

Douville-Watson, L., Watson, M. A., & Wilson, L. C. (2003). *Infants and toddlers. Curriculum and teaching.* New York: Delmar Learning.

Duncan, J. (2001). *Restructuring Lives: Kindergarten Teachers and the Education Reforms 1984–1996.* Unpublished thesis submitted for the degree of Doctor of Philosophy, University of Otago, Dunedin, New Zealand.

———. (2005). Two year olds in kindergarten: What are they doing there?! *The First Years: Ngā Tau* Tuatahi, 7(2), 4–9.

———. (2007a, September). *Kindergarten parents reflecting on their kindergartens 2006–2007: Discussion of findings—Work in progress.* Paper presented at the Ninth Early Childhood Convention, Rotorua, New Zealand.

———. (2007b). New Zealand kindergartens: Free or freely forgotten. International *Journal of Qualitative Studies in Education*, 20(3), 319–333.

Duncan, J., Dalli, C., & Lawrence, J. (2007). The changing face of kindergarten: A national picture of two-year-olds within kindergartens. New Zealand *Annual Review of Education*, 16(2006), 119–140.

Duncan, J., Dalli, C., Becker, R., Butcher, M., Foster, K., Hayes, K., et al. (2006). *Under three-year-olds in kindergartens: Children's experiences and teachers' practices.* Wellington: Teaching and Learning Research Initiative, NZCER.

Fleer, M. (2002). *Journeying back to the routes of socio-cultural theory: Rebuilding the theoretical roots of early childhood education.* Unpublished paper, Canberra University. Canberra, ACT.

———. (2003). Early childhood education as an evolving 'community of practice; or as lived 'social reproduction': Researching the 'taken-for-granted'. *Contemporary Issues in Early Childhood*, 4(1), 64–79.

Fleer, M., & Richardson, C. (2004). Moving from a constructivist-developmental framework for planning to a sociocultural approach: Foregrounding the tension between individual and community. *Journal of Australian Research in Early Childhood Education*, 11(2), 70–87.

Goodfellow, J. (2005). Researching with/for whom? Stepping in and out of practitioner research. *Australian Journal of Early Childhood*, 30(4), 48–57.

Goodfellow, J., & Hedges, H. (2007). Practitioner research 'centre stage': Contexts, contributions and challenges. In L. Kessing-Styles & H. Hedges (Eds.), *Theorising early childhood practice: Emerging dialogues* (pp. 187–207). Castle Hill: Pademelon Press.

Greenman, J. (2005). *Caring spaces, learning places. Children's environments that work.* Redmond, WA: Exchange Press Inc.

Lally, J. R., Griffin, A., Fenichel, E., Segal, M., Szanton, E., & Weissbourd, B. (1995). *Caring for infants and toddlers in groups: Developmentally appropriate practice.* Washington, DC: Zero to Three.

Loughran, J., & Northfield, J. (1998). A framework for the development of self-study practice. In M. L. Hamilton, S. Pinnegar, T. Russell, J. Lougran & V. LaBoskey (Eds.), *Reconceptualizing teaching practice: Self-study in teacher education* (pp. 7–18). London: Falmer Press.

McLeod, L. (2000). Early childhood practitioner research in New Zealand: Why? How? When? Where? and with whom? *International Journal of Early Childhood*, 32(1), 20–25.

Ministry of Education. (1996). *Te Whāriki: Early childhood curriculum. He Whāriki Matauranga no nga Mokopuna o Aotearoa.* Wellington, New Zealand: Learning Media.

Ministry of Education. (2007). *Early childhood education index, 2006.* New Zealand government. Retrieved 31 October, 2007, from http://www.minedu.govt.nz.

Mitchell, L. (2001, 24–28 September). *Early childhood education for citizenship: Using documentation to articulate practice.* Paper presented at the Teacher Refresher Course Committee course 'Strengthening the links. Learning and assessment in early childhood,' Auckland, New Zealand.

———. (2003, 22–25 September). *Children, staff and parents: Building respectful relationships in Australian and New Zealand early childhood education contexts.* Paper presented at the Eighth Early Childhood Convention, Palmerston North, New Zealand.

Moore, G. (2001). Designed environments for young children: Empirical findings and implications for planning and design. In M. M. Gollop and J. McCormack (Eds.), children and young people's environments (pp. 53–63). Dunedin, NZ: Children's Issues Centre.

Ponte, P., Ax, J., Beijaard, D., & Wubbels, T. (2004). Teachers' development of professional knowledge through action research and the facilitation of this by teacher educators. *Teaching and Teacher Education, 20,* 571–588.

Potter, G. (2001). The power of collaborative research in teacher's professional development. *Australian Journal of Early Childhood Education, 26*(2), 8–13.

Rowling, J. K. (2000). *Harry Potter and the Goblet of Fire.* London: Bloomsbury.

Wenger, E. (1998). *Communities of practice.* Cambridge: Cambridge University Press.

12 Fairness in Participation in Preschool[1]

Artin Göncü, Catherine Main and Barbara Abel

This chapter presents our conceptualization of fairness in the education of young preschool children. Our central goal is to provide a description and meaning of fair practices in the classroom experiences of children. By adopting a sociocultural approach, we discuss the construction of fairness in the classroom in relation to social and cultural contexts of children's development and in relation to institutional and scholarly context of teacher education.

Sociocultural research that expanded Vygotsky's theory (1978) has made two significant contributions to our understanding about young children's development and learning as it also guided future work such as the one reported in this chapter. First, consistent with the claims of other prominent theorists such as Piaget (1965), sociocultural research showed that children take an active role in organizing their own learning experiences. Second and equally importantly, it illustrated that children appropriate knowledge and skills that are necessary for their survival by participating in activities that are arranged for them by their cultural communities. By extension, thus, sociocultural work showed that there are variations both in the types of activities that are available to children in different communities and also the ways in which children participate in and appropriate from the same kinds of activities (Göncü, 1999; Rogoff, 1990; 2003; Tudge, 2008). For example, we described (Göncü, Mistry, & Mosier, 2000; Rogoff, Mistry, Göncü, & Moiser, 1993) how the meaning and use of play in caregiver-child collaborations vary across urban and rural communities. The caregivers in urban communities in Kecioren, Ankara (Turkey) and Salt Lake City, Utah (USA) participated in their children's play as their children's peers while the caregivers in rural communities in Dhol-Ki-Patti, Rajastan (India) and San Pedro (Guatemala) either thought of playing with their children as inappropriate or expressed constraints that prohibited them from participating in such activities.

We feel that this kind of contribution is significant. However, the sociocultural approach has not yet addressed the following four points that have relevance for the construction of fair classroom practices leaving them open for future work. First, the existing sociocultural views rightly focus on the inherently social nature of learning and, as part of this stance, consider children's participation in their communal activities without assessing it. Thus, unless qualified, the sociocultural stance can be interpreted as welcoming all cultural practices as legitimate, possibly leading to the expectation that schools should incorporate them as such. This possibility requires that early childhood educators consider what is fair practice by taking into account the priorities of both the home and the school cultures.

Second, much of the existing research presents comparisons of fairly homogenous cultural communities where variations within a given community are not examined as much as variations across communities (Tudge, 2008). Perhaps in previous research the focus on between-group differences was necessary in stressing the significance of cultural context in children's learning. However, a focus on within-community variations and their relevance to establishing fairness and legitimacy in children's participation in their activities is inevitable.

Third, sociocultural research often focused on cultural communities without paying particular attention to other communities such as classrooms. Also, as is the case in the study of cultural communities, work on the classroom communities focused on homogenous communities. For example, Rogoff and colleagues described how children, teachers, parents, and school administrators participated in the education of children in Salt Lake City, Utah where the participants shared similar values about children's education (Rogoff, Turkanis, & Bartlett, 2001). As the authors themselves acknowledged (Rogoff, Matusov, & White, 1996), their work described the practice in a middle class community in the United States. While this work illustrated the significance of participation by all involved in children's education, it has not addressed how fairness in participation in classrooms is achieved populated by children from different cultural, social class, and special needs backgrounds.

Fourth and finally, previous sociocultural research on children's schooling mostly focused on the participation of children in their educational activities in the primary grades (e.g., Cole, 1995; Rogoff et al., 2001). There has been a paucity of work on the participation of toddlers and preschool children in their educational experiences, leaving open for future work the examination how to establish fairness in young children's classrooms.

It is important to note that the sociocultural approach is not the only one that has left the issue of fairness in participation unexamined. Many approaches to early childhood education that espouse developmentally appropriate practices have not explicitly conceptualized how children's cultural, social class, and individual differences should be taken into account in constructing fairness in their participation of classroom activities. In these approaches, the extent to which classroom diversity is addressed relates to teachers sensitively guiding children according to children's learning needs. However, how such guidance takes place and what role children and their families play in this kind of guidance remains unaddressed.

In view of these considerations, our goal in this chapter is to present a framework for insuring fairness in children's participation in the preschool classrooms. Our discussion is based on our work with children aged three to five years in Chicago, Illinois, USA. We conceptualize fairness as constructing a sense of community in collaboration with children that supports children's development and education according to their individual needs rather than according to the provision of "equal opportunity." In the following sections of this chapter, we first present the philosophical stance that we take in our effort to elaborate what participation means for us and how we assure it. By drawing from Dewey (1916/1966), we discuss the significance of participation and the fair ways of assuring it. After that, we describe the features of a teacher education program in early childhood education at the University of Illinois at Chicago (UIC), construction and transformation of which is accomplished by all three of us. In this part, we state how we integrate Dewey's philosophy with the theories of Piaget (1945, 1965) and Vygotsky (1978) in order to establish a perspective that takes into account children's developmental needs in relation to their social and cultural backgrounds. This perspective describes two features of our program. One is that our program is the only "blended" program in Illinois that considers the education of typically developing children and the education of children with disabilities. The other feature is that the program is designed to address the needs of children of color who might be categorized as low income and living in underserved communities. In keeping with the goal of this chapter, this section summarizes the evolution of how we convey to our prospective teachers the philosophy of the program and ways of implementing it in the classrooms. Finally, we offer insights about specific classroom activities that we tailor according to children's needs in securing their participation. We proffer that play, conflict-resolution, group games, and group time activities especially enable children to engage in dialogue in constructing a fair classroom community where participation is secured for all involved. We end the chapter with an invitation for future dialogue.

CONCEPTUALIZING FAIRNESS IN PARTICIPATION

Fairness in participation has often been discussed in reference to democracy that has long been fundamental to defining the goals of education in the United States and in other societies. As a reflection of our constantly changing society, the discourse of and emphasis given to democracy and education in the United States have evolved and changed over the years. Even during our contemporary times, the early childhood classrooms house differing democratic practices that reflect the educational frameworks adopted by the schools. Despite the variations, however, where practiced, democracy is often understood as children's rights to voice their opinions about matters that relate to their educational experiences. Moreover, with older preschoolers (i.e., four and five year olds), democracy is understood as children's rights to vote about matters that relate to the entire class when consensus cannot be reached. As such, this tacit understanding of democracy embodies the assumption that the participants in an early childhood classroom practice it in a manner similar to that of adults.

However reasonable these understandings may appear, they do not easily apply to early childhood classrooms and call for explicit discussions of the following three points. In the first place, accepting children's rights to voice their opinions about their own education in collaboration with adults necessitates bringing discussions about democracy and participation to the fore in order to understand under what circumstances and how adults consider children's ideas. In the most ideal world, this discussion enables the teachers to examine power differences between themselves and the children. Ultimately, it calls on teachers to insure children's engagement in decision making as members of the classroom community. Second, in view of developmental, cultural, and individual differences with which young children populate early childhood classrooms, a one-size-fits-all notion of democracy without qualifying its practice according to children's understandings and needs renders meaningless. For instance, children at all ages do not know the meaning of democracy or voting and thus voting may not necessarily be a fair practice. Therefore, we need to see children's understanding of democracy as a developmental process and institute it in view of children's capacities. Third, in order for democratic principles to be functional, young children must be socialized into a world of classroom community with shared developmental goals, values, morals, and technology. Children must understand that individual and community functioning mutually constitute one another with each one influencing the functioning of the other. The shared understandings serve as a guide in determining the kind of support each child needs for him/her to reach the goals of development adopted for that group as well as establishing realistic expectations about how that child can contribute to the advancement of that classroom community. Some children may require more assistance in reaching the developmental goals or voicing their opinions than others, thus, voting or taking equal number of turns may not be the fair practice. One turn for every child is not always what's fair, for some children may not want a turn while others need more.

In our Early Childhood Program at UIC, our concerns regarding how we can best assist children to take an active role in the construction of a classroom community through which they support their own and their peers' development in a fair manner led us to Dewey (1916/1966) who viewed the school as a democratic society and the classrooms within it as microcosms of that society. For Dewey, the school had the potential and responsibility to represent the ideal values of a democracy rather than replicate the existing values of the broader society (Weber, 1984). Central to Dewey's concept of the ideal democratic community is communication. According to Dewey, "The communication which insures participation in a common understanding is one which secures similar emotional and intellectual dispositions" (p. 4).

In the way we interpret Dewey, communication is the central building block of community when it is mutual and constructed with the tacit or explicit goal of establishing shared meanings. In our view, communication involving mutuality begins with prolepsis—the assumption that the conversants are familiar with the references introduced to the dialogue and are committed to negotiation of ideas in communication with honesty (cf., Göncü, 1993; Rommetveit, 1979). In the case of working with young children, communication also involves engaging children in dialogue about matters that are directly relevant to them as well as familiar. The trust assumed in the interaction and the relevant knowledge the conversants are expected to have lead to negotiation of ideas that result in development of shared understandings and ideals that emerge through ongoing participation by all involved. Thus, establishment of communication with mutuality requires us to provide opportunities for children to share their knowledge and experiences, to actively engage in planning, inquiry, investigation and collaboration, problem-solving, play, and above all reflection. In classrooms where communication is prioritized in this way communities with shared goals for development are established despite differences among the members (Cuffaro, 1995; DeVries & Zan, 1994; Fitzgerald & Göncü, 1993; Rogoff et al., 2001).

We believe that mutuality in communication with young children requires early childhood educators to insure that children feel safe and secure in the classroom. The teachers can accomplish this both through their direct communication with the children in the classroom and through their communication with children's families. Regarding the former, as we elaborated elsewhere (Göncü, Abel, & Boshans, in press), children will engage in dialogue in the classroom only if their attachment and exploration needs are met. Teachers provide safety and security by making themselves directly available for children to refer to them and their peers at times of threat and trouble. As well, teachers insure safety by creating classroom environments that are consistent, predictable, and accessible. This will enable children to have control over the psychological and physical environment of the classroom, and thus will lead to safety and dialogue with others about their interests and needs. In turn, the communication on individual needs will branch into negotiation of how to satisfy them in relation to other children's needs. As a result, they will develop notions of fairness and community simultaneously from negotiating their individual needs and satisfying them with one another. They will understand that they have different needs that require more or less support and that meeting the needs will be accomplished in a manner consistent with the needs (Kaiser & Rasminsky, 2003). For example, a child who always gets to sit next to the teacher in order to participate in group-time will not be viewed as getting a special privilege but rather getting what she needs. Children will see this kind of accommodation not as an exception but as what is fair.

Regarding teachers' communication with children's families, this is essential both in order to understand children's attachment needs and also to understand what children's cultural communities value about children's education and how they inform and guide children's actual learning activities. Communication with families becomes especially critical when schools serve children from diverse backgrounds. As Heath (1983) suggests, communication with families allows us to understand *their ways of knowing* and the meanings behind the specific ways of knowing paramount in each cultural community. Understanding children's cultural practices and the meanings that underlie them enables us to construct bridges between home and school practices and children's participation in the classroom activities.

Unfortunately, work conducted in our program indicates that often schools do not value what families have to offer or involve families in their children's education. When families are involved they are often expected to adopt school values and practice them as passive recipients (Fitzgerald & Göncü, 1993; Pons-Clifford, 2007). That is, mutuality in communication does not exist. What Gonzales, Moll, and Amanti call (2005) funds of knowledge that children and families can bring to school from homes in constructing a school community that incorporates family curriculum is not enabled. This, in turn, results in the families' feeling of alienation from schools, and possibly children's not being able to participate in the classroom activities or benefiting from them. Thus, we feel that we need to rethink family involvement to include the development of relationships between teachers and parents that invite and honor the private and tacit sharing of goals, priorities, expectations, and values that each has for the child. In other words, we need to understand how children's direct participation in the life of their school, home, and community work together in order to help children learn the skills and attitudes necessary for their active and fair participation in school. The need to achieve this kind of understanding becomes all the more essential in view of the findings that mutual communication between families and schools lead to advances in children's social and cognitive growth and acquisition of skills in addition to learning to function in different contexts of their society (Pons-Clifford, 2008).

In summary, we claim that fairness in participation is accomplished only by considering children's interests and needs that should be taken into account in children's social and cultural contexts. When we do so, not only do we enable children to negotiate their idiosyncratic individual needs but also allow them to negotiate their cultural values and practices in their effort to contribute to the construction of a community with shared meanings despite their differences. In the words of Dewey (1916/1966), "The extension in space of the number of individuals who participate in an interest so that each has to refer his own action to that of others, and to consider the action of others to give point and direction to his own, is equivalent to the breaking down of those barriers of class, race, and national territory which kept men from perceiving the full import of their activity (p. 87).

CONSTRUCTING FAIRNESS IN A TEACHER EDUCATION PROGRAM: THE EARLY CHILDHOOD PROGRAM AT UIC

In this section, we narrate the evolution of our notion of fairness with a focus on the developmental theories that guided our work and the coursework that was designed to represent it. We first describe the Piagetian constructivist approach that provided the foundation for us. Afterwards, we state how and why we transformed our practice to include Vygotsky's theory. Finally, we describe how we constructed our "blended program" that serves typically developing children and children with disabilities.

Initially, consistent with Piaget (1945, 1965) and drawing from Kamii and DeVries (1977) who applied Piaget's theory to early education, we maintained that construction of knowledge is possible only when the need to explore the world emerges from within the learners. We believed that the learners must actively engage in the exploration in order to appropriate meaning from that experience on their own. This concept of educating young children led us to emphasize teacher's roles as providing opportunities for children to construct physical, mathematical-logical, and social knowledge in activities that were of inherent interest to children. Moreover, we encouraged the teachers to guide children's activities through open-ended questions and suggestions rather than explicit instructions. For example, in playing a board game requiring moving along a path, if the children did not count the spaces accurately, the teachers were asked not to provide the answer even if the children requested the information from the teacher. Rather, the teachers encouraged the participants to come up with the answer on their own through discussion. It was believed that cooperation among peers of equal power and status enables children to explore the possibilities, and ultimately leads to the correct answer. In this way children develop autonomy about what they want to know and how they want to learn it with minimal adult authority or direction.

We adopted this constructivist stance to educating young children based on the belief that this practice was fair for a number of reasons. For one thing, we share the conviction that young preschool children learn by actively participating in their activities, therefore, making provisions for such participation in activities of interest is fair practice. For another, when teachers presented themselves to the children as companions by reducing their authority, they agreed to function on the same fair level with children. These insights combined with Piaget's central claim that children's construction of knowledge follows universal patterns reified the perspective that Piaget's was the only fair theoretical perspective that called for its adoption.

We conveyed this perspective to our students as part of their two-year course work that included one course on Piaget's theory, one practicum, and one student teaching course. A notable feature of the program was that the students were required to do their practicum and student teaching in schools of our own choosing that followed the same constructivist perspective as ours. Usually, those schools were university based laboratory schools or private schools in addition to some select Chicago Public Schools. We felt that following our theoretical premise in schools in which we had trust as providing the best applied arena for the education of our students was also fair.

However, over time in view of increasing scholarly advances about the cultural and contextual nature of learning and development, and the needs of young children in Chicago, we began to question both our understanding and application of fairness based on Piagetian principles. We observed that the constructivist philosophy is biased towards middle class values that were accepted without critical examination. For example, primarily relying on children's initiatives may not always be the fairest practice since sometimes learners may need the teacher to initiate the activities for them (Delpit, 2006; Rogoff et al, 2001). Moreover, some of children's proposals may not be a part of legitimate preschool curriculum and are also upsetting to other children and teachers alike. For example, children's initiatives and questions about sexuality, violence, and drugs are often troubling to teachers and are therefore unfairly dismissed.

In addition, we observed that guiding children by asking questions without greater structure may be a disservice to children when they need direction, structure, and support. Not having the flexibility to work with children through different dialogic means proved to be especially problematic for children who come from homes where the guidance was provided mostly through explicit directions. In a similar vein, we observed that autonomous functioning has different meanings and is achieved through different kinds of communication in different cultural communities. We realized that unless we accept that children come from communities with varying notions of identity, inter-dependence, and agency, and achieve these with varying kinds of communication, we would not be serving them fairly by imposing our own understandings on them.

In keeping with these realizations, we also recognized that the schools in which our teacher candidates did their practicum and student teaching work may have been limiting as they did not introduce teacher candidates to the diversity of children that is paramount to living in a major metropolis. Therefore, in light of these insights, we sought to transform our constructivist stance that took into account diversity in children's and their families' functioning.

To address our concerns, we turned to the theory of Vygotsky (1978) and the work of scholars who have been influenced by him (e.g., Cole, 1995; Rogoff & Wertsch, 1984). In this process, our simultaneous considerations of the theories of Piaget and Vygotksy revealed significant similarities regarding the applications of these theories to educational practice. For instance, both men emphasized the significance of individual's construction of knowledge. Encouraged by this similarity, we maintained our commitment to constructivist approach but nuanced in the following ways.

Vygotsky's concept of the zone of proximal development and sociocultural research that expanded this concept provided a framework for us to explore what would be the fair practice in the preschool classrooms. The most significant finding that guided our transformation was that children come from cultural communities in which their learning is guided in their zones of proximal development in ways that reflect the values and priorities of their communities. Such cultural guidance may not always be consistent with the school practices, sometimes requiring teachers' adoption of a range of curricular and instructional strategies that are appropriate to the background and age of the children they teach. This may mean guiding children's learning not only in activities that they choose but also in activities chosen by families. Also, children's work with teachers and peers may take place in collaborations involving explicit guidance where relevant and appropriate. For example, sometimes the fair practice involves offering children the correct answer, for not doing so may lead children to apathy and doubt about the "availability" of the teacher. Finally, where there are irreconcilable differences between school and home practices, the schools need to engage in dialogue with families negotiating a mutually acceptable educational experience for children.

Incorporation of these insights into our teacher education program meant making substantive changes both in the course work at the University and also in the applied work with teacher candidates in the field. Long lasting dialogues among the faculty in the program resulted in the transformation of the theory course so that it included both Piaget's and Vygotsky's theories. Also, we developed a new course on collaborating with the families in order to make use of their funds of knowledge both in curriculum construction and in engaging in communication that is meaningful to young children.

Moreover, we broadened the practicum and student teaching placements so that our students have opportunities to work with children and families who are different from themselves. This way we serve the communities in Chicago in a more inclusive manner as we also aim to learn from them so that we can advance our practice in response to their needs. This expansion of placements presented us and our students with the need to consider issues of fairness beyond the classroom and the relationships among teachers and children to include the larger system of Chicago Public Schools. We expected and saw vast differences across schools with regard to physical environments, quality of teachers, support from administrators, attitudes toward parents, and levels of collaboration among school staff, community members, and parents, but it was the underlying philosophies of some schools that posed the greatest challenges and were often in direct opposition to the ideas about teaching and learning that were part of our program. Some schools espoused slogans such as "children are buckets, we pour in the knowledge," others were so heavily focused on preparing children for standardized tests that ideas and interests of the children were rarely included in any part of the curriculum. In view of these and in keeping with Dewey, we decided to see our work as ever-evolving in a system of communications that included children, their schools, their communities, and the institutions of higher education.

Our effort to provide fair practice to the children and communities led us to the third transformation of the program philosophy whereby we changed our program to include the education of children with and without disabilities together—in a blended manner. Admittedly, this decision was in response to changes in federal and state law, local educational practices, and newly created professional standards for early childhood teachers. However, it also had its roots in our commitment to provide educational experiences for children in inclusive settings where they benefit from collaborating with one another. This commitment found support in our work with early childhood teachers in schools and community agencies. They shared our conviction to educate children with and without disabilities in the same setting but they did not feel prepared to address the diverse needs of *all* young children together. For us, this meant that our job was no longer a matter of preparing either Early Childhood teachers or Early Childhood Special Education teachers, but rather teachers who were committed to and prepared to work with and include *all* young children regardless of ability. Not only did we believe that children with disabilities have the right to fully participate in education programs with their non-disabled peers, but we felt as teacher educators we had the responsibility for implementing inclusive programs for young children. This sentiment echoed Miller's (1992) argument that teacher education programs that prepared teachers to work with just one population or another were "contradictory to all legal, philosophical, empirical, economic, and moral reasoning in early childhood education" (p. 39).

In order to prepare teacher candidates who can effectively address the educational needs of children from different social class and cultural backgrounds as well as ability status fully, we engaged in collaborations with our colleagues in the Department of Special Education. This collaboration resulted in long term work of reviewing our course and applied work and carefully revising it. For one thing, we have added new courses into our program that addressed the characteristics, needs, and development of children with disabilities. For another, we have revised the course on family involvement so that it covered the needs and concerns of families with children who have disabilities. As well, we have completely revised our foundation courses such as the history and philosophy of early education to include all the relevant scholarly, legal, psychological, and educational knowledge that is relevant to the education of children with disabilities. With regard to practicum and student teaching experiences, we now place our teacher candidates in a variety of settings that include children from different ages and communities as well as children with and without disabilities. The expansion of settings that include children with disabilities further challenge us and our students as we navigate working in classrooms where behaviorism is often the underlying theory for teaching and learning. Moreover, the IEP process often prioritizes achievement of individual goals without consideration of the child's life within the classroom context. This raises issues of fairness both in terms of segregation (e.g., pull-out) and with regard to providing the kinds of support that help the children to be more active participants in the classroom community. It also challenges teachers in working toward achieving fairness in the ways we've presented throughout this chapter.

In summary, our commitment to establish fair educational experiences for children of Chicago led us to consider all young children's experiences in the classrooms and schools and thus led to changes both in the theoretical and applied work we provide for the teacher candidates in our program. This inclusive model and perspective is not limited to preparing teachers to meet the diverse learning needs of typically and atypically developing children, but also to serving children from low-income urban communities whose opportunities for participation are often challenged by the very social and economic forces that espouse to help them, including the schools. While maintaining our constructive stance to early childhood education we now subscribe to a sociocultural perspective where we believe that the appropriateness and fairness of children's educational experiences and their deliverance should be determined in relation to the cultural meaning and economical contexts in which children are raised. This current stance is consistent with and finds support in the current mission of our College of Education that emphasizes a commitment to preparing teachers to work with children and families who are least well-served by the nation's educational institutions, particularly those in urban environments including children with disabilities.[2] In reflecting Dewey and sharing the College's conceptual framework we echo that democratic societies are best served by an educated citizenry of teachers who are fulfilling their human potential, who are dedicated to informed, honest, and earnest criticism, open-mindedness, and inclusiveness, and who are able to use their knowledge effectively. We work in this spirit and aim to educate teachers and children who would resonate with this view.

CONSTRUCTING FAIRNESS IN THE PRESCHOOL

We now turn to specific activities with direct relevance to constructing practices that are fair to children and their communities as well as those that encourage children to consider fairness in participation of their classroom community. Our focus is on children's peer interactions and teacher-child interactions that put greater responsibility on the classroom community in constructing fairness than other activities and interactions.

With regard to peer interaction, one activity of relevance is children's play with their peers. After over two decades of extensive work in different capacities including working with young preschool children in different communities of the world, serving as teachers of preschool children, or working as teacher educators in the program in which we teach, we have come to realize that fair practice should include affording children opportunities for play and exploration. This conviction finds support in many educational philosophies (e.g., Dewey) and in prominent developmental theories (e.g., Erikson, Freud, Piaget, & Vygotsky) that focus on cognitive, affective, and communicative aspects of human functioning (cf., Göncü et al., in press).

A shared thesis among the developmental theorists is that play is an arena of growth. In play, children re-interpret past events and anticipate future events in their lives. Play affords children the opportunity to manipulate their worlds and experiences in their effort to test their understandings of how the world around them is constructed. Vygotsky emphasized this role of play as a learning opportunity by calling play a leading activity. Play serves as a zone of proximal development (ZPD) in which children guide their development on their own without a need for more competent members of their communities. This idea of play as a ZPD is best illustrated in Vygotsky's example of two sisters pretending to be sisters in order to test their understanding of this role. This insight combined with the research findings that play leads to gains in children's problem solving abilities and socialization into the world of peers and adults require that we incorporate play as the focus of preschool education.

Additionally, a shared conviction among many theorists (e.g., Erikson, Freud, Winnicott) is that play is a therapeutic medium for children to heal their affective wounds caused by the experiences in the "real" world (cf., Göncü et al., in press). In this sense, honoring the initiatives of children is critical in order to create fairness and participation in the classroom regardless of how challenging their proposals may be. For example, Catherine Main (author) was confronted with a play scenario involving children engaged in a number of scary events including getting chased by the police and getting arrested. She discovered that the child who initiated the play scenario actually witnessed similar events the night before with his family. In recognition of the therapeutic value of this play for him, the teacher allowed the play episode to unfold. However, she worked with the school psychologist and the children in order to transform it so that it was experienced as safe and fair for all involved (for a fuller discussion of this incident see, Fleming, Lyon, Oei, Sheets, Valentine, & Williams, 1997).

As we have argued previously (Göncü, 1993; Göncü et al., in press), children's pretend play with peers often originates from their desire to share these kinds of affectively significant experiences with others. Such efforts begin around three years of age with the assumption that other children have similar experiences that they too may want to share. In testing their assumptions, children negotiate with one another the features of their experiences. Such negotiations enable children to develop play templates for their classroom community as they also familiarize children with one another's backgrounds. For example, when children pretend that they are being mothers, they negotiate their notions of motherhood with one another, and as a result, reach consensus about what this social role entails. As such, playing with peers leads to the construction of peer cultures with shared meanings.

One caveat is in order, however. Cultural communities vary in the significance that they attribute to play (cf., Göncü & Gaskins, 2007). For example, while middle class European-American communities often value play as a developmentally appropriate activity, Korean-American families see it as only as amusement, not an educationally valuable activity (Farver, 1999). Given these kinds of differences we feel that in instituting play in the classrooms, the early childhood educators should make an effort to understand what families think about play and in what contexts they feel it is appropriate. When disagreements emerge, it is the early childhood educators' responsibility to illustrate and negotiate the educational and developmental benefits of play as a fair practice and inevitable part of preschool education.

A second consequence of recognizing cultural differences in children's play is that there are many ways of engaging in it. For instance, pretend play may take place in many different ways and is not limited to object substitutions and role play activities as they are commonly observed in Western middle class communities. Research with non-Western or low income children illustrates that children from communities with oral traditions engage in pretend play using features of language such as teasing in addition to Western forms of play (Göncü, Jain, & Tuermer, 2007). By extension, in diverse classrooms we need to recognize variations in play and accept them without prohibitions in order to provide a fair chance to children from different social class and cultural backgrounds. This, in consort with Dewey, provides the potential to break social class, cultural, and racial barriers by allowing children to become familiar with and accept their differences.

In addition to play, we suggest using games with rules as part of a democratic classroom practice. Although games are a significant part of some preschool philosophies (e.g., Kamii & DeVries, 1977; Shapiro & Nager, 2000), many preschool programs do not make provisions for them. We feel that games are important activities for a number of reasons. Games with rules enable children to overcome their egocentrism by providing opportunities for children to coordinate their cognitive perspectives and developing greater capacities for empathy (Piaget, 1965). Also, as in play, games allow children to introduce features of their home culture into the classroom community. If children are allowed to introduce their home games into the classroom, they would be bringing funds of knowledge, and thus having a fair chance to own the classroom as the others.

Another area of preschool experience that emanates from play, games, and other peer collaborations that should be emphasized as fair practice relates to children's conflicts and their resolution, and the resultant development of rules by which children learn to regulate themselves. As Piaget stated (1965), conflicts with peers are an opportunity for children to overcome their egocentrism. Also, consistent with Vygotsky's theory (1978), conflicts present a problem-solving situation (Göncü & Cannella, 1996). Therefore, we feel that whenever children engage in conflict, they should be encouraged to address it by identifying the nature of their conflict and by taking into account one another's viewpoints as well as trying to reach a solution. This practice allows children to identify with one another regarding the substantive issue at stake as it also familiarizes them with one another's values and specific ways of communication on the way to constructing their classroom communities.

After having addressed the conflicts with the particular children involved, they should be presented to the entire class to receive feedback during group time. For example, when two children have a conflict over who would use the tricycle first, this should be brought to the attention of the entire class without identifying the children engaged in conflict. The group discussion then should involve fair ways of addressing and solving the conflicts and discussing how to prevent such conflicts from occurring in the future. Deriving rules from children's own experiences about matters that are relevant to them, and then posting them for their future reference establishes fair ways of participation and enables children to regulate their joint life.

With regard to teacher-child interaction, we believe that young children benefit from teaching only if it is embedded in safe and secure relationships with their teachers in activities of interest and relevance such as play and games. As a corollary, we feel that teachers need to flexibly adopt different communicative roles and acts depending on children's needs. This means that teachers should be able to move between communication as companions or as adults. For example, when playing a game, a teacher has the flexibility to act like a peer affording children freedom to make decisions. However, a teacher should assume a position of authority in insuring children's well-being in activities ranging from establishing prohibitions to taking responsibility for children's difficulties. One example of this comes from the experience of Barbara Abel (author) who was the teacher of three-year-old Samantha. When she first arrived in the classroom, Samantha appeared very comfortable, picking up classroom routines, easily engaging in the activities offered throughout the classroom, and in moving in and out of play with other children. The only sign of a possible difficulty was Samantha's high energy level and struggle to stay focused on anything for very long. After two weeks of starting in the program Samantha's attention span grew increasingly shorter and her behavior toward others often involved aggressive actions such as grabbing toys, pushing and hitting other children, and refusing to follow the routines that she seemed to enjoy so much when she first started.

Initially, these actions were interpreted as indications of her going through a period of adjustment—a process common to many children. To help her with this, the teachers followed Samantha for a few days to observe what kinds of situations provoked her aggressive behavior so that they could better meet her needs. As part of this process, the teachers observed Samantha take an interest in the sand table. She would bury the toy people and animals in the sand, completely covering them. Afterwards, she would methodically pull them out of the sand one by one, smiling broadly and saying "peek-a-boo" as she lifted them to eye level. Observing this and taking ownership of Samantha's ostensible difficulty with separation from her parents, Abel asked her if she was missing her mommy and daddy. Samantha's smile turned into a frown, she got very sad, and began to look at the wooden person she was holding in her hand. While she stared at the person, the other children started talking about how much they were missing their parents, and began to bury the people and animals just as Samantha had been doing. Slowly Samantha joined into the conversation, and resumed her play along with the others indicating that she was indeed missing her parents. This interpretation of the teacher was inevitable and allowed Samantha and other children to understand the source of their anxiety and recognize that this was a shared feeling to work through. As a result, the class began to include discussions about separation during circle-time, read books about separation, and made a concerted effort to look and talk about the family pictures on the wall that had been collected but then forgotten about.

Fairness in participation in teacher-child interaction also relates to cultural notions of what kind of communication is appropriate in different kinds of institutions and relationships. Western schooling always encourages explicit communication and instruction as opposed to nonverbal communication and tacit understandings. While we do not quarrel with this practice, we note that children's participation in and appropriation from activity may take place in nonverbal ways. As Rogoff, Paradise, Arauz, Correa-Chavez & Angelilo (2003) document children may participate and learn only through keen observation. Therefore, it is plausible that children may begin their schooling with such a cultural tradition. As a result, expecting children to participate in a verbal manner, and considering them as language delayed when they do not do so may be unfair. In view of these considerations, we think it fair to submit our proposals to children's families as what we deem appropriate for children. In turn, we listen to them about their priorities, and thus engaging in a process of negotiation at times of difference. This process of collaboration with families both enables them to understand the stance of early childhood educators and simultaneously provides opportunities to reflect on and adapt our practice.

CONCLUSIONS

In summary, our sociocultural stance to fairness in participation in pre-school classrooms stems from our concern to provide an optimal classroom environment for children who typically grow up in underserved communities classified as low-income and attend blended programs. In such classrooms, participation needs to be qualified according to the specific ways by which children can contribute to and benefit from the classroom community. For example, not all children come to school ready to address open-ended questions espoused by developmentally appropriate practices common in the United States. Children sometimes require guidance through more direct teacher assistance. Also, children with language delays or autism would require different kinds of guidance and support than that required by typically developing children. In a similar vein, we need to institute democracy and participation that is meaningful for children at different developmental levels. With young toddlers, practice of democracy may only involve a focus on turn-taking in conversation and sharing toys while with five-year-olds decisions can be reached through voting. Finally, we need to see practice of democracy as embedded in all school activities rather than in only those explicated in this chapter. Activities that do not receive major curricular attention such as transitions can also be used as opportunities for constructing principles of democracy, for they require functioning on the basis of common rules and routines.

In conclusion, we believe that early childhood educators just like the children whose education they aim to advance construct and function in a community. This community along with families regulates and guides the contributions individuals make to the study of children's development and education. In that spirit, we see this effort as our current contribution to the ongoing dialogue about how we can support children's socialization into the society in a manner that is relevant and fair.

NOTES

1. We acknowledge David Stovall for his helpful comments on an earlier version of this chapter.
2. Conceptual Framework of the preparation programs in Education under the Council on Teacher Education at UIC can be seen in its entirety at http://www.uic.edu/educ/cte/conceptframe.htm.

REFERENCES

Cole, M. (1995). Cultural-historical psychology: A meso-genetic approach. In L. M. W. Martin., K. Nelson., & E. Tobach (Eds.), *Sociocultural psychology: Theory and practice of doing and knowing* (pp. 168–204). New York: Cambridge.

Cuffaro, H. K. (1995). *Experimenting with the world: John Dewey and the early childhood classroom*. New York: Teachers College Press.

Delpit, L. (2006). Other people's children: Cultural conflict in the classroom. New York: New Press.

DeVries, R. & Zan, B. (1994). *Moral classrooms, moral children: creating a constructivist atmosphere in early education*. New York: Teachers College Press.

Dewey (1916/1966). Democracy and education. New York: Macmillan.

Farver, J. A. M. (1999). Activity setting analysis: A model for examining the role of culture in development. In A. Göncü (Ed.), *Children's engagement in the world: Sociocultural perspectives* (pp. 99–127). New York: Cambridge University Press.

Fleming, M., Lyon, G., Oei, T-Y., Sheets, R.H., Valentine, G., & Williams, E. (Eds.) (1997). *Starting small: Teaching tolerance in preschool and the early grades*. Southern Poverty Law Center, Montgomery, AL.

Fitzgerald, L., & Göncü, A. (1993). Parent involvement in urban early childhood education: A Vygotskyian approach. In S. Reifel (Ed.), *Advances in early education and day care* (pp. 197–212). Greenwich, CT: JAI Press.

Göncü, A. (1993). Development of intersubjectivity in the social pretend play of young children. *Human Development. 36*, 185–198.

———. (1999). (Ed.). *Children's engagement in the world: Sociocultural perspectives*. New York: Cambridge University Press.

Göncü, A., Abel, B., & Boshans, M. (2009). The role of attachment and play in young children's learning and development. In K. Littleton, C. Wood, & J. K. Staarman (Eds.), *Handbook of Educational Psychology: New Perspectives on Learning and Teaching*. Amsterdam: Elsevier.

Göncü, A., & Cannella, V. (1996). The role of teacher assistance in children's construction of intersubjectivity during conflict resolution. In M. Killen (Ed.), Autonomy and conflict resolution in adult-child and peer interactions: Variations and consequences (pp. 57–69). *New Directions for Child Development*. San Francisco: Jossey-Bass.

Goncu, A. and Gaskins, S. (Eds.) (2007). Play and development: Evolutionary, sociocultural and functional perspectives. Mahwah, NJ: Lawrence Erlbaum.

Göncü, A. Mistry, J., & Mosier, C. (2000). Cultural variations in the play of toddlers. *International Journal of Behavioral Development, 24*, 321–329.

Göncü, A., Jain, J. Tuermer, U. (2007). Children's play as cultural interpretation. In A. Göncü, and S. Gaskins (Eds.), *Play and Development: Evolutionary, Sociocultural, and Functional Perspectives* (pp. 155–178). Mahwah, NJ: LEA.

Gonzalez, N., Moll, L., & Amanti, C. (Eds.) (2005). *Funds of knowledge: Theorizing practice in households, communities, and classrooms*. Mahwah, NJ: Erlbaum.

Haight, L. W. (1999). The pragmatics of caregiver-child pretending at home: Understanding culturally specific socialization practices. In A. Göncü (Ed.), *Children's engagement in the world: Sociocultural perspectives* (pp.128–147). New York: Cambridge University Press.

Heath, S. B. (1983). *Ways with words: language, life, and work in communities and classrooms*. New York: Cambridge University Press.

Kaiser, B. & Rasminsky, J.S. (2003). *Challenging behavior in young children: Understanding, preventing, and responding effectively*. Boston, MA: Pearson Education.

Kamii, C. & DeVries, R. (1977). Piaget for early education. In M. C. Day & R. Parker, (Eds.), *Preschool in action* (pp. 365–420). Boston: Allyn & Bacon.

Miller, P. S. (1992). Segregated programs of teacher education in early childhood: Immoral and inefficient practice. *Topics in Early Childhood Special Education, 11* (4), 39–52.

Piaget, J. (1945). *Play, dreams, and imitation in childhood.* New York: Norton.
———. (1965). *The moral judgment of the child.* New York: Free Press.
Pons-Clifford, A. (2007). *Reexamining family involvement through the family perspective.* Qualifying paper submitted to the University of Illinois at Chicago.
Rogoff, B. (1990). Apprenticeship in thinking: Cognitive development in social context. New York: Oxford University Press.
———. (2003). *The cultural nature of human development.* New York: Oxford University Press.
Rogoff, B., Matusov, E., & White, C. (1996). Models of teaching and learning: Participation in a community of learners. In D. R. Olson & N. Torrance (Eds.) *The handbook of education and human development: New models of learning, teaching, and schooling* (pp. 388–414). Cambridge, Blackwell.
Rogoff, B., Mistry, J., Göncü, A., & Mosier, C. (1993). Guided participation in cultural activity by toddlers and caregivers. *Monographs of the Society for Research in Child development, 58* (1, Serial No. 183).
Rogoff, B., Paradise, R., Arauz, M. R., Correa-Chavez, M., & Angelilo, C. (2003). Firsthand learning through intent participation. *Annual Review of Psychology, 54,* 175–203.
Rogoff, B. Turkanis, C. B., & Bartlett, L. (Eds.). (2001). *Learning together: Children and adults in a school community.* New York: Oxford University Press.
Rogoff, B. & Wertsch, J. (Eds.). (1984). Children's learning in the "zone of proximal development." *New Directions for Child Development* (No. 23). San Francisco. Jossey-Bass.
Rommetveit, R. (1979). On the architecture of intersubjectivity. In R. Rommetveit, & R. M. Blaker (Eds.), *Studies of language, thought, and verbal communication* (pp. 147–161). New York: Academic Press.
Shapiro, E. K., & Nager, N. (2000). The developmental-interaction approach to education: Retrospect and prospect. In N. Nager & E. K. Shapiro (Eds.), *Revisiting a progressive pedagogy: The developmental interaction approach* (pp. 11–46). Albany, NY: State University of New York Press.
Tudge, J. (2008). *The everyday lives of young children: Culture, class, and child rearing in diverse societies.* New York: Cambridge University Press.
Vygotsky, L .S. (1978). *Mind in society.* Cambridge, MA: Harvard University Press.
Weber, E. (1984). *Ideas influencing early childhood education.* New York: Teachers College Press.

13 Contexts, Pedagogy and Participatory Learning
A Way Forward

Jo Brownlee[1]

This book contributes to the increasing professional and research interest in participatory and democratic approaches for working with young children in early childhood programs. It provides cross-national insights into three main themes: *political and social contexts, teacher perspectives,* and *pedagogy for participatory learning.* These insights advance our understanding about toddlers' experiences for democratic participation across a number of countries, namely the United Kingdom, Australia, New Zealand, the United States, Canada, Sweden, and Norway.

While each of these themes contributes substantially to the growing research and theory about toddlers' participatory learning, they do so in a relatively disconnected way. It is important to think about the interconnections that might exist between these themes to enhance our collective understanding about how young children engage in participatory learning. We need to know how *Political and social contexts, teacher perspectives,* and *pedagogies for participatory learning* intersect. How might policy and teacher perspectives, for example, mediate pedagogy for active citizenship and participatory values? This gap in our understanding might be addressed in future research by examining how teachers' perspectives and pedagogy mediate between children's learning and the broader political and social contexts.

The proposed linking of political and social contexts, teacher perspectives, and pedagogy for participatory learning supports an ecological approach to research into children's participatory learning by drawing together the multidisciplinary elements of policy analysis, teachers' beliefs, and child characteristics. An ecological approach is a useful way to conceptualize the relationships between these macro and micro influences on children's participatory learning (Bronfenbrenner, 1986) because it enables a broad range of cultural and social contexts to be addressed. The model described below in Figure 13.1. is presented as a way to take an ecological approach to children's participatory learning by considering the interconnections between *contexts, pedagogy,* and *participatory learning.*

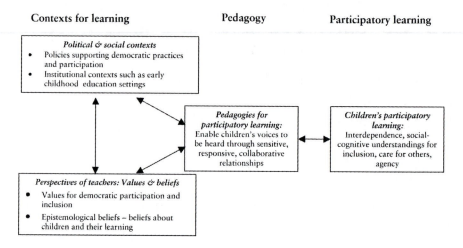

Figure 13.1   Contexts, pedagogy, and participatory learning.

Figure 13.1 identifies Contexts for learning as the first section of the model. These contexts for children's learning include the macro *Political and social contexts* as discussed in the chapters by Penn and Nyland. Penn contrasted the political and social contexts of Euro-North American and non Euro-American communities while Nyland discussed the United Nations Convention on the Rights of the Child (UNCRoC) as a policy context for participatory learning. *Contexts for learning* also include micro contexts that reflect *Perspectives of teachers*. In this model, we refer to teacher perspectives as values and beliefs. The focus on teachers' perspectives as a theme is evident in a number of chapters. Teachers' values for democratic participation and inclusion were described in the chapters written by Emilson and Johansson, as well as by Johansson. Teacher beliefs were referred to in Brownlee and Berthelsen's chapter as beliefs about learning and knowing (epistemological beliefs), while Duncan's chapter related to general pedagogical beliefs. The model shows, through the use of bi-directional arrows, that macro and micro contexts may interact to influence the enactment of pedagogy for participatory learning (the second section of the model). For example, a teacher's perspective (beliefs) on the nature of participatory learning may influence their perception of how policies should be implemented, and conversely the political landscape may impact on teacher's views about participatory learning.

The reciprocal interaction between teacher perspectives and broader political and social contexts may lead to the enactment of a range of *Pedagogies for participatory learning*, which is the second section of the model. However, the influence of contexts on pedagogy is not necessarily linear. A bi-directional relationship exists between pedagogy and contexts. For example, the pedagogical practices that teachers engage in may also influence what they believe about participatory learning (perspectives) as well as broader social and political thinking. Pedagogy for participatory learning, from a sociocultural perspective, enables children's voices to be heard through sensitive, responsive, and collaborative relationships. The focus on relationships in pedagogy was evident in the chapters written by Luff, McMullen and Dixon, Greve, Elliott, and Göncü, Main, and Abel.

Such pedagogies support *Children's participatory learning* for interdependence and for social-cognitive understandings of inclusion, care for others, and agency as described in the third section of the model. However, children also may have an influence on participatory pedagogy through co-participation. This two-way interaction means that the teacher and children are continually using each other's contributions in the process of learning (Muis, 2004). Such mutual constitution supports reciprocity in pedagogy rather than one-way, adult-oriented pedagogy. This means that the approach to pedagogy can be a factor in determining children's participatory learning but children can also influence pedagogy through co-participatory processes. The model, therefore, helps us to understand how teachers (perspectives-micro context) and their pedagogical practices mediate between children's participatory learning and the broader macro contexts (cf. Cobb, 1996, in Muis, 2004).

The model provides a framework for integrating *contexts, pedagogy,* and *participatory learning.* One particular approach that integrates these aspects of participatory learning is now presented as an example of how the proposed model might be used in future research. We know that children learn much about participatory learning through pedagogical practices in classrooms (Tomanovic, 2003); however we still do not know a great deal about how teachers enact these pedagogies in the classroom (Greenberg et al., 2003). There is a growing body of research indicating that teachers' perspectives related to children's learning and knowing (epistemological beliefs) are important in determining how a range of pedagogical practices are enacted (Entwistle, Skinner, Entwistle, & Orr, 2000; Hofer & Pintrich, 1997). Reflecting on the model presented in Figure 13.1., this body of research may offer insights into how teachers' beliefs (micro context) relate to the enactment of pedagogy for participatory learning, and ultimately children's learning.

Teachers' perspectives about children's learning and knowing may be described using a framework developed by Kuhn and Weinstock (2002). This represents just one of many frameworks that report on a similar range of epistemological beliefs (see also Baxter Magolda, 1994; Belenky et al., 1986). *Objectivism* refers to beliefs that absolute truths exist and can be transmitted to others in a one-way, instructivist approach to teaching. In addition to objectivist beliefs, individuals may also hold *subjectivist* viewpoints in which knowledge is characterized by the development of personal opinions. Learning from this perspective is often based on intuition or "gut" feelings. While individuals with subjectivist beliefs may construct a personal opinion, they do not evaluate a wide range of evidence to do so. Individuals with *evaluativist* beliefs, on the other hand, construct informed opinions by weighing up a range of different types of evidence. This means that knowledge is changeable and judgments are based on evaluation of evidence (Kuhn & Weinstock, 2002).

Teachers with *evaluativistic* perspectives about children's learning are likely to support democratic values based on connections with others and sharing of power with children because they believe there is no ultimate authority on knowledge. Further, knowledge about moral values are socially constructed through a process of weighing evidence from different points of view, including those of children. Such perspectives of learning are necessary in the promotion of participatory learning. Alternatively, teachers with more *objectivist* perspectives would be less likely to share power in learning situations because learning is viewed as transmission of information. Others' perspectives, including those of children, would be less valued. Such objectivist views about children's learning do not promote participatory learning because children are not encouraged to engage "with others in shaping decisions affecting themselves, groups of which they are members and the wider society" (Moss, 2006, p. 1).

Using the model described in Figure 13.1., teachers' perspectives on children's learning and knowing are likely to impact on pedagogical practices within broader macro contexts (political and social contexts). Although policy research acknowledges the significance of individuals ignoring, reinterpreting, and misinterpreting policy, there has been limited research investigating how teachers' perspectives, particularly in regard to children's learning and knowing, might relate to the enactment of policy. For example, how might a teacher with an objectivist epistemological stance interpret policies for participatory learning? Are they likely to interpret an imperative to promote agency as merely some form of active learning that is devoid of reciprocity in teacher-child interactions? Thus, it may be useful to find out more about how teachers' perspectives might influence interpretation of policy for participatory learning in young children.

While effective policies can enable teachers and schools to support young children's emotional, cognitive, and behavioral engagement in schooling (Fredricks, Blumenfeld, & Paris, 2004), often policy for active citizenship is focused away from the early years. For example, in Australia there is strong social and political interest in values education (DEST, 2003a; 2003b) but limited research in the early years. Rather, the major research emphasis has been on students' participatory learning in upper primary and secondary schooling. Sweden and many other Nordic countries, on the other hand, are currently leading the way in investigating how young children learn about active citizenship (Osler& Starkey, 2006). It is for this reason that further research not only needs to take an integrated approach using the model presented in Figure 13.1., but also needs to be international in nature. This will enable us to use comparative data to better understand young children's participatory learning from an integrated approach using policy, perspectives, and pedagogy.

NOTE

1. I wish to acknowledge the input of Dr. Sue Walker, Dr. Jo Ailwood, Professor Gillian Boulton-Lewis to this section.

REFERENCES

Baxter Magolda, M. B. (1994). Post-college experiences and epistemology. *Review of Higher Education, 18*(1), 25–44.

Belenky, M. F., Clinchy, B. M., Goldberger, N. R., & Tarule, J. M. (1986). *Women's ways of knowing: The development of self, voice and mind.* New York: Basic Books.

Bronfenbrenner, U. (1986). Ecology of the family in the context of human development: Research perspectives. *Developmental Psychology, 22,* 723–742.

Department of Education, Science and Training. (DEST) (2003a). *Evaluation of the discovering democracy programme.* Canberra, ACT: Australian Government.

Department of Education, Science and Training. (DEST) (2003b). *Values education study final report.* Canberra, ACT: Australian Government.

Entwistle, N., Skinner, D., Entwistle, D., & Orr, S. (2000). Conceptions and beliefs about "good teaching": An integration of contrasting research areas. *Higher Education Research & Development. 19*(1), 5–26.

Fredricks, J. A., Blumenfeld, P., C., & Paris, A. (2004). School engagement: Potential of the concept, state of the evidence. *Review of educational Research, 74*(1), 59–109.

Greenberg, M., Weissberg, R., O'Brien, M., Zins, J., Fredericks, L., Resnick, H., & Elias, M. (2003). Enhancing school-based prevention and youth development through co-ordinated social, emotional and academic learning. *American Psychologist, 58(6/7)*, 466–474.

Hofer, B., & Pintrich, P. R. (1997). The development of epistemological theories: Beliefs about knowledge and knowing and their relation to learning. *Review of Educational Research, 67(1),* 88–144.

Kuhn, D., & Weinstock, M. (2002). What is epistemological thinking and why does it matter? In B. Hofer & P. Pintrich (Eds.) *Personal Epistemology: The psychological beliefs about knowledge and knowing.* Mahwah, NJ: Lawrence Erlbaum.

Moss, P. (2006, August). *Bringing Politics into the Nursery: Early Childhood Education as a democratic practice.* Keynote address presented at the 16th Annual European Early Childhood Research Association conference, Reykjavik, Iceland.

Muis, K. (2004). Personal Epistemology and Mathematics: A Critical Review and Synthesis of Research. *Review of Educational Research, 74(3)*, 317–378.

Osler, A. & Starkey, H. (2006). Education for democratic citizenship: a review of research, policy and practice 1995–2005. *Research Papers in Education, 21 (4)*, 433–466.

Tomanovic, S. (2003). Negotiating children's participation and autonomy within families. *International Journal of Children's Rights, 11,* 51–71.

Contributors

Barbara Abel is a Research Associate and Visiting Associate Professor at University of Illinois at Chicago (UIC). For the past twenty years her work has focused on designing and directing child care programs for children from birth to five in different cultural communities in the United States. Presently she is conducting a research study with Artin Göncü, funded by the Spencer Foundation, on the development of self-regulation from a cultural perspective with the purpose of unpacking how children learn to integrate and cope with the contradictory educational and developmental demands of home and school.

Donna Berthelsen is an Associate Professor in the School of Early Childhood at Queensland University of Technology in Australia. She is an experienced early childhood researcher and a leader on three major research projects. In the Longitudinal Study of Australian Children (LSAC) she is the design team leader for educational measurement and a member of the child functioning and child care measurement teams. She is a National Evaluator on a music therapy early intervention program, *Sing & Grow,* which is a family support program for parents who have children aged less than three years. She is also a chief investigator on two Australian Research Council Discovery Grants. One project focuses on the professional beliefs and practice of child care workers and the other project is on the transition to school of young children with disabilities.

Jo Brownlee is an Associate Professor in the School of Early Childhood, Queensland University of Technology in Australia. Her current research investigates early childhood professionals' personal epistemology and the impact of such beliefs about knowing, learning, and teaching on early childhood practice. This research is important because there are implications for such beliefs on quality in child care.

Susan Dixon is part of the team at the Early Childhood Center at Indiana University's Indiana Institute on Disability and Community where she is involved in research, writing, and training pre-service and in-service early childhood professionals. In addition, she works directly with children and families as a speech and language pathologist with Indiana's Early Intervention System and in the local public schools.

Judith Duncan is an Associate Professor in Education at the University of Canterbury, Christchurch New Zealand. When this study was carried out she was a Senior Lecturer at the Children's Issues Centre and the College of Education, University of Otago. Judith is an established researcher with over 15 years of research experience, predominantly using qualitative research methods in early childhood education settings, both in national and international contexts. Judith has a background of kindergarten teaching and lecturing in early childhood education. She is currently working on a variety of early childhood research projects which examine children's and teachers' experiences, and teaching and learning in a range of early childhood settings.

Enid Elliot is a practitioner/researcher with considerable experience with babies, she is interested in the bridge between practice and theory and listening carefully to the narratives of caregivers. As an adjunct assistant professor at the University of Victoria, British Columbia in Canada she advocates for the inclusion of the practitioner voice. She has recently published a book, "We're not robots: Listening to daycare providers" (2007).

Anette Emilson is a lecturer in pedagogy at the University of Kalmar in Sweden. She is also a Ph.D. student at the University of Gothenburg and will defend her doctoral thesis in 2008. Her research focuses on the issues of fostering citizenship for toddlers in a preschool context, with a special focus on children's participation and influence in every day life in preschool.

Anne Greve is an Associate Professor at Oslo University College, Norway. For almost twenty years she has worked as a teacher in Norwegian kindergartens, mainly with children under the age of three years. Her Ph.D. theses was focused on investigating friendships among two-year-old children in a Norwegian kindergarten and more recently this study has been extended to include one-year-olds. This research uses life world phenomenology.

Artin Göncü is professor of Educational Psychology and Early Childhood Education in the College of Education at the University of Illinois at Chicago, and the Chair of the Department of Educational Psychology. His publications include Göncü, A., & Gaskins, S. (Eds.) (2007) Play and Development, LEA; Göncü, A. (Ed.) (1999) Children's engagement in the world, Cambridge, and Göncü A., Klein, E. (Eds.) (2001) Children in play, story, and school, Guilford.

Eva Johansson is Professor of Education, at the Unit of Childhood studies, Department of Education, University of Gothenburg, Sweden. She is also professor of Child Studies at the University of Stavanger, Norway. Eva Johansson is an experienced researcher in the field of early childhood education with an extensive research and publication profile in the area of children's morality. She is engaged in questions on moral learning in early childhood education, including studies on how children experience and develop morality and how teachers approach such issues in their work. Her research also includes studies on young children's learning as well as quality aspects of preschool and the relation between play and learning. Her publication record includes many books and book chapters, as well as papers all based on research.

Paulette Luff is a Senior Lecturer in Early Childhood Studies at Anglia Ruskin University, Chelmsford, England. She is a doctoral researcher in the Centre for Research in Education And Teaching (CREATe) and is currently completing research exploring early years practitioners' uses of child observation. Paulette has worked in the field of early childhood for more than twenty years, as a teacher, foster carer, school-home liaison worker and as a lecturer in further education.

Mary McMullen is Professor of Curriculum Studies in Early Childhood Education at Indiana University in Bloomington, Indiana, in the United States. Her Ph.D. research focused on the development of symbolic problem-solving skills in toddlers. Before becoming a professor, she worked as an infant and toddler caregiver and program director. Her research interests involve teachers' beliefs and practices, and international perspectives on quality care and education. She is co-creator and director of a professional development network for infant toddler practitioners, ITSI, Infant Toddler Professionals of Indiana.

Catherine Main is a clinical faculty member in the College of Education at the University of Illinois at Chicago (UIC). She has 18 years of teaching experiences in preschool, kindergarten, primary grades, and university settings. As a clinical instructor, Ms. Main works extensively in early childhood classrooms throughout Chicago Public schools and Chicago community agencies supporting student teachers and developing mentor teachers. Her most recent work has included innovative and responsive program development in Early Childhood Education at UIC. Over the past couple of years, she has presented her program work at national conferences and as an invited speaker at local conferences.

Berenice Nyland is a senior lecturer at RMIT University, Melbourne, Australia. Her Ph.D. was a study of infants in child care centers and she has presented and published nationally and internationally on the rights of infants and toddlers in group care. She is an executive member of Early Childhood Australia, Victoria and serves on the Education Committee of the Winston Churchill Memorial Trust. Present research includes young children and music in group settings and the development of early childhood services in China.

Helen Penn is Professor of Early Childhood at the University of East London, United Kingdom. She previously ran the United Kingdom's first integrated care and education service in Strathclyde, in Scotland, but in the last ten years has spent much of her time working in Central Asia and in Southern Africa on early child development projects as a consultant to a variety of international development agencies. She is the author of two recent books on early childhood: *Understanding Early Childhood: Issues and Controversies* (2nd edition due 2008), Open University Press; and *Unequal Childhoods: Young Children's Lives in Poor Countries*, Routledge (2005).

Author Index

Subject Index